The Perks of Cult Life

Or

Why I HAD to Slap Brother Ronnie 7 Times

By Prostell TJ Thomas III

Dear Mountain,
Blow me.
--The Wind

The Perks of Cult Life

Or

Why I HAD to Slap Brother Ronnie 7 Times

"When you know the plan of Allah, you will go places you don't want to go, do things you don't want to do, and talk to people you don't want to talk to."

This lesson stuck with me as I matriculated through the United Nation of Islam. As the Assistant Minister of the Detroit Temple I quoted this often to members who had occasionally met their assignment with a bit of reluctance.

It accurately summed up the idea that once you had written your Savior's Letter declaring allegiance to Royall, Allah in Person, you essentially gave up free will and agreed to do whatever was needed to be in harmony with Royall's will. The problem, oftentimes, was that by the time his will came through the many links and kinks in the chain of command, it had been manipulated by the politics that existed in the UNOI.

My most challenging experience with this came when I arrived to duty at the bakery in the Fall of 2008.

It was early in the week, so there were only two fundraiser teams going out. The first was Brother Minister Thomas: a humble brother from originally from Atlanta, Georgia. The second was Brother Ronnie's, from Kansas City. Both Brothers had been followers of the Honorable Elijah Muhammad in the original Nation of Islam during the 60s and 70s and now having joined the UNOI had been sent to Detroit to help us move things forward.

Both Brothers had been quite a bit of help, Ronnie in particular. While Thomas had quite a bit of knowledge and very friendly spirit, his lack of understanding of UNOI politics often left him paralyzed to the point of having watched his wife die under UNOI 'medical' care.

Ronnie was a brother after my own heart. In Heaven (UNOI headquarters in Kansas City, KS) he was one of the first Brothers to take me under his wing. Though he had long ago turned his life over to Allah, if you had spent ten minutes around him you could tell he was a street wise, tough guy.

In Ronnie I finally had someone willing to hurt a few feelings and say what needed to be said in order to end the lackadaisical attitudes that had made Detroit the laughing stock of the UNOI.

As the members began to trickle in to begin their duties, my phone rang. "As Salaam Alaikum"

"Wa Laikum Salaam." It was Sister Judy. "Sister Sandy wants to come in and help in the bakery. Is that okay?"

I rolled my eyes.

"Absolutely, the more the merrier!"

"Okay I will call and tell her."

We gave the greetings and got off of the phone.

Sister Sandy had been processing for the last three months. Already she was one of the more diligent and serious participants in the Temple. She regularly called to find out what was needed duty wise, gave more charity than most of the members, actively participated in class and brought visitors.

My trepidation stemmed from the fear that all of this was due to the off and on affair she and I had for the past three years.

Though this type of behavior was nothing new for me, I had broken one of the cardinal rules for Brothers that did venture outside the Nation to sow their wild oats. I had told her who I was and what I was about, even worse I began to teach her. Once she began to look for more than the intense physical trysts that existed between us, she found her way to class, and started orientation. When she cut of her long flowing locs per UNOI policy, I knew I was in trouble.

Nevertheless, once she began processing I warned her not to expect anything more from me and effectively ended our physical interactions. I let her know that what we had done was a matter of my personal indiscretion and in no way reflected the view, opinions, or values of the UNOI.

She said she understood and promptly began to apply her herself to the Nation like a woman possessed. As glad as I was to see her there, I was equally worried that she was there for all the wrong reasons.

Sandy arrived around 10am and I asked her to get the teams' baked goods together. As usual she moved out, checked with the Brothers to see what they needed, and the Brothers were promptly out on their way.

I stood in front of the bakery labeling cookies, when Sandy walked in from the back. She stood there silently for a moment so I turned and asked her, "What's up?"

"I don't think I like Brother Ronnie very much."

"Aw, Brother Ronnie's just a lil misunderstood, he's good people."

"I don't think I misunderstand him. I just don't want to be around him anymore"

"What you mean? What happened?"

"He just kissed my hand."

I paused not sure if I heard her correctly. She repeated it. I cursed. She said that after helping to put together his order Ronnie had stopped to thank her and in doing so, grabbed her hand and kissed it. I sighed and weighed my options.

The justice system in the UNOI, much like that of the world, oftentimes worked differently depending upon who was in the know about a particular crime.

In this case, a married brother kissed the hand of a sister that was processing, and here the sister was telling me about it. I would just as soon tell her to forget about it, it won't happen again, but then all I needed was for the Sister's military to think I was trying to hide or protect Brothers who sexually harassed Sisters. Not with my reputation.

"Okay well you need to call Sister Judy."

She hesitated, "I don't want to get him trouble"

"Well, at this point you have already told me, and I can't address it without directing you to the proper channels so..."

She said she understood and that she would call as soon as she got home. I walked her to the car and called Brother Kaaba, the National Lt.

"As Salaam, what's up Pros?"

Kaaba was a Brother who I had grown somewhat close to while at Headquarters (Heaven). He was generally pretty friendly with a hilarious sense of humor, but fiercely ambitious. Though he and I were somewhat cool you never wanted to be on the wrong side of his political aspirations. He could just as soon make you laugh with his sharp wit as he could be standing over you as you dangled from a cliff. Metaphorically speaking.

I think.

I sighed.

"Aw shit. What happened?"

I explained the scenario to him. He replied this didn't bode for Ronnie, who apparently had a reputation himself. These days they were putting people out the Nation for less. I stressed how vital Ronnie had been to our success and how losing him would set us back greatly. Kaaba said he would do what he could to get ahead of the curve on this one. I thanked him and told him I would be waiting on his call.

The rest of the day passed pretty much without anything of notice.

The beat down look on Ronnie's face when he came in let me he had already seen the first wave of conference calls that typically unfolded, courtesy of Kaaba and the other National Officials anytime there was any major scenario.

He didn't say much other than him turning in the funds for the day and heading home. I closed the bakery at 9pm and headed home.

The scenario was just about out of my head, when I walked through the door to the customary calls of "Daddddy!!!" from my three sons. My wife appeared at the top of the stairs with the house phone.

"Kaaba asked you to call him."

I took the phone and stepped back out onto the porch to dial Kaaba's number.

"Okay here is the deal..." "Yessir."

"In order for Ronnie to stay he is going to need to get popped in the mouth seven times."

Seven was the God number, and corporal punishment was not a new idea in the Nation.

I pulled my coat back on and called Kaaba from my cell as he tried to explain the proper way to smack Brother Ronnie.

",,,hard enough to make his mouth bleed, but not hard enough to swell his lip. Use the back of the hand; make sure you can feel his teeth through his lips with your knuckle. Hard enough to where he can't talk, but not so hard that he can't go to duty tomorrow."

If I didn't know what we were talking about, I would have thought he was joking.

I parked in front of Ronnie's home, went to the door and asked him to step outside for a minute. I walked to the back of the house and waited on him.

When Ronnie finally arrived I called Kaaba on three-way, and he then connected Bro Captain Rodney of Kansas. We all exchanged the greeting and Bro Kaaba began,

"Alright, Ronnie we all spoke earlier; I hope you understand the severity of what you did today."

Brother Ronnie spoke in his characteristic Midwestern twang, "Yessir. I definitely understand and this will not be happening again. I can guarantee you that much."

Rodney spoke, "The problem is Ronnie, we had this conversation before and you said the same thing, so something is going to be needed to stress the point."

Kaaba picked up the conversation," Ronnie you can either leave right now, pack your things and get out of the Nation's home, or Bro Minister is going to have to smack you in the mouth seven times."

Ronnie didn't hesitate, "Oh yes, sir. I don't wanna leave so I will have to take the smacks."

"You're sure?"

"I mean I don't want to get slapped but if that's only way I can stay..., "

"Alright, Brother Prostell you there?"

"Yessir."

"You can go ahead and get started. Be sure to hold the phone up so that we can hear."

I walked over to Brother Ronnie. Holding the phone up with my left hand, I brought my right hand back, and delivered the first slap to Ronnie's mouth. POP!

I could feel his rough skin and moustache recoil against the back of my hand. POP! POP! POP! He seemed to flinch uniquely with every hit. POP! POP!

I felt myself becoming more comfortable as I finished. POP! POP!

"That's it" I said.

"You started? I didn't hear anything?"

"Did you hear anything Rodney?"

"I didn't hear nothing. I don't think he did it."

Now I was getting irritated. "Do I need to do it again?"

"Ronnie, he hit you?"

"Yeffr" Ronnie responded sucking his lip.

"Is your lip bleeding?"

"Yeffr"

"Maaaaan, are you lying, Ronnie?"

"No sir, I am not. That hurt."

"Damn Prostell, you slapped him all seven times that quick?"

"Yessir."

"You must have been on the speed slapping team in college or something."

I was speechless.

Ronnie spoke up again," He definitely hit me and it definitely hurt"

"Yeah, right."

"Look I did it, if you need me to do it again slower, just say that..."

"Alright, alright, alright, alright, Ronnie you need go ahead and get ready for tomorrow and I will call you and let you know what the verdict is. Prostell we will call you right back.

"Yessir" we both responded.

As we walked back toward the front of the house, Brother Ronnie apologized repeatedly for putting me in this situation. I assured him that I had been in my share of the same type of scenario, but that we needed to put this situation behind us and do what we came to Detroit to do.

The irony of a man who was like an uncle to me apologizing for me having assaulted him, for kissing the hand of a sister I had carried on a three year affair with was not lost on me. I repeated to myself as I got in the car, "When you know the plan of Allah... "

As I drove away from the house I dialed Kaaba. He answered in a surprisingly pleasant tone that belied the circumstances we had just spoken under. "Yes"

"Please tell me you have good news."

He laughed, " Maaan Ronnie not in trouble," I could hear Captain Rodney laughing in the background.

"But once they find out we made this one up, we might be."

Orientation

I was in a cult.

I know right?

There is no casual way to bring this up. It's not a very good ice breaker. Mention it at parties and watch any conversation screeeeeeech to a halt. People who moments ago were waist deep in a flowing conversation with you, now silently stare. Looking into your eyes quizzically, almost as if to say, "Wow, he sure didn't SEEM like a circus freak at first".

Others wait apprehensively for the punch line that never comes. Or perhaps mentally scramble to come up with excuse to decline the invitation to your next cult meeting which undoubtedly will be the next thing out of your mouth.

But be all of that as it may, I was in a cult.

I have only recently come to terms with the reality of that statement. This despite the United Nation of Islam defining ITSELF as a cult, on the center pages of its own website.

While I was in the Nation, family or friends would face fierce rebuke or alienation for even insinuating such a thing. Even long after I had parted ways with the UNOI, and recognized the positive and destructive effects that the organization had on former and current members, including its attempts to destroy me professionally and eliminate me from the lives of my family, I would still shy away from the cult label.

From Jim Jones, to Waco to Charles Manson, and even Mitt Romney there is an obvious stigma that is given to cults and the people who find themselves willingly or unwillingly in their ranks. The stereotypical image we have of a cult follower is of a weak-minded individual, who is operating entirely under the will and at the pleasure of some charismatic 'nutjob' (medical term not mine).

In some cases it may be as simple as some hippie-love-revolution, strolling the country side sharing good weed and free love, forsaking the government and general hygiene.

The other end of the spectrum is some mysterious figure who has managed to convince a group of people that he is God almighty and that they should turn over all their worldly possessions to him immediately, and live in the tool shed behind his house, with thirty other followers and wait on his beck and call for their next instruction or to let them know when the mother ship has come.

I cannot say that my 10 years in the United Nation of Islam was either of these extremes, but it was much closer to the latter than the former.

Two things are ironic about this.

The first is despite being on call 24-7, and at duty for an average of 16 hours a day, having to check with 'the structure' for the most basic of wants and needs, being under constant emotional, mental, and even physical pressure, I couldn't have been happier and can't think of a greater time of progress in my personal development.

My departure from the UNOI was a hard and ugly episode from which I have still not fully recovered. Be that as it is, I recognize it for what it was. Call it growing pains.

Many of my experiences and lessons in the Nation continue to shape and direct my worldview today. Even the many ideologies which I have come to disagree with have deepened my perspective, patience, and understanding for even the most extreme and different patterns of thought.

In the ranks of the FOI (Fruit of Islam or the Men of the Nation), I learned invaluable lessons on being a Father and Brother; how to organize and mobilize people and ideas; how to come into a city full of strangers and build a support system; everything from Culinary Arts to Accounting to Carpentry to Holistic Healing and more.

While I don't give the UNOI credit for me being the Man I am today, I do recognize the important role the Nation played in revealing me to me. It was a controlled environment designed for me to grow into knowledge of self. At an age where many of my peers were becoming more and more entrenched in the pitfalls of growing into a Young Black Man in Detroit, MI, I can think of a hundred worse places to be.

The second surprising thing is that, as I began to reflect on the things that many would consider abnormal about my cult experience, I began to see significant and numerous parallels between cult life and groups and activity that many consider perfectly normal.

In other words, YOU are probably in a cult too.

Yes, you. The one holding this book.

Don't look around, I'm talking to you.

Hear me out.

"When you know the plan of Allah, you will go places that you don't want to go, you will talk to people that you don't want to talk to, and you will do things that you don't want to do."

This was an often quoted principle to the members of the UNOI, but its meaning is common among most religions, military doctrine, political parties, and society in general. It plays on the noble notion of submitting one's self to a cause or idea that is far greater than the individual.

Sometimes this is purposefully done by the individual, for instance when a soldier agrees to become a part of the armed forces. He is submitting himself to become part of a culture that is greater than his own tastes, opinions, motives, and values. In most cases his values will be shaped by the 'who, what, where, when, how, and especially whys' he learns as he is prepared for duty. In the occasion where his values differ from that which he is being taught, he will defer to the overall goal of the group as given to him from those in authority over him.

For example, if your acquaintance called you up to tell you that he has decided to travel across the planet and randomly kill men and women he has never met before in all likelihood you would be taken aback by such a statement.

If that same person told you that he or she was enlisting in the Army or Marines, then even if you didn't like the idea you could accept it a lot easier. Based on societal norms, the fact that he or she may have to eventually travel to another country and kill strangers may not even enter your conscience, but ultimately that is the reality for many.

This isn't a judgment of whether said action is right or wrong; that is a question for another day. This is merely an observation of the way our culture can influence our perception of what is right and wrong.

For all the grief Mormons got during the recent election nowhere is the cult mentality more prevalent than in the ultra-polarized gridlocked environment that is the American politic system. Here in this land of countless versions, of countless religions, all types of varying economic realities, diets, cultures, sub-cultures, pseudo-sub-cultures, and the like, we are somehow sold the notion that politically there are two schools of thought we must back one or the other and whichever we back is all encompassing.

You are either all Democrat or all Republican (or even the increasingly popular all neither, which I must admit these days is looking more and more popular).

We determine their political affiliation, religion, sexuality, and then out of fierce loyalty stick to which ever guns are given to them by that group. Metaphorically speaking unless for of course the NRA members, then its literal.

In the chapters that follow I have compiled some experiences of my ten year journey through the cult called UNOI and how through that journey I gained greater understanding of the world at large, but most importantly myself as a human being.

I began in search of peace and happiness, and experienced everything from violence, peace, adultery, love, drug trafficking, community revitalization, philandering, freedom, oppression, deceit, understanding, confusion, politics and more.

What makes these events significant is not that they happened to me, but they are the HUMAN experience. They are happening in some form or fashion every day to millions upon millions across the globe, who in search of peace and understanding find themselves knowingly or unknowingly immersed in the cult experience.

"When you buy into something that seems to explain everything, you can soon be coaxed into doing almost anything." –Marc Sageman

The Other Shoe Drops

I was at duty at the bakery late December 2008 when I got the phone call that would begin the series of events which lead to me leaving the Nation. I remember like yesterday being in the front of the bakery cleaning and setting up the display cases for the day. The phone rings and its Sister Sandi.

" You're probably going to never want to speak to me again, but",

I knew what she was going to tell me before she could get the words out.

Despite our previous improprieties Sister Sandi and I had a very good relationship. She had shown through her motion a genuine will to see The Idea successful in Detroit. She had cut her locks and came into the bakery to assist every chance that she got. That previous day in fact, Sandi had come into the bakery to volunteer.

As usual, we were the only ones there when she came in. This was typical, but for whatever reason, this day was different.

Perhaps it was our history coupled with the intimacy that comes with working side by side with someone. Or maybe I was just a little horny that day, who knows?

At any rate, on this day the normal conversation turned to flirting, then flirting turned to touching, then touching turned to an embrace and before you know it we are on the very edge of erasing whatever progress we made in the idea of staying on the straight and narrow.

We alternated between one of us instigating the action and the other trying to be the responsible one. As we went back and forth, I am not sure what made us finally stop but when we did, perhaps from the testosterone mixed with guilt and anger in myself, I reacted rather strongly.

I told her that behavior was completely unacceptable and could never happen again, too much was at stake. She abruptly left the bakery. After taking about twenty minutes to cool down, I called her.

I told her that I wasn't trying to be cruel or mean, I just didn't want things to go back down that road. I had made such progress and even more importantly the Detroit Study Group was at a very critical point and the last thing that was needed would be me falling off.

If I fell or got caught up in a scenario, especially one of that nature, then it would affect not only my family but essentially the whole study group. I wasn't willing to take that chance.

She said that she understood and respected that and that she would just talk to me a little later.

To be honest, at the time I felt like that was a battle with myself that I had won.

Had that been a year ago, the closest I would have come to discretion is making sure that the door was locked to the bakery before I got into whatever I was going to get into.

I had nothing but very good memories of my rendezvouses with Sandi, however it had been close to a year since we had been intimate. I was working hard to clean up my image and renew some sort of confidence in my being able to be a leader in the Nation.

In my mind the conversation was another sign that all of that was behind me.

And then I got that call.

" ....when I got home I was still feeling some kind of way about the situation. Sister Wendy was there and we talked about it. And I told her everything."

At this point a chill ran down my spine. I had gotten myself into some really bad spots since being in the Nation and I can tell you that a lot of times, what determined how far a scenario went, was who was in the know of the scenario.

If, for instance, just officials knew about a scenario and it was not productive or in accord with anyone's agenda to let a scenario be known to the general public/nation, then it may stay amongst the ones who were initially involved.

In this situation the words "I talked to Sister Wendy" made that prospect impossible. Sister Wendy was the queen of reporting transgressions, real and perceived. She would not only report to the proper officials, but also would waste no time getting information circulated on the gossip circuit. Like most gossips, the inaccuracy of the information was secondary to the need to get it on the wire as fast as possible. Gossip was so rampart in the Nation that there multiple entries addressing in the FOI/MGT Manual, which amounted the UNOI Bible.

Sister Wendy had a well-known record of taking the most innocent situations and twisting and magnifying them into huge dramatic problems. Imagine what she could do in this case where I was clearly in the wrong.

Sandy continued, "She asked me if I loved you. I said yes. Then she told me that she didn't see anything wrong and that I should put in a bid for you and that if I didn't do it then she was going to report the scenario. I put in the bid however she still reported the scenario . . . . . "

I must have said the same four-letter curse 200 times in a row as I stared out the window of the bakery at East Warren Avenue.

"This is it.......... my whole life is over." I declared in a rush of emotion. I could feel my very salvation and sanity slipping from my grasp.

She continued on telling me what happened and apologizing repeatedly but to be honest, I couldn't hear a word she said after this point. My heart was in my gut, and I felt like cement was trudging through my veins. Everything just felt so dull and dark. I was immediately overcome with the feeling that my world was coming to an end.

My mind started to travel a million miles a minute and I had that all too familiar feeling of having let my family, the study group, all those who believed in me, down. Mentally I fast-forwarded to what was probably happening on another phone call somewhere in the Nation. Having been here before I realized that if I was going to go down, then it was best to do it on my own terms. I quickly rushed her off the phone and dialed Kaaba's number.

"Yes"

"As Salaam Alaikum."

I gave him the greetings he returned them. " Y Laikum Salaam. What's up Pros?"

"Okay if you asking me that, that means you haven't gotten that call yet."

"What call?"

I broke the whole thing down for him, detailing my affair with Sandi, its end, everything that happened the previous day at the bakery, and what happened between Sandi and Sister Wendy.

"Aw shit Pros. That's not good at all. Especially not for you."

"Yeah I know, I just wanted to call and give you a heads up."

He repeated.

"Yeah that's not good at all... " I could sense he was scanning his mind to see what angle to take in this situation. By this time Kaaba had become a master politician, which meant he was capable of greasing the wheels of justice, and at the same time he was wise enough to know when a situation was beyond even his political tinkering.

And this was certainly one of those.

"OK I'ma have to call you back"

"Yessir" I responded as I prepared myself for the inevitable. I had survived some pretty bad situations in the Nation but I could see no escape from this one. Too many people where involved and affected by it. Amanda, Sandi, Wendy, even the fact that Sis. Judy was the one who actually ended up taking the report made my heart ache.

Members continued to mill about the bakery as usual. Since it was my ass in the ringer, I figured that Bilal, my Brother in Law and the Detroit Lt., would mostly get a call to perform the execution.

It was a Tuesday, so all the members would be coming to the bakery, the Brothers for FOI class and the Sisters for MGT Class.

I moved about the bakery like the walking dead, doing my best to keep my happy cordial spirit as the members walked in and greeted me in the usual enthusiastic way, small talking about this, seeking guidance about that.

Just before 7pm Bilal came to the front of the bakery.

"We need to call Kaaba and Bro. Minister"

I picked up the bakery phone and called Bilal's cell. He in turn called his Father, Minister Joe, while I called Kaaba.

After the obligatory greetings and acknowledging that everyone was on the phone Kaaba began,

"Alright Prostell, you are on 90 days away from us. You are to remain in the home with your family, but you are not permitted to come to classes or to any of the Nation's businesses. Father also said you are to go get a job and to keep up your charity."

A wave of relief rushed over me.

Mercy!

I don't know what I was expecting but it was certainly harsher than this. Hell I had been instructed to lay hands on Brothers who had done less. Tears began running down my face and I fought being choked up as he asked me to repeat my instructions.

I repeated them.

"Yessir. Bilal you will get the vehicle and the bakery keys from Prostell."

"Yessir"

Kaaba asked did anyone have any questions, I asked him to tell Father I said thank you and just that that quickly it was over.

I was still crushed but I knew it could have been a great deal worse. I felt like Father had thrown me a bone by allowing me to stay in the home. I figured the emphasis on getting a job was there to make sure I didn't go out and get caught up in any hustle.

I understood.

It brought to mind a conversation I had with Kaaba shortly after I had first arrived in Heaven. I had mentioned that my will was to return to Detroit and help move things forward. He assured me that would never happen, because the easiest place for a brother to get caught up was where he was from. In other words he knew all the right places to get into all the wrong things. Now a few years later I was a case study in that principle.

I turned over all the keys, other than my house keys. I was offered a ride home, but turned it down, thinking it best that I figure that out on my own since I was now officially out of the Nation for 90 days. I had been on the other side of the scenario plenty and the last thing you wanted to do was appear to be helping a brother that had gotten on Royall's bad side.

I walked around the corner to my sister's home and borrowed a couple of dollars in order to get on the bus home. I knew the long bus ride would give me time to sort out the million or so thoughts buzzing around in my head.

My children: I would have to figure out how I would break the news to them, I wondered how many times a child can see their Father fail so publically before they are embarrassed by his presence.

My wife: I knew words could never describe the pain and embarrassment she would feel. Again. If nothing had been the final straw, I knew this was it. I knew people had been in her ear for years that she could do better. She was a very good sister, so my body wouldn't even be cold before the Brothers would start putting their bids.

In the Detroit Study Group, as much as I had been in trouble, very little of it actually ever became public record. This scenario would surely change their perspective of me.

As the Minister, my absence would have a huge impact on the daily motion in and out of the bakery. At the very least it meant an increased work load for the more diligent members.

For those on the fence it meant potentially falling off altogether. For lost-founds/regular civilians who may have never even heard of us, it would greatly jeopardize their only hope for salvation. After all, that was the point of all this motion, to save the Black Man and Woman here in North America. Now their blood would be on my hands.

As an FOI, knowing I would be the latest casualty of the last 'few good' Brothers that was left in the Nation hurt. Me, Carter, Emory, Morris, Daniel, and a handful of other FOI often kept in touch, and pledged ourselves to make sure that the few Brothers who were not politically motivated would do whatever was necessary to protect the overall integrity and brotherhood of the FOI. Yet more and more it seemed like we were dropping like flies.

Judy: I knew she was happier than she had been in long time. Even though she had been ordered to go back to Alabama and her husband against her will, I knew she liked it in my home and my family loved her, so I held onto the idea that maybe things would work themselves out. Amanda trusted her and had grown extremely close to her. Judy's respect for me was helping Amanda to begin to look at me in a new light. The possibility of her being a permanent part of my family evaporated with Sandi's phone call.

Sandi: I felt sorry and hated her all at one time. Sandi was a great sister who had shown more dedication in her six months or so processing than most of the members had shown in a lifetime in the Nation. She was a real soldier. Even after we ended our affair we remained close. She was always a very good and genuine friend.

On the other hand, I wondered how she could fix her mouth to tell Wendy of all people what had gone on. She had told me a million times that the main thing she learned from living with Wendy was that she could not keep her mouth shut.

With all of this buzzing around in my head, I walked out my sister's home, and looked at the red brick house almost directly across the street.

5220 Courville.

Poetic Justice.

My journey was slowly coming to an end; right where it had first began. This is where I had first learned of Royall, the UNOI, and Mathematical Thinking Class. This is where it had all started for me 10 years ago.

LESSON C-1

(Detroit)

How can a story about a life changing experience not start with a woman?

Her name was Amanda.

She was straight out of central casting for my dream girl. Dark skinned, big beautiful eyes, killer smile, modest dress, but not modest enough to hide those legs, and most important to me, she was a revolutionary.

But let's back up for a moment. It was Spring of 1998. I was a sophomore at the Wayne State University in Detroit, MI, majoring in Elementary Education.

As a child I had regularly moved back and forth between my mom-- a native and lifelong Detroiter-- and my Dad-- who moved often due to his job as an Air Traffic Controller with the Air Force and FAA.

It became clear early on in life the dismal condition that the city of Detroit was in. These days every time you turn on the television there is some 'expose' or 'breaking news' about the bad situation in the D. But in reality Detroit has been on the steady decline for decades, including most of my life. I heard one activist friend of mine aptly describe the conditions of the city as a slow motion Hurricane Katrina devastating the city gradually over time.

In Detroit, the first thing everyone notices is that the city's population is primarily Black, and that is only slightly before noticing the great disrepair much of the city is in. One can only imagine the subconscious correlations those visiting and those inhabiting the city draw from this.

Liter is strewn across much of the landscape like indigenous plant life and potholes riddle the streets with such frequency that some roads appear to be victim of saturation bombings. The city has made significant strides since my childhood, but growing up, there was nothing noteworthy about seeing entire blocks of vacant or ram shackled buildings; residential, commercial, even on what should be prime real estate in the center of downtown.

Too many students and too few resources had long ago turned our schools into preparatory classes for street life. You did your best to remember why you came, but spent much of the time trying not to get caught up in any of the foolishness that was going on.

I had moved back to the city after somewhat of a tenuous split from my Father's home. I came ready for a change and eager to reconnect with all of the family and friends I had been missing after an extended stay away from the city.

I was leaving the peaceful, middle class neighborhoods in Columbus, OH and the laid back country atmosphere for the blighted crime-ridden urban center of Detroit, MI.
And I couldn't get there fast enough for me.

When asked as a child I used to say that, "I like the city of Columbus, but I love the people of Detroit."

So while those around me, like my Mom, had hesitation for bringing a teenage black male into an environment where things were dangerous for us, at best, I couldn't have been more excited.

In order to create somewhat of a buffer for me or ensure that my idle hands wouldn't find their own interests I was immediately sent to the church.

Sacred Heart Catholic Church to be exact.

Looking back I cannot overstate the impact this move had and continues to have on my life to this very day. My experience there shaped my closest friendships, and laid the foundation for the very thing I dedicate my life to.

Now hold on.

Before you get to thumping your bibles, if you don't know me or my story, let me tell you now this is not a send-the-kids-to-church tale. This incredible impact that Sacred Heart had on me had far less to do with what was going on in the church than what was going on in the Activities Building not thirty feet from it.

Let's explain.
Sacred Heart Church is a Catholic Church.

Now when I say that, I need you to immediately forget everything that you have come to assume about a catholic church.

Because Sacred Heart is a Catholic church in Detroit.

Let me not mince words.

Sacred Heart is a Catholic Church in Detroit, across the way from the Brewster Projects...with about a 75% black membership.

So let's just say they were not doing it like the old Catholic Church just up the street. That means they were playing straight up gospel music with a full gospel choir rocking the house on Sundays.

Soloists getting the Holy Ghost and all.

Yes in a Catholic Church.

There was an old Motown artist Mr. Prince directing the choir. Chicken and grits in the kitchen on Sundays.

Basketball Teams.

Not impressed?

How about this one; in the art on the church on the ceiling there is not just a Black Jesus but EVERYBODY is Black; Jesus, Mary, Judas, Peter, Paul, even the little guy bringing the food to the table, at the Last Supper, they're all Black. Don't tell the Vatican I told you this, but I digress.

The most pivotal thing about Sacred Heart that had an effect on me, even more than Black Jesus, was the sense of community involvement. This is what touched me and shaped me.

As I stated earlier, Detroit as whole was in a constant state of turmoil, and there was and continues to be an ongoing war for the land, resources, finances, and yes the very souls of the people in the city. Many forces conspire to exploit every resource that is valuable in the city/people and in return for little to nothing.

That is where places like Sacred Heart become so vital. I have been blessed to have traveled to more than my share of cities in this country, so I say with full confidence that no city I have been to or heard of has the community activism that there is traditionally in the city of Detroit.

It is a topic worthy of libraries but I will mention briefly here. Detroit has been the breeding ground for legendary champions of the people such as the original Nation of Islam, The Republic of New Africa, Focus Hope, Shrine of the Black Madonna, The Honorable Elijah Muhammad, Malcolm X, Rev. Albert Cleage, Imari Obadele, Coleman A. Young, Yusef Shakur, and countless, countless others.

I would like to say my immersion into activism was all me, but as soon as I hit church grounds I was promptly grabbed by the lapels and dragged to every youth group meeting, retreat, choir rehearsal, homeless sleepover that was going on.

I didn't have a choice.

29

No one asked me if I wanted to go.

And I loved it.

Because it was one thing for everyone to recognize the problems and struggles of the city, but it was a whole different, inspiring thing to be up out and about putting your hands on it.

So if there was an activity being set up for the youth, I was there, and if there was youth that couldn't afford to go, we were there finding a way to make it happen. There were whole weeks we would open the Activity Center to the homeless of the city and for that week, feed, clothe, provide shelter, cut hair, play dominoes, spades and most importantly commune with the homeless of the city.

My Grandmother, Loretta, who had the greatest hand in burning the love of service in my heart, was one of the elders of the church. On the board of numerous organizations around the city, she was responsible for handing out breakfast tickets to the homeless on Sundays, along with her being the chair or on the board of many outreach and charity groups across the city.

She would work tirelessly, on the phone all hours of the day and night taking calls from random persons, groups, and of course family members, about something that NEEDED to be done, usually right then. Never fixing her lips to say no, very rarely even saying not now.

She's had chronic problems with her feet for decades, but more times than I care to admit, I watched her labor down the stairs of her home at some God forsaken hour of the day or night, struggle to climb into her car, to carry some money, food, transportation, clothing, very pieces of her soul across town to those in need.

She now lives some 1600 miles away from the city, which seemed to be the only thing that could stop a) those distress calls from coming in night and day and b) her from answering them.

Perhaps this dedication and passion was born from good will, but surely a good part of it came from understanding that as Detroiters, our fates were inescapably tied. I am sure somewhere in the faces of those recovering substance abusers, homeless, and those in need, she saw her own children.

The systemic blight that gripped Detroit during the 80s and 90s, was no respecter of persons so indeed many of those distress calls came from within the family.

Someone needed money to get the heat and lights turned back on. The kids needed school clothes. Auntie is having a hard time breathing and needs to go to the E.R. Uncle Raymond had been arrested needs bail money. Again. Some anonymous person just called; he's disappeared and left the boys at some crack house, we need to come get them. Again.

I was only 13 years old when I got one of the most important phone calls of my life.

My mother called me into her bedroom to tell my uncle was on the phone and wanted to speak to me. It was Uncle Raymond. He had one simple instruction. "Take care of your cousins. Protect them."

Before I even responded with a simple, "Yes sir," his instructions had been all but burned into my heart.

With my own Father miles away in Ohio, my Uncle Ray was a fitting father figure/role model/superhero whenever I was in Detroit. His sons Ray and Alan, one and four at the time, had been the boy cousins I had been impatiently waiting on all of my life, so nothing else needed to be said.

Over the course of the next decade, I watched as this man who was once the closest thing to Superman, was reduced to the walking dead. He went from being a reliable anchor in an already suffering family, to

31

disappearing for months at a time. Every time he came back you could see the chunks of his humanity missing.

He used to routinely pick up me and my cousins up to take us to Belle Isle Park, now we were getting anonymous phone calls that the boys had been left in a crack house and we needed to come get them.

It is one thing to deal with the death of a loved one. The problem with the crack epidemic is that so many of us had to watch people whom we loved and die slowly before our very eyes. It didn't take long to realize that the Uncle Ray that had taught me how to shoot a basketball, or drive a car was gone forever.

Day after day, violent episode after violent episode, drama after drama, caused his memory to grow fainter and fainter in my mind until it was eclipsed with this dark soulless monster. It was not long before all fondness for a man whom I idolized was gone forever.

But even in the presence of this zombie, my uncles instructions resonated, loud and clear. "Take care of your cousins. Protect them."

Against a world that was already identifying those who looked like me as suspect, against the cocaine addiction that the younger of the two boys had been born with, against a city that was going to have no sympathy, nor time to even hear their sob story of a childhood.

"Protect them."

Most ironically from their father himself.

It was a regular routine for me to hide them deep within the bowels of my mother's basement, with the TV turned up loud on cartoons, while their father is upstairs trying to tear the metal door off of the hinges in some primal cry for help and/or money.

Even my best attempts to buffer them from the harsher realities of their life proved in vain. They would casually tell me of the horrors that growing up around two drug addicted parents had already shown them.

They were my passion, the living personification of this battle for my people's survival that was unfolding before my consciousness every increasingly. I decided by 15 years old that I would be their guardian and made it my business to make this clear to the entire family, who fully supported the motion.

Even before going to court once I reached the age of 18 to become their legal guardian, I had already stepped up as their caretaker, leaving my school, Detroit Northern High School, in time to make to their school for PTA meetings, or field trips.

Like my Grandmother, I saw what I was doing in the community at Sacred as an extension of being a father figure to the boys. Not only were they seeing me immersed in positive activity, but they were in it as well. I was well aware that I was still being shaped and molded myself, so the things that I saw as good activities for me, I just assumed would be beneficial for them.

Now being in all of this motion was a great thing for me and I loved what I was doing at church. It fed and nurtured my soul and gave me an outlet to feel like I was doing my part to make life better for a few people.

However it was still a church. And as much as I was in love with everything that went on in the Activities Center I had questions.

Being in Detroit made me painfully aware of the juxtaposition of being African descended people in America practicing Christianity. As easy as it was for someone to explain to me what time the youth dance or the canned good drive was, too often answers to spiritual questions didn't come as freely. Many times spiritual conversations would end with the familiar Christian fodder: 'You just have to have faith', 'you just have to believe', and to put it plain I was struggling with that.

Struggling with understanding how if we were brought over in slavery, how is it that the religion they gave us when we got here is okay for us?

And how if Christianity came from Judaism, then when did it become cool to eat pork?

I recall once letting it be known that I was going to stop eating pork until I better understood if or how it was right to do. Before long I got wind of a rumor that I had decided to become Muslim.

In retrospect maybe they knew something I didn't know about my future. I couldn't get over how asking what I thought to be simple questions got me labeled as a dissenter.

So the more difficult it became to the get those answers at church the more I began to look elsewhere.

Where?

Well I looked where a lot of people before me have looked.

I asked Huey P Newton.

And he told me to check with Malcolm X, and Malcolm, well he told me a few different things depending on when I asked him. At one point (book) he told me to look to the east in the Quran, and then at other points (books) he told to seek out the Honorable Elijah Muhammad and the Nation of Islam.

Like people from many backgrounds and walks of life, I read just about anything that I could get my hands on to make sense of it all. I wanted answers not just for myself but I wanted to know answers for what ailed us a people, spiritually, mentally and physically.

And that's when I met HER.

I strongly believe that our lives are a series of predestined forks in the road, at which we have the option of choosing the direction we go thereby shaping the story of our lives.

It was during this period of intense spiritual soul searching that I met Amanda.

I found it hard to imagine that it was just a matter of coincidence that this family of Muslims moved in right across the street from my mother's home at the precise time in my life when I was exploring Islam of all things.

At the time I was living on Courville on Detroit's east side. Compared to some of the rougher places we had lived before, this neighborhood was calm and peaceful. Other than the occasional skirmish that came along with having a neighborhood full of teenagers (and adults for that matter,) things were relatively quiet.

That is until the Hassans moved in.

It's funny to think back of my first impression of them compared to what I would come to know. They moved in seemingly overnight.

The first thing that struck me about those people across the street was the amount of activity going on at that house. No one over there seemed to be older than me, 20 years old at the time, and everyone was driving a late model car with nice rims and sounds.

And people were coming a going all of hours of the night. And I mean pull up in front of the house, leave the car running, run in, five minutes later run out, and speed off. So at the risk of sounding like a hater, my first thought was drug house. At the very least.

On my block?

Across the street from my family?

Right where Ray, Alan, and all their friends played every day?

Aw HELL naw! I had seen what having a drug house had done to blocks in my old neighborhoods and I wasn't having it.

The last thing I needed was for some knucklehead to come by shooting up the place and one of the kids getting caught in the crossfire, so at the risk of sounding like an even bigger hater AND a snitch, I had already mentioned this to a friend of mine whose Dad was a Narcotics Officer.

Well, fortunately for Detroit taxpayers, the Detroit Police Department, and me a drug bust never materialized before I actually got to meet the Hassans.

It didn't take long for me to learn that I couldn't have been more wrong.

I had seen Amanda from across the street going from her car to her house several times.

She was pretty hard to miss.

She was dark skinned about 5' 6 shoulder length hair, radiant smile, very womanly.

What struck me most about her was the way she dressed. Usually she wore long flowing sun dresses or skirts and moved with such grace you could see she had a very womanly build, without showing you everything.

Exactly my type.

Unfortunately for me I was still stuck on shy when it came to talking to girls. And this was no girl; she was a full-fledged grown woman.

So even after she stopped to offer me a ride on a rainy day, I was pretty resigned to the fact that I had NO SHOT of getting any real attention from her.

Nevertheless we became fast friends, and ended up spending hours upon hours talking, whether on her porch, or when we would cross paths at the kids' school. Her daughter Tammy, who was her spitting image, went to the same school as Alan.

It wasn't long before we would find ourselves at one of the various waterfront parks on the Eastside, talking until the wee hours of the morning.

We'd chat about everything from our children, her relationships, my relationships, love, school, dreams, careers, music, religion, you name it.

I knew from her last name that she was likely Muslim, so when she learned of my interest in Islam she was more than willing to share all that she knew.

Up to that point I had only known one person that was Muslim, Marshood, a brother from the neighborhood. My only spiritual conversation with him came during an episode when he tried to strangle his younger sister on his porch after she did something that he took as disrespectful and against their upbringing.

I didn't necessarily think that to be an accurate representation of Islam, but I knew I probably would want to find another source to learn about it.

I did know that Marshood followed Eastern Islam, and quickly learned that was an entirely different idea from The Nation of Islam.

Amanda told me that she was raised on the Teachings of The Honorable Elijah Muhammad. She spoke of the big black book from which her Father taught her and her six siblings; ideas such as the black man being the Original Man and rightful rulers of the Earth, the white man being the devil, God being a man, and how she would go head up with her teachers anytime they contradicted what her Daddy had taught her.

She also told me of her parent's divorce and how that subsequently led her and her Brothers and Sisters away from the path of Islam as laid out for them by their Father.

Her Father ruled his home with an iron fist and was the major force in their lives. With his departure from the home, they began the troublesome balance of being able to now indulge in things they saw other children do while at the same time holding onto the values instilled in them.

When we met, he was just now coming back into their lives. Unfortunately for them this was after over a decade of growing up on the Eastside in one of Detroit's roughest neighborhoods. They never lost the strong sense of identity and self-confidence instilled in them by their Father. Tragically they weren't entirely successful in avoiding some of the more deadly elements of the East side.

Their Father's return was marked by the loss their oldest brother Ragman.

Needless to say there was a major swirl of emotions when he returned; from burying his oldest son; unresolved feelings from a rather tumultuous departure; the always difficult task of trying to resume a paternal role in his children's lives after an extended absence.

Add to that to the fact that he was coming with news that would test the faith of even the most loyal of his children: God was here and he had met him.

My response to Amanda telling me that she personally knew Allah was not different from the hundreds of people who I have told the same information to since; I kind of acted like she just told me that she knew Bobby Brown.

Like, "Oh Okay, that's interesting."

Or "Wow, cool. Good for you."

Like "I'm familiar with his work, but hadn't really considered meeting him."

It really is an interesting experience and if you have the gumption, I insist you try it.

Seriously, at least once in your life, tell someone who you only know casually, that you not only know God, but are driving to Kansas to see him or are expecting a phone call from him later. It's really quite an experience.

For my part, I knew she was a Muslim, and though I had been studying Islam, I just figured I misunderstood, what or who Allah was. I THOUGHT it was supposed to be, like God himself, but clearly it must be like the Muslim president, or Dali Lama or something.

But no, it was just what she was saying. This man was calling himself Royall, Allah in Person, styled as Solomon.

As Amanda and I began to court and I started to attend the Mathematical Thinking Classes held by UNOI, I began to have a better understanding.

Let me be clear; better is a relative term, which in no way means firm or clear, just better than completely confused; slightly better than completely confused.

Mathematical Thinking Classes were classes held once a week to teach one how to think according the "Mathematical Thinking" developed by Royall and the UNOI.

While the principles of Mathematical Thinking in themselves are interesting and useful, (always check, never assume, be specific etc.) what they had in common with the most religious truths/teachings is they were open to interpretation.

Even to my pedestrian body of knowledge at the time this was apparent.

Much of the time we spent in class, in fact was spent not so much discussing the virtues of Mathematical Thinking or the UNOI, but actually pointing out the fallacy in other religious groups- what I now call spiritual player hating or the "right by default" doctrine. Essentially propping up your group by tearing down the another, this is the spiritual expression of Willie Lynchism or if you from the hood just general spiritual cock blocking, for example;

Christianity was given to us by the same people who enslaved us, and after praying to a blonde hair blue eyed Jesus for over two hundred years, the only thing the church has ever done for black folks was build a bigger church. (The church of course at the time was paying for my education and had just given my uncle and Grandmother houses but that was aside the point).

The white man was the devil and had caused nothing but bloodshed and mischief in every corner of the Earth that his hand touched. (This of course did not stop Solomon/Royall from utilizing the positive attention the UNOI had garnered from white folks in government and the media on the UNOI website and in speeches to prop up his or the UNOI's standing.)

But no target was more regularly in the scope of Solomon and the UNOI than Louis Farrakhan and the Nation of Islam.

No, they are not the same group.

I know that's what I thought too.

Yeah, I know right?

Just listen.

One of the first things that had to be explained to anyone who came to class or was introduced to the UNOI was the difference between NOI and UNOI.

So much so that it was actually part of the UNOI's formal introduction on its flyers and website:

The United Nation of Islam, which is a separate and non-related entity than the similar sounding "Nation of Islam".

This is because of obvious reasons. As soon you explain to a person that you are member of the United Nation of Islam, people often begin to ask you about or heaven forbid *tell* you what a powerful and dynamic leader Louis Farrakhan is.

Bad idea.

Royall no like Farrakhan. No like him a lot.

The divide, like so many other religions, laid in the interpretation of the original teachings or in this case the teachings of the Honorable Elijah Muhammad.

Elijah Muhammad, of course, was recognized as the Messenger of Allah and the Seal of the Prophets within the Nation of Islam. When he died the Nation splintered into many different groups, each one staking claim to be the true heir, or fulfillment of the Messenger's teachings.

For the record, Elijah's son Wallace was the official heir to his father's throne. Once in power, Wallace began to slowly turn the Nation toward Eastern or Orthodox Islam. This brought to surface many underlying tensions and politics amongst the leadership of the NOI. One by one followers of the Messenger began to break off and resurface with their own new version the NOI.

And just like every other major religion each new group used some part of the teachings to show themselves as being the rightful heirs to the Messenger's legacy.

The UNOI was no exception; one of Elijah's most famous and debated over teachings was when he said, "After me comes God himself. I do not say that I will live so long as to see that day, but if it pleases him I will be with him."

According to NOI theology, Allah had originally come to Elijah in the person of Master Fard Muhammad also known as WD Fard in Detroit, MI in 1921. And that generally is where the most NOI sects began to disagree.

Now if you ever read any of the Messenger's books you recognize that he refers to Allah, as God in the Person of WD Fard or Master Fard Muhammad. In a few places you will even see it as WD Fard, God in Person.

It was the contention of the UNOI that Fard was but a vessel to house the entity of Allah and that after the Messenger did his duty, then Allah was to come back." In his own royal robes", or "Royall robes."

Get it? Geeeeeet it?

To support this position, it was pointed out that before he passed, the Messenger shared with the Members of the Nation of Islam that his National Secretary Abass Rassoull was to let the members of the First Resurrection (the original followers of the Messenger) know what was to be done with the coming of the Lord. Abass was a major force in establishing and legitimizing the UNOI in the eyes of the many of the Messengers original followers.

The NOI under the leadership of Farrakhan countered that this entire argument was ridiculous and that the Messenger said from the rostrum that the members of the NOI should go where they see Farrakhan go, and stay away from where they see him stay away from. To put it mildly, Farrakhan wasn't going anywhere near UNOI, and he wasn't looking to invite them over for tea either.

In 1993 Abass Rassoull sent a letter to Farrakhan informing him of the arrival of "Solomon, The Prepared One." This letter thanked the Minister for his years of service and 'requested' that Mosque Maryum, essentially headquarters for the entire NOI, be made available for Solomon to speak to make a MAJOR announcement and that further instructions were to follow.

Yeah, THAT was gonna happen.

After the predictable denial by Farrakhan, the UNOI moved forward with their meeting at another location in Chicago. This meeting was to announce nothing short of the reincarnation of the Honorable Elijah Muhammad.

Let's pause here for a second.

Right now I want to talk to you about a thing called commitment.

One thing I learned early on about the UNOI and cult life in general is you don't go lukewarm with nothing. See that whole Son of God thing, it's been done a million times, man.

While all these other kooks are out here talking all that 'Jesus said this, Jesus did that'?

You?

You go over their heads.

You book God Himself.

Oh, so the Nonprofit up the block wants to make the news for a little community revitalization? They want to open a rec center?

You?

You open Heaven. (UNOI headquarters in Kansas City, KS was known as Heaven, meaning 'having everything you need to be successful')

And when the NOI, and NNOI, and the others splinter groups are dissecting the books of the Messenger?

Guess who gets the reincarnation of the man himself? You do.

In your face, Farrakhan.

Royall proclaimed that not only was he Allah, but that he had brought back the entity of The Honorable Elijah Muhammad in the body of this man, Joseph Kelly who was now standing on stage with him. His reward for doing a wonderful duty as Elijah the Messenger, was to come back now as the eventual ruler of the Planet, King Joseph.

This bold declaration defined the UNOI in the eyes of many.

If you were anti-UNOI it was all the proof that was needed to show them to be phonies. The Messenger taught that there was no such thing as coming back from the dead. He had illustrated this point many times when debunking the story of Jesus being resurrected.

Now here was a New Allah, Royall, standing on a stage in Chicago with a New Messenger.

To UNOI supporters this was equally strong proof that Royall MUST BE ALLAH. After all, the Messenger said that if it pleases Allah, that when Allah returned, he would be with him, and here he was.

Allah was to come and make all things new, and was this not what he was doing? Who would dare to make such a bold statement and be making it up?

As fantastic as these events and ideas may be, it is important to remember they are not at all unique to the United Nation of Islam. These are my experiences and things that happened to me, but how many lives have been ended or dramatically altered because two people read the same line, from the same book and got something different from it? How many wars have been fought, how many suicide bombings, how many families divided over another man's interpretation of what another man's relationship with God should be?

In Mathematical Thinking Class we would sit for hours and discuss what Farrakhan was or wasn't doing and how that proved that;

a)   He was purposefully misleading the members of the NOI.

b)   He had gone against the teachings of the Messenger.

c)   He had the members of the NOI worshipping him instead of Allah and his Messenger.

Mathematical Thinking was the system through which the UNOI sought to change the damaged and self-destructive thinking of the Blackman and Woman in North America. If applied properly this way of thinking would systematically reverse the effects that 400 plus years of oppression had on the minds of our people.

 Mathematical Thinking Class in Detroit was held on Sundays at the Butzel Center on Detroit's east side.

Joe, being the only person in Detroit familiar with The Idea (UNOI speak for the UNOI), conducted the classes in the beginning. As His oldest son Bilal became more versed in the knowledge of the UNOI, he began to assist in the administration of the class and the study group in general.

Class would be scheduled to start at 11am but everyone would typically start to roll in around 11:15-11:30, with some stragglers picking up the rear as late as 12:15-12:30.

I wasn't aware of it at the time but these first classes were an early indication of the rift that existed in the thinking of the ones who had been followers of the Honorable Elijah Muhammad (or the first) and those who were being developed in the United Nation of Islam.

In Detroit, these early classes were a mish mash of what Joe knew of Royall's teachings and the great deal of knowledge that he had gathered in his studying and travels.

It's safe to say we covered the basics, like what is Mathematical Thinking (The gathering of facts to come to the absolute answer without putting a person to it), what is personalism (the act of taking partners with Satan) or what being defensive means (defending self). The

45

problem lied in gaining understanding of what those things actually meant.

When it came to the answering questions that required more than a prima facia knowledge of the idea, then usually that began the journey into Joe's knowledge more so than Royall's.

This was especially the case when it came to dealing with scenarios. Scenarios were the opportunity to apply Mathematical Thinking to an everyday life situation.

This usually manifested itself in the form of a dispute between two or more members. Usually, the person that was offended or felt they had the best case decided to bring the scenario in front of the class. One of the members first would explain the scenario.

In Detroit, this process also indicated the divide between advanced mathematical thinkers and those who were only casually familiar with these principles.

Math Class was to be conducted devoid of emotion, opinion, or anything that could be considered remotely personal. If it was not a fact or did not relate directly to the solution it had no place in the conversation. Questions were to be asked for understanding purposes only, NEVER to argue or debate.

Yeah Right.

Instead of gathering facts to come an absolute answer, most scenarios would devolve into

a) a tar and feathering, point by point breaking down of how many ways a brother or sister was wrong for their actions complete with loaded questions and an absence of any real solution,

b) A tug of war with the members of the class becoming more and more personally invested in one side or the other as the scenario was discussed.

People would ask questions that not only did they know the answer to, but that didn't even really relate to what was being discussed. Brothers would quote laws and principles that didn't apply to the discussion in an attempt to seem deep. The conductor of class would often 'tell' or indicate very clear hints and clues as to his/her personal leaning in a scenario, which would unfailingly impact how others viewed the scenario.

Add to that the trademark Hassan sense of humor that would lead them to smile widely or flat out laugh uncontrollably in direct proportion to the sensitivity of what was being discussed, and you had an experience that was less help than it was stress.

By the time a scenario was completed, no real solution had been reached as much as each scenario served as a raising or lowering of the some person's status within the Nation. That is not to say that this process was exclusive to Detroit. Though the methods differed greatly, this principle I would come to see repeat itself with great regularity as I advanced further into the UNOI, but that is later in my journey.

We would come to class, and if there were no scenarios to cover, Bro Joe would go into teaching from his knowledge gumbo, mish mashing and mixing ideas he understood from Royall, with things that were clearly from his own experience. Some of it was enlightening, some of it just came across as hateful rhetoric about the Whiteman/devil/Yakub, about the church and how all they have done is build bigger churches, about black people and how crazy they are for not being there at the meeting with us, and of course the UNOI favorite target, Farrakhan.

Despite all of the confusion coming from Mathematical Thinking Class, the constant soap opera that was the UNOI, despite even the constant shots at Farrakhan and the Nation of Islam, there was one major factor of the UNOI that kept my attention: the activity/motion.

You will find no limit of revolutionary minded groups/people in the city of Detroit, and all of them can and will endlessly point out to you, the numerous fallacies in the 'system'.

The public schools are a joke, failing more than half of the children who enter them, and the rest that it doesn't fail only find themselves indoctrinated into a lie of a culture that is diametrically opposed to their success/freedom.

The Police are terrorists, who will drive past an old lady getting mugged in order to pull over a car with a cracked windshield. The good cops on the force whom aren't desensitized to youth violence or confused about who they are supposed to be protecting and serving, find their hands tied in bureaucracy.

Government wasn't ever going to do anything about it because the biggest crooks were in City Hall. They were all out of touch, too busy lining their own pockets and making their friends rich by privatizing city services and selling off the city's assets for backroom basement bargains.

This only leaves the citizens.

Ah yes, the citizens. The violent, drug addicted, unemployed, crab in a barrel, house squatting, warrant having, food stamp selling, spend my whole check on some new Jordans, gold digging, four baby daddy, generationally impoverished, mentally enslaved citizens.

Even if you did want to save them, they were so happy at the bottom of the barrel it would be an exercise in futility.

Now I would be remiss if I didn't point out this was the PERCEPTION and not at all the reality. As I would come to learn, oftentimes the ones that come in the name of saving a people had the lowest opinion of those they were claiming to save.

In my experience, though, Detroit has its obvious problems, more than any of the 20 or so cities I have lived in, my experience with the people of Detroit has been the most genuine, passionate, and easy to connect with.

I recall as a young father in Columbus, OH, my car breaking down one night at dusk. In the car I had three small children, a baby and my wife. We were in a very nice neighborhood and it had just started to snow. I knocked on a few doors to ask if I could just use the phone to call my father to come pick us up or if I could get a jump. They all said they couldn't help me. Feeling I had no choice I began to push the car with everyone in it the half mile or so to the service station up the street. As I pushed not only are cars going around me, some actually have the nerve to honk at me. (In their defense I was pushing a little slow after my other hand went numb).

On the other side of the token I have been on the side of the road countless times in Detroit, never more than ten or so minutes without someone pulling over to see if I needed any help.

I know this to be the experience of countless others, but these aren't the stories that will make the National news reports about the state of things in Detroit. You also won't hear it from a person who is trying to sell you on the idea that you need the salvation that they are selling.

But look at me on a tangent.

What was so novel to me about the UNOI, was that they were to taking the standard line, "This is what's wrong," and adding the not so common, "and this is what we are doing about it"

After all It was almost a crime to point out to a person how everything in their world is wrong, and then provide them with no opportunity to do anything better.

More than anything else this kept my interest in the UNOI. Though at the time there was little actual motion in Detroit, the weekly announcements would outline a bevy of activity in the study groups and temple across the Nation.

Occasionally we would even have visitors from Heaven stop through Detroit, bringing in orders of groceries or good from the farm or Heaven. This brought it all to reality. We may have heard the announcement about the Nation opening a bakery, but to lay hands on bread actually baked there. They may have told us the UNOI made its own Peppermint soap, but here it was and the guys delivering it to you smelled like peppermint themselves.

In addition to the products and the latest news and knowledge coming straight from Heaven, it was something to see how those who would normally pose as know-it-alls would fall all over themselves in fake humbleness whenever someone came to town.

For the whipping boys of the class, like me, what could be more entertaining than watching the one who would normally be doing the mental and spiritual bullying, being corrected and schooled every time they opened their mouth?

It was during one such visit that I got my first close look at the hierarchy of the UNOI.

It was at Royall's first speaking engagement in Detroit, and I was nervously looking forward to laying eyes on the one UNOI member called Allah.

This was the first of many times I was exposed to a chapter in the UNOI FOI book, entitled PROPER TREAMENT OF THE ROYALL FAMILY.

The Royall family was of course the wives, children, grandchildren, and adopted family of Royall, Allah in Person. If the title itself carried the slightest hint of promptitude, then once you read this list of do's and don't-you-dare-do's you would be speechless.

At least you better be.

I will list just a few of my favorites

1)   Never speak in a tone higher than a Royall Family Member.

2)   Never eat meat in the presence of a Family Member.

3)   Ask for permission before speaking to a Royall Family Member.

4)   Ask for permission before exiting a conversation with a Royall Family Member.

5)   Never turn your back on a Royall Family Member; back away until you are at a respectful distance.

6)   Never spit in the presence of the Royall Family.

Like many things that I learned to stomach and even believe over time, I will never forget the incredulous look on everyone's face the first time we heard it, superseded only by the collective unwillingness to actually say how ridiculous what we were hearing actually was.

The Royall Family, it was explained was doing the work of Allah. They had been prepared by Royall to guide us, the members, in and out of our affairs. These instructions were a mercy to us, because Royall would not tolerate ANY disrespect towards his family.

Right.

I know.

Same thing I was thinking.

In order to ensure that proper treatment of the Royall Family was being practiced, they had their own personal security that made sure that everyone and thing was to their liking. In general you were never going to get closer than within a few yards of a Family member.

In addition to their security, you had the members constantly seeking to get in good/be of service to the family or ask them some question that they probably already knew the answer to.

For this particular visit, we had been afforded the blessing of a private FOI/MGT class with Mother of Civilization, Royall's biological daughter, Moreen, and her teenage son, David.

Second in rank only to Royall, Moreen was referred to as the Mother of Civilization or M.O.C. She was Mother to the whole Nation and more specifically responsible for the Sisters, or MGT, which stood for Muslim Girls Training.

David came across as the most down to Earth of the Royall Family members. A teenager, he had been placed in authority of all the Nation's men, the FOI This made him responsible for reprimanding and instructing Brothers as much as four times his age. Despite this, he maintained a very good relationship with most of the FOI, never seeming to throw his rank in the face of the soldiers.

It was determined a relationship class would be beneficial since most of our regular scenarios centered on or stemmed from our relationships. The class was held in Joe's home, where Mother, as Moreen was called, and David had been staying.

Joe had turned over his house to the visiting Royall Family members, in a show of generosity that was promptly thrown back in his face by Mother who took every opportunity to take digs at the inadequacies of his home. Joe was a minimalist so even the best sprucing up and decorating of his humble abode were far below the amenities she had grown used to as the daughter of Allah.

As expected, class mostly consisted of members unskillfully bringing up questions about old scenarios that had supposedly been resolved in prior classes. Anytime members from Heaven were around, their perceived higher knowledge served as an appellate court for members who felt they had gotten a raw deal in previous Math Classes.

Moreen and David did a masterful job of feeding into all the attention, giving both sides of the scenarios just enough slack to save face and feel justified, but still straddling the fence enough to not clearly take either side of a scenario that they had little knowledge and even less interest in delving into. We didn't know at the time but all the while things were happening behind the scenes that would change the face of the UNOI drastically.

The following day was the big day with Royall arriving in town to speak at the larger public meeting, which was being held in the ballroom of the Butzel Building. If members were busy trying to please Moreen and David, then you can imagine the buzz when Royall and his wives arrived.

Laborers couldn't tell on each other fast enough.

The brother who never wanted to hold post any other time broke his neck to be seen on door post as Father walked into the building. It was a relief for underlings like me as I was too small a blip on the National radar for it to matter what I had botched that week.

The People of Detroit did their part to make it a lively meeting. During the open of the meeting, Moreen had posed the question to the large gathering, "What question would you ask Allah, if you had the chance to ask him anything?"

She must not have known where she was.

When the mic was opened up for questions, Royall was asked everything from, "Why did my Big Mama have to die? Why did you have to take her?" to

"If you are God what am I thinking right now?"

and my personal favorite, "You God right? Well what size shoe do I wear?"

Classic Detroit.

You can ask God any question you want, so you ask the same thing you would ask the manager of a Footlocker, but I guess I know where he was coming from.

One visiting brother even got out of his chair to answer a question that was asked of Royall as though the question was asked to him (and then almost got physical with the FOI who was on mic post when he wouldn't give up the mic so that he could answer the question.)

All of which drew the customary admonishing from Royall about how they were asking all the wrong questions, how is Royall telling him his own his shoe size going to help that brother and just how crazy and hopeless the black was in general.

I had to admit it was exciting to even be playing a small role in the background of an event that was such a big deal. It was fascinating to be around Brothers and Sisters who actually LIVED this knowledge that we had been talking about in classes. Everyone traveling with Royall seemed to have a glow and self-assuredness to themselves, a sense of purpose and direction that separated them from the lost-founds and even us.

Just as quickly as they had come, they were pulling out of town, greetings were exchanged and a reminder that everyone was expected to be in Heaven for the annual Independence Day Celebration that was fast approaching. We had been sending charity, we were reminded, so it's important to come and see what is being produced with that charity.

VISITING HEAVEN

For all its criticisms of the church practices, the buildup to the annual UNOI Independence Day Celebration had the feel of Easter at a typical church. But instead of one Sunday this was a few days.

Much fuss was made about members buying a couple of new suit or dresses for themselves and their children. Class topics turned more heavily to civilization or etiquette so that members didn't go to Heaven and embarrass the whole Study Group by behaving in a savage or uncivilized manner.

Those who had been to Heaven previously would warn the class with horror stories of what would happen to members who did not behave in a way that was in accord with what was being taught. Punishments were said to run from being stood up in class and addressed in front of the 'whole nation', grown men and women being made to stand in the corner, to extra duty at one of the Nation's businesses, to the ever popular and legendary FOI or MGT Beatdown.

All of this, of course, ignored the fact that the other 51 weeks out of the year members rarely showed up to class in uniform or practiced proper civilization amongst each other to say the least. But if being visited in Detroit by Royall was like a visit from the Pope, then going to Heaven was like visiting the Vatican. Everyone sought to live up to the adage 'when in Rome'.

For people that were supposed to be convincing you that you really should move to Kansas, there was an awful lot of time spent trying to paint pictures of how strict and no nonsense Heaven was.

"Brother, keep talking like that, you gone find yourself in a scenario. Them Brothers in Heaven will have you crying at the mic, like they did Bro. Henry."

Finally the day arrived and we were on our way.

I suppose what I felt on that long drive out to Kansas was some mix of anticipation and trepidation. By this time Amanda and I were expecting our first child, which meant the pressure to come to class, participate, get my X and of course, marry the sister was mounting by the day. She would be showing when we arrived in Kansas for Celebration-not exactly the impression she or her family was looking to make.

55

Amanda was an extremely beautiful sister, intelligent and eager about participating in the Nation. Plus she came from what was recognized widely as a powerful family, which made her a great catch in the eyes of any Brothers who were looking for a wife.

Without question it was frowned upon for Sisters in the Nation to talk to, much less date, much, much less have a baby out of wedlock with a scruffy, rough looking, lost-found brother who wasn't even taking the idea seriously.

Like I said, not a great look.

All that being said, almost from the instant we arrived I had one of the most amazing and fascinating experiences of my life. I had never seen, nor even really imagined so many clean, apparently happy black people in one place at one time. Hundreds of beautiful brown people milled about exchanging love, peace and smiles.

 The Sisters were breathtakingly beautiful, like nothing I had ever seen. Long flowing dresses and gowns with bright vivid colors, hair adorned with flowers and bows, graceful to the point of almost not touching the ground.

The men varied, some serious, seeming to be in perpetual motion, always on the way to do something of grave importance, others, more friendly, stopping to laugh or ask where you are from.

The elder Brothers usually took the time to enlighten you on some teaching from Royall or the Messenger or some other history of the Nation, especially if you told them you were from Detroit. Everybody had a story about Detroit.

Even today when reflecting upon this experience in Heaven for the first time, one particular event sums up what the visit meant to me.

We had been on Quindaro Blvd. for the Independence Day Street Festival on Saturday. Home to a majority of the Nation's businesses,

Quindaro served, fittingly, as the centerpiece of Independence Celebration Weekend.

Part of the festival included live music by the Nation's band, which required that a portable stage be set up in front of the Diner. As dusk approached, and the performers had come and gone, Bro. Jessie, (who I would come to know well) announced loudly to no one in particular, "This stage needs to be broken down and taken to the back of the diner."

And then the most amazing thing happened.

As if by remote control or by some advanced wifi signal that connected their minds, Brothers came from everywhere to begin breaking the stage down and take it behind the diner. Men who had just been leisurely strolling along Quindaro with their wife, or loading their family into the minivan, immediately stopped what they were doing and went to work.

Equally breathtaking was the unspoken precision and harmony with which the duty was executed. Brothers from opposite ends of the country and varying generational and economic backgrounds, many of whom had never met a day in their life, or at best just met that day, moved in unison, some breaking the stage down, handing each piece to four waiting hands who hauled the heavy 8x4 pieces behind the diner where they were handed off again and stacked neatly.

No one was barking out orders. No one held any official ranks or titles that they felt the need in mentioning. We just moved.

More than any of the businesses that the Nation had bragged about opening, or any of the knowledge that had come from Royall, THIS is what left the greatest impression on me.

I had always been a person who was eager to help, whether it be around the neighborhood doing odd errands, or at the church cleaning up after a wedding. But even at church that behavior was out of the ordinary or forced me to fend off labels like goody two shoes or a kiss up.

In Heaven there were many more experiences like this one; Brothers and Sisters doing what needed to be done, not for accolades but for the sheer joy of doing it.

These businesses and homes, this Nation, this activity was theirs and they jumped at the opportunity to invest in it. Like in all things, you always had some who had ulterior motives, but by and large most of the members I would come to meet were genuinely there to be a part of something positive.

We had come from various destinations across the globe with the hopes of finding something that was true and real. We sought to replace the generational depravity we lived with the picture of Heaven that Royall had been painting for us. In moments like these it seemed to be all too real; a place for, by, and about the Black Man and Woman.

No one followed us around or told us we were not qualified. We didn't need a membership card or ID badge. We were in fact our own ID. This was all ours; The Diner, Supermarket, Service Station, Buses, Vehicles. These Men, These Women, These beautiful, beautiful Children, they were just like us. We were not alone and we had an activity to participate in a Nation to build TOGETHER. And all praise was due to Royall.

I returned to Detroit a changed man.

Well, somewhat.

That year and every year after we would all return to Detroit, charged up spiritually, mentally, emotionally from the experience. That annual visit to Heaven elevated the pressure to go full-time or at least move to Kansas.

Unfortunately (or perhaps fortunately), this feeling quickly dissipated for most of us, much in the way of a New Year's Resolution. The further we got away from that inspired feeling of being around all those like-minded individuals and got back in the hustle and bustle of Detroit, ideas like going full-time or opening up a temple or business in Detroit became a distance notion.

That didn't stop members from continuing to talk a good game. I recall one year after returning from celebration the conversation in class had inherently turned to what we needed to do get things going in Detroit on the level they should be going. Reports had been pouring in from across the Nation about progress being made in other cities.

Maryland had opened a Temple, a restaurant, and was in the midst of building a home for the Royall family, Connecticut had opened a temple and had a television show, and Wichita had a temple and a sandwich shop, and so on.

Meanwhile in Detroit, we had just recently started getting SOME Brothers and Sisters to come to class in dress code, and only ten to fifteen minutes late. As the conversation went on in class as to why things had not progressed at the same level, one of the Brothers rose to his feet, pounded his fist on the table in frustration declaring, "If Detroit doesn't start making some progress soon, then I am taking my family and moving to Heaven by the end of the year!"

Needless to say by the time I moved to Heaven, then to Connecticut, then to Cincinnati, then back to Detroit, eight years later he hadn't gone anywhere.

One thing that we learned in building a nation that certainly has stood the test of time, is that you can tell a person's thinking by their actions. In the case of the Detroit Study Group, we spent as much or more time and energy trying to figure out how to stay ahead of the curve on the latest hustle as we did in class.

Joe had taken pride in the fact that he had rarely, if ever worked a job for 'the white man' and was able to able to make money 'standing on the corner with nothing other than myself' as he put it. He attributed this largely to his upbringing in the Nation of Islam, where Brothers would often sell everything from papers to fruit to hosiery as fundraisers. This produced in him a business acumen that led him to become a successful businessman at an early age and travel the world.

He was one of the very first black store owners in the city by his early twenties, and had crisscrossed the globe on countless business dealings from real estate to wholesaling.

This was a skill that he looked to pass on to his children and those close to them, which included me.

It was during this time I began to take my first baby steps at hustling; the art of looking a set of circumstances and knowing how to shape them to your benefit. Detroit has always been known as a hustler town. If there is a hookup to be had, or way to scheme the system, trust and believe I can find five to ten guys who do it for you 10-20 ways.

And Joe, while managing to keep things legal was among the finest of them. In his early fifties, he had been hustling so long that he knew how to make moves like a master chess player with his head first. He would school us on everything from asking for a manager to get a discount because you showed up to bowling with 14 people to calling corporations to get free coupons for faulty product.

I recall one occasion going out to eat at a restaurant after math class. On this occasion, our server somehow hit his leg on a table as he walked near us, and crumpled to the ground yelping in pain. While the majority of the study group struggled to keep from laughing, Joe promptly made his way to the manager to ask for a discount for having had to watch such a spectacle; which of course he got.

Watching this man negotiate was like watching a torture scene from Saw. He would just slowly, methodically wear a person down until they just gave him whatever he asked, even if just so he would go away.

At first, all of this was foreign to me and I was very uneasy about participating in any type of hustle of any kind, whether it be selling purses or mix tapes, or even asking for discounts or deals for perceived slights that I would normally allow to roll off my back.

Like most people the idea of approaching random people on the street or walking into a room full of strangers and getting them to give you money for whatever product you might have was slightly less painful than having my teeth removed thru my nose.

And for the ones who get past that initial shyness, its entirely different thing to be able to really connect with people in that less than one minute you have to get their attention and trust. So I was naturally apprehensive.

That was until the realities of going from a flat broke college student to being the sole provider for a wife and four kids in less than a year caught up with me.

Amanda was a natural mother and would do a wonderful job of making sure that everyone ate and was healthy, clean, and happy. I had been a father figure for some time, but was learning fast there was a huge difference between being a father and a father figure.

Me and all of the children were very close. Ray and Alan, despite the ten year gap that separated us, were very much my best friends and we spent a great deal of our time playing ball at the various basketball courts around the city, playing video games, and talking. Tammy and I would spend time, and she was a welcome touch of sweetness and softness in my life.

PJ's birth was one of the most scary and amazing moments in my life. His entrance was sudden and dramatic. His Mother would go into labor at 9:15pm at home and he was out by 9:45. It was a lot so I will give you short version:

The doctor yanked on his head.

I wanted to deck him.

I didn't.

The baby was huge. So big I thought something was wrong.

I picked him up.

He didn't cry.

I did.

I had no idea how deeply this child would impact me and perhaps that is a subject for another day, but suffice it to say I have never been closer to another human being than I was to my new born child. I would find peace and refuge in those little eyes that couldn't say a word but told everything I needed to know.

We were a family and all was right in the world.

All the good intentions and high morals in the world can't explain to your wife, who was doing well as a single woman taking care of herself and her child, why she has to ask her Dad, or Brother to borrow a few hundred dollars to do what needs to be done. We would go week after week of the money not adding up to the bills, and having to borrow to put food in front of the kids or pay rent.

At some point when the pantry and icebox is bare the only thing left to swallow is your pride, and you do what must be done.

I would like to be able to say that I was an instant success at hustling but that wasn't true, either. I did excel at establishing relationships with people, and thinking quickly on my feet. I had established myself at a few spots around the city where to this day if I go back there they know me.

Where I did struggle, however, was in the ability to manage money and ultimately to lead my household. Money would come in and either it would go out to wrong places or it just simply wasn't enough. Hustler's rule 3: It's not what you make, it's what you keep, but again, that's another book.

So here we are moving from home to home, staying with my Grandmother, then her dad, then her brother, never experiencing any type of stability, which is affecting the way Amanda views me, which is naturally having a major effect on other aspects of our life.

In one corner she had this young brother, who she knew at heart was a good Dad and husband but simply wasn't living up to his potential, as her family would be all too quick to point out.

Which brings us to the other corner, where you have Allah himself, promising you peace of mind, contentment of heart, money, good homes, friendship in all walks of life. Perhaps things would have been different for Amanda had she been in the cozy or at least palatable position that kept most of the other members from going full-time.

But the more we struggled, the more attractive the idea of going to Heaven became.

As I grew more familiar with nation members and their different stories, this pattern began to bear itself out. As I become more familiar with cults, nations and movements, (good and bad) that came before the UNOI, it became even more familiar; You come to a people who are experiencing their own deep, personal, and generational hell, and provide them with some measure of understanding and peace. This works particularly well if you can point to something outside of them as being the root cause of their problems.

Conservatives: It's the welfare recipients that are destroying this country.

Liberals: Corporate interests are decaying American values.

UNOI: The Whiteman is the Devil and this system is set up for your failure.

Wutang: Waka Flacka is the downfall of hip hop.

They are often all too willing to disassociate themselves from a world that has shown them nothing more than hurt and disappointment after disappointment. In many cases in exchange for that smallest sliver of hope they are willing to commit amazing acts- those of the atrocious nature and otherwise.

As our marriage went further and further down the wrong road, our scenarios in class would eventually lead to phone conferences with officials from Heaven and ultimately, Royall's wives. Not that the outcome would be any different. I would stumble through the conversation unable to articulate my point, while Amanda recalled everything from the type of gum I had chewed on the offending day to how I said what I said and the face I made whilst saying it.

It got to the point where the calls were so predictable that I would pretty much jump to the end of the conversation, " Yes Maam, Sister National, I know that if I just do what it is that I'm supposed to do as a Brother/Husband/Man then scenarios like this wouldn't happen. I just need to do what Father is teaching, and everything else will take care of itself."

Sometimes I really felt this way.

A lot of the times, I didn't.

I had resolved to take the path of least resistance when it came to any conversations with Amanda, her family or the Nation. My priority was being around my children and I would just have to figure out the rest eventually.

So rather than argue, I would plead guilty or no contest and get back to finding some escape from it all.

...which always seems to be where the trouble comes in, doesn't it? Trying to escape what you are afraid or simply unwilling to face.

Some of the time my escape was my kids, other times it was my music. I even began to find enjoyment and peace in being out amongst the people when I was working.

Ultimately, with the perpetual problems in my marriage spilling into the bedroom, and my inability to deal with what was broken in my and Amanda's relationship, that propensity for taking the path of least resistance led me to begin to seek attention outside.

I reasoned, if my woman doesn't respect, appreciate, or desire me then I know plenty of woman who do/will.

Although I didn't set out with the intention of cheating, I deluded myself into thinking that I could just get some friendly attention and everything would be okay. I would learn later that the worst kind of liar is the one who lies to himself.

Things carried on this way with regularity. I would get up go hustle, bring the money home that still never seemed to be enough for what we needed, spend time with the children, steal whatever moments I could to go hoop, make music and sneak some occasional face time from some old female friend or whatever supplemental attention that came from the females my homeboys brought around. Never quite cheating but certainly not being faithful either.

Within the study group things pretty much stayed the same. By this time we had added a couple additional members, but the general malaise of Detroit still marked our meetings.

Since nothing of consequence was going in Detroit (other than whatever the latest hustle was), class centered around the progress and happenings in other areas of the Nation, and of course whatever scenarios members managed to get themselves into.

My reputation began to precede me in this area, as visiting members from around the country had heard of me before they got there. Which couldn't mean anything positive since the only reason to mention my name in Nation's business would be for the hare-brained scenarios I was getting myself in with alarming regularity.

Additionally, we were constantly reminded that our scenarios were now being reported to Allah, himself, and that everything was going on our record. For a group that considered itself the cure to the problems of Christianity, tactics like these were strikingly familiar to those who had grown up in church. If you didn't have the good sense to do right for the right reason, then you better do right because God is watching and he might send you to the hellfire!

And then all hell broke loose.

We walked into class just like any other Sunday.

I recall thinking about some scenario I was hoping Amanda didn't bring out in class, which is why I almost missed it when Bilal opened up class, reading a mandatory national announcement.

Almost. Announcements were usually reserved for the end of class. Once he started speaking it was clear why this one couldn't wait.

"Per direct instructions from Father, Mother of Civilization is now on class F. No members are to accept any phone calls from Mother of Civilization. She is not to receive any assistance of any kind. Any member contacted by Mother is to contact Brother National Secretary James 2X immediately. Does anyone have any questions?"

At first I didn't understand. I thought maybe my ears were playing tricks on me. I scanned the room to see any sort of response from the members. He read it again.

"Per direct instructions from Father, Mother of Civilization is now on class F. No members are to accept any phone calls from Mother of Civilization. She is not to receive any assistance of any kind. Any member contacted by Mother is to contact Brother National Secretary James 2X immediately. Does anyone have any questions?"

I looked around the class again. It felt like I was in the twilight zone.

In the hierarchy of Nation, Moreen, Mother of Civilization was second only to Royall/Allah himself. When she walked into a room full of members, the crowd would part like the red sea as she floated by followed by an entourage of security and her daughters. Paintings of her were sold at Independence Day celebration right alongside Royall's. In fact, they sold at a higher rate. She was the only one other than Royall to have tapes circulated around the Nation that were mandatory listening for the members, the only one whose birthday was acknowledged other than Royall. Even Royall himself was on record as saying that she was prepared by HIM to teach the members and that if she gave an instruction it was as good as him giving it.

And now she was on class F. The worst distinction that could be placed on a member.

THIS.

WAS.

HUGE.

Slowly a few hands began to raise. The couple questions asked just to be clear on 'the what' were answered with such vitriol, that it was clear if you got around to asking for 'the why', you were asking for a fight.

67

But at the end of the day what really needed to be asked? Here was a woman that Royall had placed before the entire nation as being the example of what he was making us into. Not only was she his second in command, she had been taught by him personally. She had authored the MGT and FOI manuals that every member was taught from.

She was the biological daughter of Allah. He had outlined in great detail her duty in final stages of Armageddon; explained how her heart had been hardened against wrong BY HIM, and that she was a perfect reflection of him.

Despite all of this, whatever the details may have been, she had done something so bad that she went being from being 2nd only to Allah to being on Class F, designated for the hell fire.

While the 'hear no evil, see no evil' approach was in full effect during class, light was about to be brought to the many questions that swirled in minds of everyone.

Though the UNOI had its own website on which it documented its many meetings, as well as business openings and posts from Royall and sometimes Moreen, its representatives spent a large amount of time posting and advertising on the sites of its rivals, like FarrakhanFactor.com and Seventhfam.com. Both of these sites were run by followers of the Honorable Elijah Muhammad that were highly critical of the UNOI and Royall.

Despite this fact, UNOI members and officials were permitted to post their meetings and positions without fear of editing or removal by the sites administrators. This was ironic, because on the UNOI website, any posting that ran contrary to the UNOI agenda would be removed post haste. This backfired in the UNOI site being less frequented than its peers.

The internet had added an entirely new element to the ongoing war between these various factions of the NOI. Instead being bound to discussing or oftentimes arguing with those who you might cross paths with in the line of duty, one could engage mindsets from all backgrounds, from atheist to 'orthodox' Islam, to any of the offshoots of the original NOI, anytime, from just about anywhere across the globe.

Like the internet often does, it also added a new level of bravado that many of those posting might not normally have in person. Very few of those posting would use real names, and would make incredible, improvable claims about their knowledge and qualifications as a scholar of Islam. Though most claimed to be a follower of the Honorable Elijah Muhammad, at least half of what was posted was 'slack-talk', gossip, insults, or faith baiting.

By the time the news of Moreen's clash with Royall made it to class, it was already all over the internet.

Many of the questions that we didn't have the freedom to ask were right there on our monitor for the whole world to see. Moreen was going about the business of airing out the Nation's and Royall's dirty laundry much to the delight of their online critics. For people like myself, who were on the fence with the Nation, it proved to be a very valuable look behind the curtain.

In class we got the Secretarial Department approved version of the Nation; the businesses, the FOI, the MGT, to say nothing of the Royall Family and the structure, were all perfect in every way. To put it mildly, we were shocked to find out that things in Heaven were sometimes wilder than what we might have been doing back in the hood.

She wrote:

(posted on farrakhanfactor.com 7/30/2002)

This is Moreen Jenkins/Kelly,
a.k.a. Mother of Civilization (MOC) – TITLED by
Royall. To "Truthbetold" and all others, it is
most certainly time for the truth to be told. Why

has the question not been asked, "Why
did Mother leave?" Royall shared on a mandatory
tape made in California that I wanted to be a
Lost/Found, however it was never shared *why*.
Think over this: math does not allow one to be
lost. I, Moreen Jenkins/Kelly, know math and have
therefore left The United Nation of Islam
because of the practices that were contrary to
what was taught to me from the beginning.
Everything that I have taught under the
title Mother of Civilization was because of what
was taught to me by Royall. However, as things
began to change from these teachings, and the
reason for the changes was shared with me
"[because Royall is Allah, so don't question
him]," caused me to just observe. The more I
observed, the more I saw that the math of what I
was taught is true, however the practices were
not. When you teach someone that 1+1=2 and then
teach them the formula HOW it is true, you cannot
come and share with that same person that has
learned the formula that 1+1=3 because "I said
so, being Allah." The things that were
asked of me to do by Royall - pertaining to the
members, in getting with Royall's wives to
deceive the members because of the members' love
for me, I was to put on a front, to merge with
Royall's wives, to abuse the members - I refused.
I do not need to receive any power, material
wealth, or fame by stepping on anyone.

As far as Brother Jerry leaving to be
with Mother, Brother Jerry left first. As far as
Brother Jerry being the father of Mother's
youngest child, that was sanctioned by Royall, to
show Joseph F. Kelly, a.k.a. The King, that he
could not leave and turn his butt up to Royall

*without a consequence. Joseph F. Kelly never
could accept the fact that he is Elijah returned,
and due to his extreme personalism against Moreen
and Royall, he left several times, and it was
explained by Royall that The King was "off on
assignment." Further, the one thing Royall taught
that Allah *cannot* do, which is lie, was done.
So in that happening, this must be the time that
He (Royall) taught that a clone of Himself would
come – to deceive and test the members – and
attempt to dismantle the UNOI.*

*When I witnessed this for myself, I had nothing
left to hold onto, so I shared with Father
(Royall) that I wanted to leave. On several
occasions, He (Royall) shared with me (MOC),
"No," and if I did leave (run away), that I would
meet him "out there." So I remained, for the time
being. In my moment of going through the mental
fear and turmoil, I confided in a few members.
They were of the same thinking as me – that I
should leave, one being Laota Rassoull Favors.
The pressure continued, and the threats of my
life increased by Royall Elliott Jenkins, so to
escape momentarily the pressures, I consumed some
alcohol, supplied to me by my son, Daniel Aubrey
Jenkins. He (Daniel) attempted to offer me some
marijuana, saying the alcohol was no good for my
organs. I refused to take the marijuana, however
he (Daniel Aubrey Jenkins), indulged – and
indulges heavily – in marijuana, along with
drinking and frequenting various nightclubs.
Royall's wives, Dana Peach and Etenia, a.k.a.
Sister National First Lieutenant, participated in
partaking of the alcohol also.*

After the flag raising ceremony at the past

Independence Day Celebration, Royall Elliott
Jenkins shared with me (MOC) that if I did not
merge with his wives - to perpetrate a fraud on
the members - that He would take everything that
He gave me back, starting with the death of my
daughter Ra-kiia, or "whatever her name is," as
He said. When that was shared, it left me no
choice other than to do what a mother would do,
which is to protect her children. So I left on
July 10, 2002 with just a few credit cards that
were in my name. I, being over the Nation's
checking account in Kansas City, Kansas, left it
alone, did not take *a penny*, proving that what
Royall taught concerning my character - that my
heart was hardened against wrong - would not
allow me to do so. I took a few clothing items,
my daughter (Ra-kiia), and the 1987 Chevrolet
that Royall gave to me. He (Royall) instructed
the car to be reported stolen. After Laota
Rassoull Favors shared with Him where I was
located (at a hotel), Ihsan Mahmoud and Douglas X
came to the hotel, removed the tags from the car,
called the police in Kansas City, Missouri, and
reported the car stolen. Further, they shared
they did not want to press charges, and because
they did not want to press charges, the cops knew
it was personal.

The next day after I (MOC) left, Royall
instructed that the locks on the house in which I
resided be changed, ensuring that I could not
return. He then instructed that all of my
belongings - clothes, jewelry, shoes, etc. - be
collected and removed from the house, and taken
out of town via UNOI transportation. He then
called upon Joseph F. Kelly to return to the home
on 810 Troup Avenue. Joseph F. Kelly refused.

72

After his refusal, Royall spoke to him directly
and made him an offer he could not refuse, after
he was gone close to two years, enjoying monies
from the UNOI account, monies from his SSI,
living in the Q45 that a member gave Joseph
during a raffle, per Royall's instructions,
working out at the YMCA daily, and going to the
doctor for MRI scans to see if there was
something wrong with his head as to why he,
Joseph, could not understand how he, Joseph, was
Elijah returned, taught by Royall. Question: why
is nothing said, positive or negative, about
Joseph F. Kelly? Could it be that he is a partner
with, or the supplier of, information in recent
posts (concerning the UNOI and the Royall Family)
that exclude himself?

So, after 17 years of complete loyalty and
dedication to the UNOI nation building, the end
result for Moreen Jenkins/Kelly is having
all of her children except for Ra-kiia taken from
her, her clothes and possessions taken from her,
her home taken from her, her bank account closed
out and taken from her, her being ostracized and
excommunicated by the very members against whom
she would not perpetrate a fraud, causing her to
go to the very people that He (Royall) has taught
are the enemy – the white man (devil). They (the
government) have given me more assistance than He
(Royall), and what I am posting, Royall Elliott
Jenkins shared if I go to his enemies (the white
man, his biological family members not with him,
or any disgruntled member), He would kill me in
such a way that He cannot mention. He just said
to me it would be "slow and painful."

He (Royall) taught me (MOC) as well as the

members that there would be a clone of Himself, and the only way that we could identify that the clone was not Him (Royall) would be to use the math and the formula of it. This past Independence Celebration, for the first time, He (Royall) said that He was here representing right and wrong, and that we, the members should stick with the truth and math, not a person – including Himself (Royall) – and that is what I, Moreen Jenkins/Kelly a.k.a. MOC, am doing, and encourage all others to do likewise. Royall E. Jenkins has always taught us that my son, Daniel Aubrey Jenkins' (who is the head of the FOI) sole purpose on this planet is to stop me, his mother, Moreen Jenkins/Kelly, and that he, Daniel A. Jenkins, would be my sole test. Now, Daniel A. Jenkins is having his way with any Sisters (MGT) in the UNOI of his choosing, one in particular he shared with her that Royall (Father) sanctioned him (Daniel) and her to be intimate. After this (the intimacy) took place, he shared with her that he could no longer be with her because Royall would kill her. It brought questions to the sister, and she sought an audience with Royall, under the thinking that her life was in danger, to share with Royall what His grandson (Daniel A. Jenkins) had shared.

Royall and His wives, Deborah White and Sis. First Lt. Etenia, shared with the sister that she is to look at it as though she "was blessed to experience royalty." As a result, the sister was removed from her post in the UNOI, and placed in Class F indefinitely. The excuse that was given to the members for the sister being removed from the post was that she was not *being* the post, and Daniel A. Jenkins is rewarded by getting the former Captain's (of Atlanta, Georgia) convertible while he (the former Captain) catches the school bus with his wife and child. He (Daniel) is being rewarded with clothing, shoes for every day of the year, power and position. According to Daniel, while he left and went to stay with the stripper in California, Daniel had intimate relations with the current Captain of California, Sultan's wife, and she is the MGT Captain of California, who frequents nightclub activities often (as reported by Captain Sultan to Brother National Secretary James 2X and myself, MOC).

There's much more, such as the hate crime that Daniel A. Jenkins, Aaron Carroll (son-in-law of Royall) and others participated in, that is in the media today. They kidnapped a young Black man, beat him to near-death, Aaron Carroll breaking each of the young man's fingers with a bat, one at a time. Other Brothers, such as Rodney Hadley, participated in the beating as well, yet Daniel A. Jenkins gave the final, paralyzing blow to this young man, who is still our brother, all because this young man allegedly threw a rock at the UNOI school bus.

Wayman Favors is using his clout as being an attorney to retrieve documents that Moreen Jenkins/Kelly has filed against Joseph F. Kelly and Daniel A. Jenkins to try and stay a step ahead of her, and her four smallest children were taken out oftown per Wayman Favors' counsel, although the judge in Kansas City, Kansas has given Moreen Jenkins/Kelly temporary custody of all of her children under the age of 18. Royall is using His power, prestige, and the UNOI's money to keep Moreen Jenkins/Kelly from having her children - that she birthed - out of spite for her leaving.

There's more to be shared on the ins and outs of what has been taking place in the UNOI, and even though my life has been threatened, I am willing to take the chance and share it. To reiterate, since my heart has been hardened against wrong, the wrong that has been perpetrated against myself and the members of the UNOI and anyone else involved leaves me no choice but to take the necessary steps in righting the wrong. I do not have a penny to my name, just a few credit cards. If anyone is willing to assist me in standing up with TRUTH and what is right, I can be reached at 913-636-2677. I am in the process of looking to purchase, by way of the credit cards, transportation since I have no employment to get to and from the various places that I need to visit to expose this once and for all. And anyone that is in harmony with truth, extend your will to ensure the success of what must be done.

Signing off,
Mother of Civilization

p.s. Although Royall has taught for many years that no one could replace, stand in for, or challenge the position of the
Mother of Civilization, He has now stood up His concubine, Jocelyn Greenwood, as the UNOI stand-in Mother of Civilization and asked the question "[do His new tailor-made suits and shoes that His wives dress Him in make Him look like a pimp?]." That's a hint to the wise to be able to use math

*to determine who is before them. Refer to the
Book of Kings, after Chapter IX, pertaining to
Solomon's wives, and that will explain the other
material possessions (new Chevrolet Avalanche,
Infiniti Q45, control of the members' hard-earned
charity, etc.). Lastly, Father taught on a tape
that His wives *think* that they know Him, but
they don't. Food for thought…for the thinking
ones.*

Needless to say she had the internet going nuts. The Nation did its part
in verifying the validity of her statements by having a quick knee jerk
reaction to every one of her posts attempting to refute her claims.
Moreen's initial post went up a little after 5am. Five hours later Royall
had posted his response on the UNOI website. Knowing little to no one
would see it there The National Secretary James 2x posted a link to
Royall's response on Farrakhan Factor:

*This apparent treachery and the attempt to stab
the Nation in the back is clear evidence of the
success that we are stepping into. Since I,
ROYALL, Allah in Person, Have taught and Am still
teaching one to think Mathematically, read over
the post carefully, and then answer the question:
"Why was this done in the manner in which it
was?" Placing this message on another board other
than our own cannot be proven that it is the
members of The United Nation of Islam who were
trying to be protected.*

*I Am Placing this on the UNOI Message Board so as
to bear witness of the seriousness and the
need of a house-cleaning By Me of The House that
I Am Building.*

All who have studied and learned will see this for what it is -- a spoiled brat, kicking and screaming, regardless to what damage they do to their Brothers and Sisters, they are pitching "a fit to the high heavens" because she cannot have her way.

I, ROYALL, Allah in Person, Am not a liar. I will accept no partner. And when it comes to Me, the only partner that could be one is Satan. And regardless to how he shows up -- whether in my daughter, or whoever -- Satan will not be accepted. The majority of what is posted by Mother (Moreen) has been twisted to reflect other than Truth. It is an emotional plea to receive help from the sympathizers of Satan. So I shall repeat, that will not be a wise thing to do.

This is a matter between Me --- Allah -- and Satan, and my spoiled daughter. So be very careful how you place yourself in it.

Signed,

ROYALL, Allah in Person

This of course set into motion or intensified an already raging cyber war of words. On one side you had Royall and the UNOI, and on the other you had Moreen and the bevy of critics and detractors of the UNOI .

This would go on to include Royall's own sons, Hanif and Clint, who had long ago left the UNOI after short stints, and had now come to the aide of their sister. Before long former members of the UNOI began coming out of the woodwork to pile on.

This was all to the delight of Royall's critics and those outright jealous of the progress he had made.

Most took every opportunity to twist the knife, or pour salt on wounds that had been opened up by the appearance of Moreen, her Brothers, and other former members on the website.

The UNOI did itself no favors by reacting to nearly every comment or insult that was hurled at them. Then they started making things worse.

On one side you had Moreen and the Detractors (sounds like hot 60s soul group almost). On the other side you had the UNOI and those who saw the divinity in their work.

And then somewhere in all of this chaos there was the third group. That group, which included me, that was far from fans or devotees of the UNOI, but weren't quite buying everything that the UNOI haters, especially Moreen were selling. After all, if all of that was going on, she didn't seem to have an issue with any of it when the members were lining up to touch the hem of her garment.

 The situation provided us with the opportunity to ask a few questions to gain understanding about what was being stated from Moreen and the Nation.

The anonymity of the web, along with a working knowledge of mathematical thinking allowed me to ask questions in a manner which would not be offensive, and not have to worry about being looked at as being a detractor. At least that was my hope.

Wrong.

Unfortunately UNOI officials were so in the mode of being on the defensive that ANY question presented was being met with hostility.

If the circumstances of Moreen leaving backed up whatever doubts I had, then my subsequent interactions with UNOI representatives served as the final nail in the coffin as far as I was concerned.

Officials who I had heard speak with intelligence and insight in front of hundreds of people, not to mention personal audiences I had been granted, now flailed wildly into the darkness of the internet, accusing me of being devilish, cowardly and even twice of saying that I was Moreen.

The questions I had were not much different from the other 'detractors' or members who had left or were in the process of leaving the UNOI; if Moreen had been taught and prepared by Allah himself, was a sister who according to the UNOI, could only reflect the ideas of the man she was with (Royall), then how was she now suddenly the author of the confusion that was now being exposed?

This was not to say she wasn't complicit, or even the source of some of it, but the bar Royall had set for himself was that he was Allah, the all knower. We had been taught that Allah either does a thing or permits it to be done.

Hell, the bar that had been set for the Brothers was that the women in our charge represented our thinking, and if they went wrong it was a reflection on us. These facts alone justified at least some sort of explanation.

After a few days of going back and forth with UNOI ministers and the National Secretary, my mind had been made up; I didn't need any convincing. The UNOI was a sham and I was getting out before they started passing out the Dixie cups of funny tasting Kool-Aid.

That of course was easier said than done. Although Amanda and I had continued to have a very rocky relationship, we both had resigned to stick the situation out for the sake of the children. For me that meant compromising by participating in the Nation. For her, that meant dealing with my wishy washy ways and my lack of ability to bring income into the home.

For all of our turmoil, the thing I always admired about Amanda was that she was a dedicated mother to not only our children but she fulfilled a very much needed maternal role for Ray and Al. Though our friction was apparent to any adult who was around us for five minutes, the kids had the first semblance of a stable home environment that any of them had ever had.

Despite my best wishes, the turmoil going on in the Nation had no effect on Amanda's will to go to Heaven and be full-time. If anything it seemed to only strengthen her resolve.

Whatever drama was going on within the Nation was not nearly as bad as the drama and turmoil going on in her own life. It's one thing to read about rumors of someone's troubles, yet an entirely different one to be trying to escape the reality of your own.

In the Nation we had been offered friendship in all walks of life, peace of mind, contentment of heart, even good homes and money. All of this at a time when our life consisted of plenty of past due bills, no sense of direction, moves in and out of the homes of our family and the straw that would break the camel's back: infidelity.

Even today it's hard not to feel like an asshole when I say I never cheated in any relationship until I got married, but unfortunately it's true. I was always the hopeless romantic; the guy who would take extreme umbrage when people would say things like, "All men cheat."

How dare you sir!

I had seen men I looked up to cheat on their wives and KNEW I would never be THAT guy!

To be clear, I still am of the opinion that not all men cheat, but I now know unfortunately it is not something I can say I never did. (Understatement Alert)

It had far less to do with my wife and our relationship than it did with my lack of development as a man. Not different from many young couples, as our financial, emotional and marital struggles began to pile up, home life began to seem like work.

Rather than confront the issues that I didn't like, I sought refuge in things like playing ball with the fellas, writing and performing in hip hop with a few local cats I grew up with, or even going to Wayne State to do more studying about the things I was hearing in class.

By this time I had become a far better hustler than when I started out. I had established myself at a couple spots around town; on the Westside at Seven Days West and on the east at the Shoppers World Plaza. I was also learning quickly that being a hustler in the city of Detroit had its benefits.

Again, Detroit is a hustler's town, and there is nothing that was respected more than a young brother skillful at getting out there and making money for himself. At this time I was selling everything from bootleg movies and CD's to fireworks to weed to ladies jeans and purses.

I was out amongst the people making connections, meeting and greeting for at least six to eight hours a day. A great portion of this population was young women on their way to buy a cute a little outfit for the club, some air force ones for their baby, or grabbing a 27 piece on the way to getting their hair done.

My work was the perfect excuse to stop and talk, even if they had no intention of buying anything, though many did. Numbers were often exchanged, and calls under the guise of business would turn with regularity to what I or she was doing this weekend, if we could hook up, if I had any friends for her girls, did I have a woman, etc. etc. etc.

At first these talks consisted of just some flirting over the phone, whenever I could get away to a pay phone. (Everybody didn't have a cellphone yet, OK.) Unfortunately or perhaps fortunately, I was as new and poor at cheating as I was at marriage.

Amanda would inherently find and confront me about numbers she found in my pockets, answer my phone if I had a 'buirn-out' phone at that moment, or even one occasion catching me on the phone with a female suitor when I was too dense to leave the neighborhood to find a payphone.

This of course intensified the vicious cycle that was our relationship.

The notion that I would be struggling so mightily as a provider and then turn around and have the audacity to seek refuge in the arms of other females was unfathomable to Amanda.

Catching me in the act only caused her attraction for me to wane even further, while also causing our affection in and out of the bedroom to grow even colder, which in turn would leave me even more susceptible to the advances of female suitors.

I would leave a house where my wife would have and show little to respect, only to be showered by the attention and affection of females who would be more than happy to have some of my time.

Eventually these brief emotional and mental getaways began to turn more and more physical. Not quite sex but well across the line, some kissing, some making out, etc.

Sometimes I would get away with the crime, often I did not. When I did get busted, my misdeeds would lead me to yet another phone counsel session with structure in Heaven. After thirty minutes of grilling on the phone by Royall, one of his wives, or a national laborer, not only would I lose standing in my marriage but, Royall and the UNOI would look more and more like the saviors they said they were in Amanda's eyes.

This back and forth eventually led to the approval of Amanda's long standing request to come to Heaven as a full-time member. This approval was to include Amanda, all of the children and, for some reason, myself.

Of all the things I knew, I KNEW I was NEVER, EVER in a million leap years going to Kansas permanently. Based on the horrible image of Heaven that had been painted by the members in Detroit, the drama that had just went down with Moreen, and my reputation, which I knew would precede me, I knew I wanted no parts of going there. One of Royall's wives echoed the same thing no less, after a phone interview, telling me it sounded like I wanted Amanda to go, but not me. This was true.

I was not happy but I knew neither was she. Despite all that was going on with us I still cared about Amanda's happiness. I knew that she was very dedicated to this idea and that she had experienced enough of this world to know she wanted a change.

Already in her young life she had lost a brother, her first love and too many friends to street violence. Around this time, one of her close childhood friends had committed suicide by walking into a Police Station and opening fire.

Our financial problems and my infidelity were only icing on the cake.

Now we had been approved to come to Heaven and were simply on the waiting list. Somewhere in my mind, I knew the moment of that call to come to Kansas would be the breaking point. She would take Tamika and PJ to Kansas and then it would be me and the boys just like before. I repeat: I was NOT going to Heaven. Sounds like I am STILL trying to convince myself, huh?

It is amazing how the best things happen at the worst times and then the worst things happen at the best times, though I am not sure in this instance which was which.

Amidst all of the confusion that was our lives, we had come to be pregnant again. Oddly enough our pregnancies were often some of the best and most peaceful times of our relationship. Perhaps it the beautiful promise of new life that would give us the added inspiration to get on the same page at least in this one aspect of our lives.

No matter what we didn't like about the other person or our situation, we both respected and appreciated the other as the best parent a child could hope for.

Pregnancies meant shopping for baby clothes, more eating out, more talking about the future and of course less intimacy. In case you missed it, that last one wasn't good.

No matter how much a baby on the way inspired us to work on our relationship, our bed always seemed to grow the coldest when my blood grew the hottest. Maybe I would win the battle between my conscious and my libido that first night, but eventually I would find myself making up excuses to leave the house-and then making up excuses to find myself alone with old friends.

The first time you cheat on your wife is a disjointed experience. You feel disconnected from yourself; like you are watching the entire episode from outside your own body.

This makes sense.

Your wife, your family, if you have one, is your identity. They are, in effect, you. If you have pulled together people, from various places, including parts of yourself, and brought them together to be a family, what can be more treasonous than acting against the best interest of said union?

What's worse is you know all of this when you are doing it. The various aspects of your ego and consciousness scream it at the top of their lungs. This is not to imply that its out of your or in this case my control, It is quite the opposite. You listen to this dialogue in your head as you watch your body take those steps, open that door, drive that car to that place.

You make the conscious decision to ignore the protesting of your morals and listen entirely to the faulty reasoning of your ego. 'I deserve this. It won't affect anything else if I steal away for these few minutes. This is a victimless crime'

This led to me working out my frustrations in the back seat of my Cadillac, which led to the subject of my 'few minutes' bragging to her cousin about how good it was, which led her other cousin, who happened to overhear this conversation and also happened to be good friends with Amanda, to write a letter describing in detail the events of this particular episode. And place said letter in the mailbox so that it is waiting on Amanda the next time we all returned home.

Did I mention what a horrible husband I was?

Whatever good feelings the pregnancy had brought about were shattered with the revelation of this latest indiscretion. Cloud nine evaporated and we came violently hurtling back to Earth.

I repeat: violently.

Any thoughts I had that this would be the garden variety break-up to make-up were shattered when Amanda told me to get out. Instinctively, I tried to talk my way out of the scenario, presenting her with the same BS that I had sold to myself.

She wasn't buying.

In all fairness though, she didn't get to hear my whole sales pitch as she came hurtling out of the kitchen, knife in hand, with the aggression of a world class athlete who was NOT pregnant.

Apparently, she REALLY wanted me to get out.

I have been in my share of physical confrontations in the streets with men twice my size, with and without weapons, across the country, in hoods familiar and unfamiliar to me. I have been threatened by criminals, law enforcement, and FOI the same. Yet I have never felt the sense of fear I felt in that moment with that 5'3 pregnant woman coming at me with a kitchen knife.

So yeah, I got out.

I made the necessary call and I was rooming with my family for the foreseeable future.

After a brief cooling off period, we began communicating again slowly but surely. This didn't change anything, however. We were done.

Enough was enough. Amanda had put in her request for an official divorce in the Nation. On the phone conference I, still racked with guilt, had said I wasn't in harmony with a divorce but understood why she was. I was read the riot act, and we were told that Father would get back to us with a response.

What I didn't know at the time was that Royall rarely granted a divorce unless the Brother in the relationship agreed that it was over.

So with our marital status up in the air, we continued to prepare for this new life that we were bringing into this crazy situation. Amanda would call me to let me know when the OB-GYN appointments were and I would come pick her up.

These visits would be our only opportunity to talk, which meant whatever pent up emotion she had been holding onto usually spilled out or hung silently over us as we rode to doctor's office.

On what was to be a routine visit for our scheduled ultrasound around six months, she was called to the back to get ready for the technician. I hung out in the lobby after it was made clear that my presence was not welcome in the ultrasound room. Not having much of a leg to stand on, I patiently waited for her to return so we could leave, and I could take the rest of my lashing on the way home.

The next thing I saw was Amanda standing in the doorway sobbing, tears streaming down her face. Instinctively, I went to her. She put her arms around me and began crying into my chest. My eyes began to water as I anticipated the worst. She tried to gather her words tried to explain what she had seen on the ultrasound screen.

Something was wrong with our baby.

The Doctor would come out shortly to explain. The baby had anencephaly. His/her skull and brain had failed to properly form which meant that the child would be stillborn.

I was floored. We had miscarried before PJ was born, but very early on in the pregnancy. At this point we were more than halfway to the baby's due date and developing the strong emotional attachment that comes with the months of anticipation of your child.

Now we were being told that our only options were to have an abortion or for Amanda to carry the baby for three more months and deliver this baby who not live more than a minute outside the womb.

I didn't need to think about it. There was no way I was going ask her to carry a baby for three months grieving the moment of its birth.

We were in shock.

This process of grieving for our unborn child, coming up with the money to take care of situation, and explaining it to the children brought Amanda and I together one more time. Even in this horrible moment of grief, our children seemed to be the only thing could get us on the same page.

It was during this ordeal that Amanda got the call that she was waiting on.

Bro. Mike 7x, the head of the Nation's Trucking Company would be arriving early October to pick her and her items up and bring her to Heaven.

Part of me had been anticipating that day, but now I wasn't sure why. For all of our back and forth and emotional rollercoaster, Amanda was still my best friend.

We clashed on so many issues. She wasn't the woman I wanted, I wasn't the type of man she needed. I was childish and dishonest, she was overbearing and inconsiderate. And we couldn't live without each other.

The most important thing in our life was our children. We both were very family oriented. In each other we saw an ideal parent, who would fight and scrap to the death for our kids.

The problem was most of the time we were fighting and scrapping with each other. Even still, Amanda emphasized to me that ALL of us were approved to come to Heaven and it would be in my best interest to not miss this opportunity. We had not yet received word on our divorce, and I was still not back in the home.

I assured her that I would. BUT, not before I paid back some of this debt that we were leaving behind. Yeah that was the ticket, had to pay back this debt.

She would go on to Heaven and I would follow shortly after. The Study Group supported this motion not in small part because much of the money I was to pay back was borrowed from them.

I suppose it was also an opportunity to put some space between Amanda and me. By now it was clear that I was not the first choice for their sister/daughter and even I knew they were constantly asked by the Brothers in Heaven about Amanda.

While Amanda and I were blinded by the all emotions that constantly swirled around our relationship, anyone with common sense could see my actions were those of a man who did not want to be where he was.

Even though I stated my intention to follow my family to Heaven, there was some serious doubt as to whether I would set foot in class again once they left Detroit, much less make the trek to Kansas.

This was a logical conclusion except for one factor. Because I had said I would be right behind her, I couldn't come up with any logical reason for her not to take Ray and Alan with her. While I could reluctantly deal with the fact that PJ was with his mother in Heaven, those boys were my responsibility.

I couldn't just leave them hanging.

I had given my word to their Father that I would look after them. They were my first loves and my first family, so if they were going to Heaven I had no choice but to follow, even if just temporarily.

C-2

Heaven

After weeks of foot dragging, back sliding, and day-to-day hustling, with no real agenda or urgency on my part, I began to realize that I had better get to Heaven as quickly as possible or find myself caught in the 'Detroit Trap'.

I had often shared with people that Detroit had ample opportunity to participate in whatever sin Black people may be interested in; sex, drugs, gambling, clubbing, and general thuggery and tom foolery. My life had become a great example of that.

 With my family gone, my daily ritual was waking up, smoking a lil weed, running to my wholesaler to cop whatever product I might be selling that day, then taking what money I had left from that and going to Kmart and buying my outfit for the day, which usually amounted to a pair of jean shorts and a t shirt or polo shirt.

I would promptly arrive at my 'eastside spot' around 11am. At this time I was setting up at the Shoppers World Plaza at Warren and Conner on the eastside. This was one of those bustling shopping areas that you find in most ghettos. You could find all the essential stores that tend to thrive in inner cities, i.e. Footlocker, Kids Footlocker, beauty supply store, dollar store, Rainbow, etc.

Here I would post up and offer my wares to the people coming in and out of the stores. As much as it was a means to get product off, it was also a ghetto networking paradise. For every paying customer I met, I would meet a fellow hustler who had whatever it was that I didn't sell, or some female who was more interested in me than what it was I was selling.

Most of the shops closed at 7pm, so at about 6pm I would start calling the homies or whatever females I met that day to see what was on the agenda for the evening. This usually led to me heading to my band mate's house for a smoke-vibe-bullshit session, then from there into whatever was cracking for the night, which invariably meant some drinking, some more weed, possibly hitting the studio or the club, and probably some promiscuity.

This endless cycle was my basic routine for the six weeks that I was without my family. This activity also coincided with me attending Mathematical Thinking Class less and less. Although I failed to see any real benefit in attending and rarely felt like I was learning anything, I realize now Math Class had provided at least some pursuit of self-enrichment or spiritual enlightenment that I would have otherwise not had at all.

However with no one at home to force the issue, the lack of any real motion or activity in Detroit, along with the great controversy that was still unfolding between Royall and Moreen, let's just say I was less than inspired to get up on Sunday morning and make that trek to the Butzel center. I wouldn't attend and I really cared less and less about what those in class thought about it.

At the same time, as I was slipping deeper and deeper in the nothingness that was becoming my life, my mind could not escape the thought of Ray and Alan. They had left with Amanda and the rest of my family with the understanding that I would be arriving shortly thereafter. After Amanda left and I became accustomed to seeing myself as a single man, I resigned to the idea that she would be in Kansas with Tammy and PJ. But Ray and Alan were supposed to be where I was, in this case in Detroit.

I had given my word to my family, myself, and their father that I would take care of them at all costs. In fact they were my family before I even had a family. So even though I knew Amanda had taken them on as her own children, and would never allow anything negative to happen to them, I knew I had to go get them. That was my mindset. Not that I was going out there to live or stay but I was going out there to get my boys and coming right back.

To everyone I talked to about it, I would phrase it just that way. I would drop my personal effects over my homeboy Jay's house and say, "Hey I will be back to get this in a couple months." I would let my family know I won't be gone long and the boys will be right back with me. I told everyone; family, friends, customers, women. Unless you were with the Nation, you understood I would be back in no time.

Had I known then that it was commonly discussed and expected amongst the Detroit Study Group members that I wouldn't last long in Heaven before getting kicked out, perhaps I would have been just as up front with them.

My plan was to leave with a brother named Ricky who was from Romulus, MI and had been approved to go to Heaven the same time as me. His was another classic case of how things went in Detroit. He had been thoroughly lectured, sold and convinced on all the reasons as to why he should go to Heaven and be full-time under nation's care by a bunch of people who could name 1001 reasons why that same logic did not apply to them.

Ricky and I were originally scheduled to leave late November, but we had pushed back our departure date several times, once or twice due to financial reasons and a couple more times due to probably not wanting to let go. However, I called one Sunday and he said he really needed to leave, and I told him I felt the same. I was short on funds but he agreed to spend his last money (literally) on my ticket so that we could leave the next day. And so we did.

Other than missing a connection and somehow ending up in Omaha, our bus trip was relatively uneventful.

We arrived in Kansas City, KS at approximately 10pm one evening early December 2002. Bro. Kaaba and another brother met us at the bus station, with an unenthusiastic greeting, helped us put our luggage into the 80s model Ford Taurus and we were whisked off to Quindaro Blvd.

Thinking back now, I recall riding in the back of the Nation's vehicle with a million thoughts and emotions running through my mind, body and soul, a million miles a second; anxious to see my family again as soon as possible, wondering what my treatment would be in this place that all that the Detroit members were scared to go, the peculiar feeling of still being a little high from my going away party, curious how my reputation would precede me, if I would see any of the effects of the Moreen gossip on the web, along with thoughts of what would happen between Amanda and me once I arrived.

Despite all of this my overall attitude was to remain calm and open minded. Contrary to my many negative experiences with the Detroit Study Group and my confrontations with UNOI on the web, I had nothing but positive memories from my two visits to Heaven. The Brothers had always treated me well, I was always learning something new, and more than anything else was inspired by the experience of being around a large group of my people and having positive activity to participate in. Even though I had already had my mind made about the Nation and my will to not be a part of it, I knew that I would enjoy this particular aspect of being in Kansas.

We had put in a request to stop by the MGT house where Amanda and PJ and Tammy were staying.

The MGT house was the house set up specifically to house the single Sisters. Like most of the homes in Heaven it housed an unusually large number of the members. The house was at the bottom of a hill that dead ended next to the cemetery. There were no street lights at the house which, when coupled with the neighboring cemetery gave it an almost cryptic appearance.

We pulled up in front of the house and before we got out of the car good, Tammy was at the door giving us a couple of much needed big hugs.

We stepped into the front dining room as Sisters scrambled to ensure that they were properly covered since there were Brothers in the home. The Sisters who weren't scrambling peered curiously from around corners or found some reason to come through the living room to get a look at us. There seemed to be a million people in the house. I heard Amanda's familiar voice from upstairs.

As Amanda came to the top of the stairs, she instructed PJ to come with her and they began to make their way down the stairs. Now up until this point I had been relatively calm, simply taking things as they came. However, with each step they took down those stairs I began to feel something I can only describe as nervousness.

Only thing I have ever felt close to it was the feeling I had when each of my children were born; that feeling of being excited to see the most important person in the world, mixed with the fear and apprehension of not being sure if everything is going to be alright.

As they turned the corner Amanda gave me a hug, and then the oddest thing happened. PJ didn't budge.

Well to be exact he did budge; where his Mommy's leg went he followed. He was hiding behind her as if he didn't even remember me. My heart sinks in my stomach even now I simply recall the moment.

I instantly began to regret every moment that I had stayed behind.

I was close to all of my children. I took pride in the fact that I had developed a unique relationship with each of them, each one having its own particular nuances. But I would be lying if I didn't say I have a special bond with PJ. He was my firstborn biological child. From the moment he came from his Mother's womb, we had an uncanny closeness. As an infant he would rarely cry and when he did all I had to do was pick him up and he would stop instantly.

In many respects he is a best friend to me, and probably the person I am the closet to on this planet. Anyone who had ever seen us together would marvel at the closeness we have.

Well at that particular moment, someone looking on would not have even been able to guess that the little even boy knew me.

It took major coaxing and a bit of scolding from his mother to get the boy to simply hug me. We said a few pleasantries and then made our way to the FOI apartment.

The FOI apartment was above the donut shop that the Nation rented. The long stairway at the door between the Donut Shop and the Diner led up to about a 15x20 foot space that was split between a kitchen and a living room. Both portions of the room were unspectacular, with a wooden dining table with about five chairs around it sitting in the center of the kitchen.

It was at this table where the Brothers would break bread of the physical, mental and spiritual nature, sharing everything from bean soup, to a discussion/debate as to what was the true meaning of English Lesson C-1 in the problem book or more often than not going over a scenario that had taken place amongst the Brothers.

The living room had two chairs on either side of a couch that sat directly across a 20 inch television set. The whole setup was just as one might expect it to be for a group of full-time Brothers who had little to no time nor concern for aesthetics.

Connected to this large room were three bedrooms that would house as many as 13 Brothers, often with another spare brother or two crashing on the couch in the living room for good measure.

The bedrooms mirrored the rest of the house in that they were set up for optimum use and not at all for prettiness. They each had two bunk beds on either side of the room and the largest of the three rooms had an additional bed. Each brother was responsible for the area on and around his bed. Closet and dresser space was shared. The rooms typically stayed pretty clean, depending which Brothers were staying in the room and if inspections were going on at the time. However, all things considered, things went pretty smooth and if a brother got too out of line we would have an impromptu math class or in some cases civilization class on him.

One of the major concepts the Nation emphasized was civilization. This is what made what would normally be too many people in one space work.

There was a system to everything in the home. The cleaning of the home, the cooking of the food, the school work of the youth in the home, what would be watched on the television, even all the way up to the appearance of the Brothers. Everyone was charged with the responsibility to make sure that these systems were enforced at all times.

If a brother transgressed the system and you were present and did nothing about it, you were liable to get addressed as much or worse than the brother who broke the law in the first place. This created a very no nonsense environment and gave each brother a boost of confidence to know that if he took a stand on someone breaking the law he would most likely, be backed up.

In most cases this boost was enough to get said offender in check. Other times it would depend entirely upon which brother was doing the checking and which brother was doing the transgressing.

In Heaven, Royall had set up a society based entirely upon Mathematical Thinking. So everything in Heaven was run on the principles of Mathematical Thinking.

This meant the greater a person's understanding of Mathematical Thinking, the greater their ability to know, be in harmony with, and in some cases, circumvent the law.

As with any other method of thinking, government, or religion, Mathematical Thinking was a great system. When used in its purest form, it would solve many if not all of the problems we face on a day to day basis. However, just like every one of these other systems, when used with the wrong motivations it could quickly become very dangerous.

For instance, if I caught a brother transgressing the law, however I was not as sharp as he was in either knowing, or simply expressing the math, then he had a very good chance of escaping any real consequence. Similar to how a man who has a better lawyer has better chance of getting out of a murder case than the guy who has the public defender.

On the other side of the coin, if a brother had a particular agenda, whether it be not liking another brother, trying to make himself appear wise, or even if he was just misguided or had some predisposed personal prejudice of some kind; if he had a greater grasp of Mathematical Thinking than I, then he had the very strong potential to dictate the outcome of scenarios. Much in the way a sitting judge's personal prejudices often color the verdicts they render.

This created an environment in the barracks, and largely across the Nation of what was called Brothers "beating each other up" with the Math. Brothers would spend hours on end discussing, debating, and analyzing a scenario that may have only taken a matter of seconds to happen.

This was because more important than the event that actually happened was the thinking that went into said action. None of the World's thinking would be accepted in the New World that Royall was creating. It was of extreme importance to point out weakness in one's thinking when and where it happened so that it could be addressed and eliminated.

This process brought with it another effect. Often at stake in these debates and discussions was a lot more than who left the beans out or who was supposed to turn off the television. Each scenario also represented an opportunity to express some level of knowledge, which in the Nation represented power.

Amongst each other we didn't operate off of money, but knowledge was the currency of the UNOI.

After the back and forth of a scenario was over and the smoke had cleared, the one who had put a period to the scenario would essentially appear to have the higher level of knowledge. Each time this took place, and the more people that could bear witness to this process, the "victor" left the scenario with a slightly elevated status.

The "loser" would see the opposite result and oftentimes turn inward to either sharpen his Math or set his sights on the next opportunity to show his level of knowledge.

Now if this all sounds a bit like Shaolin warriors walking around the village battling for supremacy, that's because it was very much that way.

You could often tell a brother's level or mastery of the math by how members related to them, especially during scenarios. If a brother had a higher ability to express the Math, then members tended to submit to them without much of a fight. No sense in getting burned up unnecessarily.

The majority of the time these Brothers would take the lead in scenarios and dictate which way the conversation would go. If the other participants of the scenario were of a particularly low level of Mathematical Thinking, they may simply oversee the scenario and allow the participants to work their way through it, only interjecting when they see things going off course. Conversely if they, consciously or subconsciously, felt that they were in a scenario with a person that was a threat to them, they expressed themselves with higher degree of energy.

It wasn't until you reached a certain level of maturity in your Mathematical Thinking that you understood that calmness is power and that your ability to keep a cool, even temperament during scenarios was an indication to those around you that you were in fact, in control.

On the other side of the coin, if you found yourself in a scenario and did not have the answer, it was very wise to understand that submission is the key. Many times people found themselves in much larger situations because they were constantly in the mode of defending or trying to make themselves clear, rather than submitting to the truth they heard coming from the other person.

This was of course personalism: paying more attention to the person that is sharing something with you instead of paying attention to the truth of what they are sharing.

This may become even more of a challenge if you suspected, accurately or not, that the person bringing something to you had ulterior motives. That person may be screaming at you in front of the entire class (which in Heaven would mean a couple hundred people) but if you got more caught up in how things were being brought to you, than WHAT is being brought to you and WHY it is being brought to you, then you would find yourself losing almost every time.

What you had to come to realize is that it didn't matter what a person's motivation for bringing something to you was, at least not to you. The only thing that mattered is that you would find the truth in it, submit to that, and then utilize it for your growth and development.

Again, this was a process that required some patience and discernment. Many times members could find themselves looking for the 10 % right so hard that they missed the 90% wrong that was being expressed by the person that was speaking with them. And then mess around and find themselves being addressed for letting the other person get away with that.

So it was not only a matter of knowing and understanding the mathematical principles and formulas, but also knowing how and when they applied and having the intestinal fortitude and confidence to stand on those principles while at the same time being open-minded enough to submit to the right that was being brought to you.

Simple enough right?

If all of this sounds complicated on paper, imagine one utilizing this process to go about their everyday motion and make decisions that would not only effect that motion, but would be judged by everyone around as right or wrong.

The better one became at striking a balance between all the moving parts of Mathematical Thinking, the better their capability to move about the Nation with some semblance of self-determination. If you were skilled enough you could justify control of not only your life but eventually the lives of those around you.

Again, knowledge was the currency of the UNOI.

It is very much similar to a man who has built up a great deal of personal wealth growing from the point of expressing control and stability in his own life, to being in position to influence the circumstances of in the lives of those around him.

The same way he can employ people in need of his finance to perform his will, a person with the proper mastery of mathematical thinking can manipulate those around him/her to exact his/her will.

Coming from the 'weekend warrior' Detroit Study Group to a place where Mathematical Thinking was the order of the day 24/7 was a major transition to say the least. What probably made it a smooth transition for me was the understanding that I didn't know the first thing about Islam, Mathematical Thinking, or how things were to go in the UNOI.

This kept me constantly in the position of a student being open to learn which was optimal because in Heaven teaching was all anyone ever wanted to do.

But what assisted me even more than that was having living examples of not only what to do but, what NOT to do.

My first duty upon arriving in Heaven was on the construction crew. Other than the little bit of work I had assisted with around various family members' homes every now and again, I had very limited construction experience. I understood this so I made it clear that I didn't know much at all, but was more than willing to do whatever task I was asked to do.

On the construction crew there was a brother who had arrived in Heaven shortly before me, named Charles. Charles had slightly more construction experience than I, which is to say he had almost a little.

To his detriment and much to my advantage, Charles' approach was the polar opposite of my own. He missed no opportunity to let everyone how much or, in most cases, little he knew. If the Brothers tried to correct him, well that was an entirely larger production. The Brother(s) assisting could barely get their words out of their mouth before Charles was into an explanation of why he did whatever thing he was being corrected on.

When the Brothers would let him know that the explanation was not only unnecessary but out of order, Charles would attempt to use some principle that usually didn't fit the scenario, in order to show Brothers that it was their fault. By then it was pretty much off to the races with the Brothers addressing Charles with increasing intensity and Charles accusing the Brothers of everything from being enemies of Allah to violating his civil rights.

Charles was about 40 years old and from Newark, New Jersey. You could tell he had been through a lot in his life. He was a dark skinned brother a few inches shorter than me and his body had a slight tremble when he spoke like he was going thru withdrawal.

Charles was everything that embodied my image of New York/New Jersey Brothers. He was aggressive, he was bold, and he was arrogant and had a general distrust of authority. He had a great warrior spirit and was enthusiastic about building the righteous kingdom. The problem came in anytime anyone tried to correct him.

If he viewed you as being on equal ground with him he was a loveable brother with a very friendly and playful spirit, no different than any city cat you might meet. He may tell a couple jokes, talk a little trash, and play around a little. He wasn't lazy at all and always willing to take on an extra security shift or help you out at duty.

As soon as you tried to make even the smallest correction on him, well then you may as well have declared war. I recall one incident that stands out vividly in my mind.

One afternoon in the barracks, it was Charles, Ricky, a few youth Brothers, and a Puerto Rican brother from Connecticut named Hector. Hector was in the kitchen cooking beans for all the Brothers. Charles was in the kitchen as well. I was in the living room sitting on the couch waiting to go to duty.

Hector was a man that was definitely passionate about the idea. He was very, very spiritual almost to the point of at times being a little spacey or what we called in the Nation being 'off in the ether'.

At any rate Hector goes to correct Charles on some idea, Charles delivers his usual rebuttal which Hector dispatches with relative ease. As this back and forth is going on Charles is becoming more and more irrational/emotional as he is apt to do in these situations.

When scenarios start to get heated in the home, the Brothers would generally come from the various parts of the house to assist.

Ricky and I, still relatively new, had come into the room but had yet to interject anything into the situation. This is when Charles comes with the gem of all gems. He turns to Hector and in a raised agitated voice says at the top of his lungs, "You know what? I think you're a god damn racist! That's what's this shit is about! You're a fucking racist."

Now thinking back I had to have been laughing/ gasping a millisecond after words came out his mouth. Now I do not purport to know what is truly in the heart of any man, but let's just say I was not the least bit concerned about finding any white hoods in Bro. Hectors closet.

Here was this Puerto Rican man, there in Kansas City KS, a full-time member of the United Nation of Islam. In order to even get here he had to write a letter to a Black man recognizing that Black man as his God Almighty.

The lessons that he studies next to us in class and at home every day are that the Black Man is the Maker, Owner, Cream of the Planet Earth, and God of the Universe. He sits right there and recites these ideas with or in some cases better than the Brothers.

But wait, there's more!

Just before coming to Kansas, Hector had been in prison on the east coast and as he learned more and more of the teachings, he was not shy about declaring what he had learned. Needless to say, this did not go over too well with the Latin Kings, of which he was formerly a member. Hector spent his final months in prison with a price on his head for declaring that the Blackman is God and standing up with the United Nation of Islam.

Keep in mind this is at a time when you have some Brothers, Black men, who couldn't miss a day of work, or miss having cable TV in order to support the Nation. Some Brothers in Heaven might just as soon stab you for waking them up to go on their scheduled security shift.

And now here he stands in this living room, in the FOI house being called a racist of all things.

The irony was apparently lost on Hector, who now has this absolutely mortified and hurt look on his face and for some reason begins to defend himself against these charges of being a racist. By this time we had jumped into the scenario to assist in quelling Bro. Charles' latest uprising.

 These types of scenarios were so common coming from Bro. Charles, whom I seemed to always find myself at duty with, that my learning curve was incredibly accelerated.

I found out later that my reputation had preceded me to the point that Brothers in Detroit weren't the only ones who had all but taken up a pool to see how long it was before I found myself kicked out of Heaven and back in Detroit.

In the gun slinger like atmosphere that was Heaven, a slacker like me would be an easy target for Brothers looking to make a name as being upstanding, no nonsense soldiers. Charles proved to be such an easy, obvious target, that the amount of pressure and attention that normally would have greeted me never came.

I had such a poor reputation that though many of the Nation's businesses where short staffed, no one really wanted anything to do with me, so after a few weeks on the construction crew, doing busy-stay-out-of-our-way-work, I was shuffled off to the Diner for duty there in the dish room.

Your Diner on 18th and Quindaro was the crown jewel of the Nation's activity, though there was not a great deal of business coming from the public.

More than any other place, this was the hub of activity in Heaven. Most transportation runs stopped through the Diner, the school buses brought the youth who lived in the barracks there for breakfast, the Royal Family would send for a couple orders on a daily basis, and Brothers from the FOI apartment next door above the donut shop would make up excuses to stop in and find out what food they could beg up on.

It was there in the tiny dish room, where I would have a first class view of the motion of Heaven. It was also here where I began to make a name for myself.

The dish room was a very humbling duty. Though there was very little commerce taking place in the Diner, there was always something to be done. Garbage taken out, groceries picked and up walked back from the Nation's Supermarket up the street, floors mopped, rat traps set and cleaned, fryer oil changed. It was the sort of position that if there was something not clearly covered by a particular duty, then we would just ask the dishwasher to do it.

This was not limited to duties inside the Diner. For instance, if there was a work detail where a couple of Brothers were needed, and the Captain called to find out if the Manager could spare a brother or two, well, the dishwasher may as well suit up.

And whenever you returned from whatever odyssey that you found yourself on, of course out of respect for the sanctity of a man's labor, the mountain of dishes that had been accumulated in your absence would be there waiting for you. Along with the day's trash and whatever detailed cleaning and/or minor repairs that fell under the ever expanding list of duties of the dish washer.

It was one of several duties that seemed to be setup almost entirely to test the humility and will of a soldier. If not done properly, then the entire Diner would schreeeech to a halt, because there would be no clean fork for the Royall Family, or cup for the one random patron who happened to mosey in that day.

If you were on your duty, well then no one would even really notice you were there. This suited me just fine, because the dish room kept me out of the line of fire for any scenarios that might come with another more glamorous, 'important' position. In essence, it was grunt work.

So my first couple of months were spent in the Diner, doing very little talking and a whole bunch of listening. When you were new in Heaven, what usually happened is if members (young or old) saw you doing something less than ideal, they would go into a teaching, right on the spot, as to why you should do it another way, and the spiritual, mental, and physical meaning behind doing it said way.

The combination of me not knowing much, plus the members' need to share the knowledge they had, created an opportunity of constant growth for me.

The expectation of my short run in Heaven also meant that no real effort was made to provide housing for my family. Amanda and the two younger children continued to stay at the MGT house, while the older boys and I were living in the FOI apartment.

This meant that other than class, I would only see Amanda a couple of times a week at the most. This also probably was in my favor. Not that I didn't miss her, but Amanda was rapidly developing a reputation as a rebellious Sister, which was only partially true.

The reality was that in Heaven they were not at all used to a member, much less a sister, questioning ANYTHING that came from the mouth of an official. Amanda was a Detroit girl through and through. And on top of that had been raised Muslim in a Christian world, which is to say she wasn't having it. She was not afraid of conflict. Quite the opposite, her natural reaction was to question those in authority.

Royall had spoken at length on the fiasco that was Moreen's exit from the Nation. He said that Moreen's crimes against the Nation and the members were partly the fault of the members. All of that never would have happened, he said, had anyone had the courage to speak up against her.

Amanda made it clear that no such thing would happen as long as she was around. She made it her business to question anything that didn't add up to her.

This made her a role model and heroine in the eyes of many members who lacked the gumption to do so. But in the eyes of those she was questioning and their ever faithful underlings, it was an irritant at best. At worst it was outright disrespectful and treasonous.

Because I spent most of my time in some duty or another, she would end up dealing with the structure directly on a lot of those issues. By the time we would see each other, three or four minor scenarios had come and gone. Many I would never hear about. Occasionally some brother would ask me about a scenario with my wife that I had never heard of.

Not that I had a major problem with that setup. This worked out for me because my natural instinct was to go with the flow. Even though I didn't agree with everything that went on in Heaven, I didn't disagree with everything either. Beyond that, I knew we were both new to this experience, so I wasn't looking to get into any knowledge contest or power struggle when I was essentially unarmed.

Barrack life had all but relieved me of the concerns of managing a household, and though I would see the boys nightly, they were just as busy as I was. So that left me concerned with the one thing I did absolutely LOVE about the UNOI.

The work.

Regardless of whether or not I knew/thought/felt/believed that Royall was Allah, what I did know is that I had never been involved in such a fulfilling activity as what we were doing.

If you can, imagine the concept of waking up in the morning, in a home full of people who are about what you are about: building a better tomorrow for your people.

Then walking next door or getting on transportation, which is being driven by these same people. Then going to YOUR business, or YOUR University or YOUR medical center to actively participate in the building and manifestation of this idea of independence for your people.

Coming from Detroit, I had seen and lived the worst of the Blackman and woman's condition in America: broken families, drug addiction, blight and disenfranchisement everywhere.

In Heaven I was not just seeing, talking about, or theorizing, but living with my people in a new light. Everything thing we did, everything you can think of was our own activity. Save for a few designated people who dealt with the business of the Nation (shoppers, secretaries, etc.) you NEVER even had to interact with ANYONE outside of the Nation.

This aspect of cult life is often pointed out as detriment, and I appreciate the importance of being exposed to cultures outside your own, but consider for a moment being an endangered species, which Black men in this culture certainly are, living that reality for most of your life, and then finding an oasis. Where there is an entire Idea/Nation/structure/activity setup for, by and about, your progress.

Instead of constantly being bombarded with overt and subliminal messages of your impotence and shortcomings, you are in an environment where everything beautiful about you is lifted up and magnified.

Even now the image that plays over and over in my mind is the Nation's school bus pulling up in front of the two large picture windows in front of the Diner, and seeing the school bus full of clean, happy, beautiful Black people, children, smiling and waving. The very memory of it continues to take my breath away. I feel blessed to have ever been able to witness and be a part of such a Godly spectacle.

I suppose this is just a good a time as any to go into the other major aspect of Heaven: class.

According to the UNOI, the entire motion of Heaven was setup to be a classroom. No matter where you were at any point of the day, be it in the barracks, in the Diner, in the Nation's barbershop, walking down the street between nations businesses, there was always something to be learned or, more specifically, taught.

In other words, the entire purpose for the activity was not for us to have a Diner or Supermarket or Service Station, because after all, these things were going to be destroyed in the Hellfire. The purpose was for us to have a way to put into practice the knowledge that Royall was teaching us.

That knowledge, of course, usually came to us for the first time in class.

Class was an activity unto itself. As a member coming from Detroit, you would think the intensity experienced during Independence Celebration was once a year, only when the entire Nation is in Heaven. And you would be wrong.

There were four major classes in Heaven. Mathematical Thinking Class on Friday's, Temple on Sunday, FOI class for the Brothers and MGT class for the Sisters on Mondays and Wednesdays respectively.

All classes were held at the University, unless there was a work detail in lieu of class.

The Nation's buses would transport the full-time members in from the various homes and businesses. Part-timers, most of whom we would rarely see outside of class, would show up looking the part of the model member, wearing their snazziest suit and bowtie or dress.

Full-time Brothers would be milling about the University in various security posts, helping the Sisters and elders in and out of transportation, up and down stairs, and ushering everyone into the auditorium for class. As usual, the Royall Family would have their designated security team, escorting them about the building, attending to the Family's whims, and making sure that everyone else kept the proper distance.

Once in the auditorium, Sisters sat to the immediate left of the stage, Brothers in a separate section directly in front of the stage, and a final section to the far right reserved especially for the Royall Family and friends.

On stage there would either be a rostrum or a table, depending on the nature of the class. At either side of the stage there were two microphones set up. These were for those participants from the 'body' to come up and speak. It was at these mics, many Brothers and Sisters would find themselves, fortunately or most often, unfortunately, the center of attention for class.

During Sunday Temple, scenarios were rarely gone over, as this class would be more of a spiritual teaching conducted by the Ministers, one of the Instructors at the University or The Royall Family. Occasionally Royall would surprise the members and show up himself, at which point class took on an even greater intensity.

This would rarely be announced, so we would be all settled in for a normal class, and the familiar call "ALL RISE" would sound out as Father entered the auditorium, and the entire place would go nuclear. The large already echo filled auditorium would vibrate from the sonic boom of clapping and cheering that now filled the air. Shouts would come sporadically from the raucous crowd,

"Allah U Akbar!!"

"All praise be to Father!"

"We love you Father"

"All praise due Allah, styled as Solomon named Royall!"

Most of the full-time Brothers would roll our eyes silently as many of these calls would erupt out the mouths of members, usually part-timers, who couldn't be bothered to take up a couple hours of duty at the Service Station. The UNOI equivalent of CMEs, (you know the church goers who only show up on Christmas, Mother's Day and Easter but insist you are sitting in their seat), they became the most holy of the holy, the most devout of the devout, the upright of the upright when it came to showing out in front of Father or the Royall Family.

One of the great juxtapositions of the Nation was Class vs. Duty. Though duty was where you could earn the respect of the soldier next to you, class was the stage where you could make a name for yourself in front of the whole Nation instantly.

Participating in class not only meant having your name called, but also standing up front of everyone, walking up to the microphone, and speaking before the body. And more so than any other place in the Nation, EVERYTHING was analyzed and corrected if you did it wrong. By whoever might feel like getting up and saying,

"Why are the Brothers walking so unspirited up to the mic?"

"Brother why are you facing the stage if you are speaking to the class? The right thing to do would be to face the ones you are speaking to."

"Do the Brothers know the dress code for Temple?"

"Why is the Brother standing like that?"

"Look at the Sister's posture!"

All of this before you even spoke. Between your appearance, body language and what you actually said, you had the opportunity to either establish yourself as a sharp up and coming brother or sister, or someone whose mastery and understanding of what was being taught was still at a very low level.

This was great for those looking to show their progress toward being Gods and Goddesses, those looking move up the political ladder in the Nation, or even those younger and older Brothers and Sisters looking for a potential husband or a first or second wife. Since interaction between the Brothers and the Sisters was so closely monitored, class would often be the only and ideal place for a young brother to strut their stuff in front of the Sisters.

Of course, just as quickly a brother or sister could embarrass themselves beyond all recovery.

Usually because Temple was more for spiritual teachings or introducing new teachings from Royall, the more intense scrutiny was reserved for Math classes.

Math Class in Heaven was the stuff of legend.

If you came from one of the outlying Temples to Heaven for Math Class you were warned to keep your mouth closed and your eyes open. Not only was the majority of the knowledge coming from Royall being presented to the body in Heaven well before rest of the Nation, it was also where that knowledge was being practiced 24-7.

Back in Detroit, you might come to one, maybe two classes and discuss Mathematical Thinking for 1-3 hours out of the week, but after that you were right back out into the world with the rest of the lost-founds and the white man's way of thinking.

There were countless cautionary tales of Brothers who were Ministers in other temples around the country, coming to Heaven for Math Class and having their heads handed to them, metaphorically, speaking of course. (Only slightly metaphorically though).

Though there was occasionally time allotted for members to bring scenarios in the beginning of class, usually the conductor of class would know ahead of time what scenarios or topics would be gone over. This would usually be at the instruction of Royall or the Royall Family and done ahead of time to ensure that none of the persons relevant to the scenario found a way to skip class.

Things would be open the same as in the Detroit area, with a brief explanation of what Mathematical Thinking was and a review of the steps of the mathematical formula, laws and principles of Mathematical Thinking, and then finally class would start.

Gossip was so rampart in Heaven that usually half the class knew what scenarios would be discussed before Math Class began. This led to a somewhat charged and anxious atmosphere since everyone knew what was coming. Kinda like the school yard when everyone knows there's about to be a fight.

If you were one of the ones in the scenarios, the knot in your stomach would be the size of a small boulder. In the early days of the Nation, when Moreen was still Mother of Civilization, scenarios would be duked out on the spot. The interested parties would share would happened, and before they could even get the story out, questions, many dripping with accusation and innuendo, were flying. This would lead to classes that ran on for well past the four hours mark.

Perhaps it was the emotion of the scenario, coupled with being questioned aggressively by a couple hundred people, but though the outcomes were often inevitable, the majority of those 'at the mic' rarely went down without a fight.

This only served to work the crowd into a greater frenzy. Each time a question was not answered properly a sea of hands would shoot into the air. If you answered one question wrong, each person who had something to share would speak before you had the chance to correct yourself and move forward.

This process made for great theatre, and included, men, women, and yes, even children. More than a few times, a child of less than 6 years old has toddled up to the microphone to share "Bwava" Captain is being defensive, or technical or outright devilish in the way he is responding.

And of course while all of this is happening, you are still standing at the microphone, so if for whatever reason your body language was now not right, then THAT had to be discussed and analyzed and used as evidence to show your thinking was in error.

And while all of these members are pointing out how you used a word incorrectly, or how you were purposefully being deceptive in your use of the language, or how the way you are standing is disrespectful to Allah, the one thing you don't ever want to do is respond with anything other than your understanding of what is being shared with you. Preferably in a 'yes sir' or yes 'ma'am'.

No seriously.

The last thing you want to do, ever, ever ever, ever, is start to explain yourself.

 For the love of God.

Named Royall or otherwise.

DON'T

DO

THAT.

An explanation, aka a justification bka making yourself clear, fka "what had happened was" is like blood in the water to a hungry school of piranha.

This is even harder than it sounds when you KNOW in your heart of hearts that you didn't say what they just said you said, and certainly didn't mean it in that way, but now you have been standing at the mic for forty-five minutes, after a 12 hour shift at the Service Station, listening to the Brother who EVERYBODY knows is one of the laziest and sloppiest bums in the Nation, lecture YOU about how Father is not going to accept such behavior in the hereafter and you NEED to get it together.

You learn early on that submission is in fact the key, and oftentimes it is your only way out of these moments.

The plus of this process is that in reality, even if you were not 'wrong', you learned you were responsible for everything that does or doesn't happen to you. This lesson has served me well long after I walked away from the UNOI.

You may have been set up by an incompetent manager or even a member who is outright lying on you to further their agenda or cover their ass. But what you ultimately learn is that you had to take responsibility for everything that happened around you.

If a brother or sister could lie on you then it was your fault for putting yourself in a position to be lied on. The saying for this was, "God either does a thing or permits it to be done."

You come out much better in the eyes of the Nation accepting responsibility for something that was not really your fault than you do for trying to explain your way out of it.

For those serious about Nation-building, this attitude did not go unnoticed and that was the other part of it all. Class, especially the classes like Temple and Math Class, were largely for show. So much so that the officers and structure in the FOI would invariably schedule themselves for duty away from the University during class, because they saw little value in the pageantry of it all.

If you were an officer responsible for getting things done, you knew that the brother with the slick style when it came to explaining why Brother Keith was being coward on the mic in front of his wife and children would be same brother begging off of duty at the Service Station. While that brother he was busy roasting, the one who couldn't seem to get his words together, was at duty 18 hours a day and on call the other six.

As a new brother, class was intimidating and helpful at the same time. I admittedly didn't know much about this knowledge Royall was teaching, I didn't see much value in raising my hand and getting flambéed, but the tidal wave of information coming forth served to accelerate my learning curve, and I began to truly understand how misguided and misinformed the Detroit Study Class had been.

Now FOI Class?

FOI Class was different.

 This was the class strictly for the Brothers. The formality and grandeur that accompanied Math Class and Temple was absent from FOI Class. The Brothers still wore suit and bowtie most times, unless it was a work detail or exercise, but FOI Class was purely about getting shit done.

This was the class where you did not have to worry about having perfect diction or being polite or even civilized. At my first FOI Class, there was a brother at the mic who was receiving heat for some deviant behavior or another. The investigation and question answering was going pretty much the way I had become familiar with scenarios going.

The brother, one of the most notorious smooth talkers in the Nation, deftly danced around question after question, skillfully pleading ignorance or innocence to the increasingly intense queries from the Brothers.

You could feel the anger building in the room, because Brother Dino was bullshitting, everybody knew Brother Dino was bullshitting, and we

117

all really wanted Brother Dino to stop bullshitting. Then all of a sudden bellowing from the back of class, was Brother Mason,

"STOP BULLSHITTING DINO! STOP FUCKING BULLSHITTING!"

Yeah that'll do it.

I turned around to scan the faces of the Brothers knowing that this clearly uncivilized and unrefined outburst would change the direction of class and that Mason would be the new 'star of show' as the subject of scenarios were often called.

Other than a couple of nods in agreement, smirks, and some scattered, "Hell Yeah!"s no one even blinked. I knew right then FOI would be my favorite Class.

FOI was the class to put an end to all the politics and bullshit that was the undercurrent of so many interactions in Heaven.

If you had a beef with a Brother who was being lazy in the barracks or at duty, call him out. Felt like one of the officers was not living up to the standard his rank and title demanded, call him out. Felt like a Brother was mistreating you, or his wife, or even himself, man call that shit out.

"Steel sharpens steel" was the policy.

Conflict and aggressiveness were tolerated, even encouraged. Brothers would stand at the mic and duke it out spiritually, mentally, and if things went far enough even physically. And if you were present during the scenario that was being covered, then you may as well come up to the mic too. There was no such thing as innocent bystanders in the Nation. Seeing and allowing wrong to happen was just as bad as being the one doing the wrong in the first place.

Even the conductors of class were more aggressive, demanding input from the Brothers. Again no innocent bystanders even in class, even if you did not raise your hand and had nothing to do with the scenario. There was no such thing as neutral or middle ground in FOI Class. "Allah spits out lukewarm water" and "If you don't stand for something, you will fall for anything."

So a Brother sitting silently was just as or in some cases more likely to be called on as the Brother jumping out of his skin to comment. This was an opportunity to let it be known amongst the men what type of man you were.

What principles did you stand for? What could you be counted on for? Were you going to stand with truth or just go whichever way the wind blew you?

One of the worst things that could be said about a brother was that he had been around us for years but we did not know who he was, what he does, or what he could be counted on to do. Even amongst the 'trouble makers' and riff raff of the Nation at least we knew where they stood.

Brother Rodney might not be the sharpest pencil in the box, but we know if there was some ass needing kicked he could do it. Brother Kinte might be trying to sleep with the entire MGT but if we sent him out with the sandwiches he will get em sold. Brother Ramon might be lazy, shiftless, might have bad hygiene, might not really have a redeemable skill in any way but, well, um, he could hold the hell out of a door.

Yeah Like I said you had to make a name for yourself.

This set the tone, even outside of FOI class, for a very strong sense of brotherhood. It was one thing for you as an individual to find something you were willing to dedicate your time and energy to, but to find a group of men willing to show that same level of dedication to that idea was true divinity.

The systemic spiritual, mental, economic, and physical blight I had experienced growing up In Detroit was unfortunately not unique at all. We had hailed from places all across the map, Detroit, New York, Chicago, Long Beach, Tallahassee, Houston, even Africa. Each of us with the different experiences that added up to the same thing- WE were an endangered species. The only thing lower than our opportunity for success was the expectation for us to be successful.

Even if I was not sold on Royall being Allah, I had never, nor have I since, experienced anything more fulfilling than being a member of the FOI. In the world, you might experience one or two guys you could get close to who were about what you were about. But as an FOI you stood shoulder to shoulder with literally hundreds of Brothers that could be counted on to do whatever needed to be done as it related to this idea.

We had our share of glory hounds, political puppeteers, and general fuck ups (raises hand) but for every one of them I met ten Brothers who would work past the point of exhaustion and then cringe at any glorification of their name. The way we saw things, we were only doing what we needed to do to create a future for ourselves and our families.

Add to that the opportunity to meet and work side by side with many Brothers from the First Resurrection, who had soldiered under the Honorable Elijah Muhammad to build the Original Nation of Islam. As a fledging revolutionary I was in absolute awe at the living, breathing legends that had labored and struggled at much risk to themselves, during the 70s, 60s, and even 50s when they were stringing black men for far less than having the audacity to be men, much less claiming to be Gods.

Well into their 50, 60 and 70 years of age many of these same Brothers were some of the UNOI's mightiest soldiers. In fact, 80% of the UNOI Construction Company, responsible for the monumental task of building, repairing, and maintaining the Nation's many properties, was made up of Brothers from The First.

They would rise at the crack of dawn and be at the duty before many members were even out of bed. Then in the evening you would see them returning home at dusk at the earliest, without as much as a complaint.

If the idea of providing a better future for your children and those who would come after you were not enough to inspire you to work hard, then certainly the example set by these Brothers and Sisters HAD to motivate you.

After all, no matter what duty we had, no police were busting into the businesses pulling weapons on us like they had during the 60s and 50s. None of us lived under constant threat of lynching or assault for trying to improve our communities.

The only thing we had to do was master self and do the work. And there was no shortage of work to be done.

In addition to my primary duty at the Diner, there were additional work details, mandatory security shifts, shopping runs, helping out at the bakery, etc. If you had another duty that you had an interest in, then you were usually free to take on extra shifts at that business in order to learn the duty.

As all of this activity also meant that I had less and less time to concern myself with the issues that had previously troubled me i.e.; finances, my marriage/infidelity and the ideology of the UNOI.

My food, clothing, and shelter were being provided. Other than that, I could care less about old bills since this all was going to burn up anyway.

As for the Royall being Allah, that was something that never came up. It was simply never up for discussion amongst the members in Heaven.

After all, they were members.

And this was Heaven.

Anytime anyone even thanked another person for doing anything, the proper response was, "All/The praise be to Father. "

If not, then as always there would be a conversation about why you should say it, and a thorough examination as to why you did not say it.

After all, this motion that you were in, that you enjoyed so much, that you learned so much doing, was all because of what Royall was producing. If you did something praise worthy, surely you were not looking to accept credit for that. And so, "All praise be to Father."

So I began to say it.

After all, I understood the reasoning.

Yes, I was very happy doing what I was doing.

Yes, I was learning so much about myself, and life.

Yes, all of this was a result of the environment set up by Royall.

Looking back, it is impossible to pick the moment or even the day, week, or month when you go from saying praise be to Royall, because you know it's expected, to really thinking, " Man, this is beautiful, and thank you Father for this situation."

Or the moment you began to stop saying to yourself, "I can't find any reason to believe he is Allah", and begin saying "I can't think of any reason why he isn't Allah."

I suppose so much of it has to do with your reality. When everyone and everything around you bears witness to a thing, how long before you start to see the same thing?

How many aspects of our everyday life do we accept as normal simply because the society we are surrounded by says it's normal?

Things like birthing your baby at home, home schooling your children, or growing your own food are considered revolutionary or of off the beaten path, yet less than a hundred years ago it was unheard of to NOT do these things.

Though I still could not reconcile with all of the theology of UNOI, one thing I could bear witness to was things being different. In addition to my own personal growth and development, I could see a 180 degree turn in how the world treated me as a member of the FOI.

There was a respect from the people in the neighborhood that was tangible. Respect even in the absence of admiration.

Many of the locals, especially the youth had had a frequently violent relationship with the UNOI.

As an FOI it was completely unacceptable to ever take ANY flack or back down from one of the lost-founds. Lost-found was the term we used to describe those of African descent who didn't have knowledge of self.

Though we were in the process of building Heaven in the heart of the ghetto of Kansas City, KS, the hood was still the hood.

We still had our share of vandalism, break-ins, theft, and other general activities that are a part of ghetto life. In the tradition of the Brothers in the First Resurrection, our M.O. was to whoop ass first and ask questions later.

After one particular bad patch of aggressions by the locals, it was the strong recommendation of one senior official who happened to have been an official during the Messenger's time, that we needed to grab one of the lost-founds and set them on fire in front of the Diner in the middle of the day as an example to the rest of them. It didn't even need to be one that had done something to us; any lost-found would do. This was seriously discussed in more than one FOI class, but luckily (to my knowledge) was never put into action.

That is not to say we didn't ever get our hands dirty. Anytime lost-founds would cross the line, or Moreen had been sighted stalking the Nation's properties, a hand-picked squad of bothers would be dispatched to apply the proper attention to said issue.

It was a great honor to be selected for one of these squads. It was the UNOI's version of being Black Ops. Being a part of one of those teams meant you needed to be able to think on your feet but also be very capable of handling yourself in a battle. It also required discipline and strict adherence to the laws and principles that governed FOI military action.

Once an instruction was given, no matter how brutal or impossible or extreme it might seem to you, there could be no hesitation in carrying it out. Our instructions were coming from Allah himself. If a lost-found needed his hand broken for throwing a brick at our school bus, or the police were at the door to take one of the children (with the constant exodus of disgruntled members, custody battles were a constant) and Royall said they are not to leave with that child, then it was simply to be as Royall stated.

These were not requests, these were instructions and if you could not be trusted to carry them out, there was a line of capable Brothers behind you jumping at the opportunity.

Our attitude was that we had our own Nation, so there no need to call the police. What kind of Nation calls the military of another Nation, in particular its enemy, to defend it against its own people?

If situations needed investigation, we were fully capable of doing such. If suspects needed to be apprehended, interrogated and eventually punished, who better than the right hand of Allah, The Mighty FOI?

What was all the more impressive is this was understood and respected by the Kansas City Police Department. They had no luck in cleaning up the neighborhood, so when we came and not only opened clean, crime free businesses and homes, but also put a stiff boot in the ass of those who attempted to infringe on us with their wrongdoing, they had no problem looking the other way.

Though the Nation often bragged on the relationship they had with the police in Kansas, at first I was skeptical. I was a young guy from Detroit who came to KC with more than a couple warrants.

Many of the Brothers can relate to that sick feeling you get any time the police show up in your review mirror or if you are posted up on the block.

Much ado is made of 'Driving while Black' that many of our people fall victim to. What many fail to realize is to be harassed you didn't have to be driving a certain type of car, in a certain neighborhood. Hell, you didn't have to be driving at all. You could even be standing outside of your own home, and if the police wanted to give you a hard time, then you would just be having a hard time. Call it Existing While Black.

Though I looked a far cry from my hood days, dressed as an FOI, clean cut, sober and moving with purpose and direction, I still felt like the same kid from back off East Warren when I saw police cars.

It wasn't long before my experience in Heaven began to challenge even these deep seeded notions.

One night in the barracks we got a call from Brother Charles who was doing security at the University.

"I need Brothers here now! We got a break-in here at the University!"

Five Brothers hopped up, threw on sweats, jean shorts, everything NOT befitting an FOI, scrambled down the stairs and smashed into the tiny compact vehicle sitting directly in front of the barracks.

In the mad dash, none of us had grabbed a lick of ID as we sped off into the night toward the University.

Tires screeched, and the car bouncing as we took turn after turn, speeding thru whatever lights sought to slow us down on our mission. That is until the red and blue lights got behind us.

Yeah this is a wrap, I thought to myself.

Here is this car full of big burly black men, speeding through the streets of KC at 3 o'clock in the morning, not an ID amongst them. Completely understandably, the cops stepped out of the car, weapons already drawn. Knowing what was next; I took a deep breath and waited to be told to get out of the car one by one.

Just then, before the cop can say another word, Brother Doug leans his head out of the window.

"We are with the United Nation of Islam, we just got a call about a break in at our University, and we need to get there."

The cop took a step back, raised his hand to his partner, and said, "You fellas drive safely."

And off we sped again.

I wonder if Heaven got Ghetto indeed.

All this time had been wasted trying to convince me that Royall is Allah, and that the UNOI was the fulfillment of prophecy when all they had to do was tell me I could get pulled over speeding thru the hood, run lights, have no ID and just say who I am with and not only will the cops let me go, but will wish me safe travels.

That experience in itself was divine intervention where I was from. Hell, you could have ALL of your paperwork in order and the police would still find some reason to hassle you.

It was moments like these that I began to truly buy in and see the divinity in what was being done in the United Nation of Islam.

Between the respect we got from the cops and the lost-founds; between that unspoken bond and unity that came with being in the trenches with your fellow soldier; living day after day after day with those who looked like you, working in unison toward a common goal, a common tomorrow, learning and practicing a knowledge that produced happiness, peace, and unity. No violence, no drugs, no crime; maybe this really was Heaven.

There was a system to resolve the disagreements or problems that did arise. More and more the understanding that Heaven meant having everything you needed in order to be successful became clearer and clearer to me.

My relationship with Amanda was still rocky, but even that was turning around as I gained a greater understanding of the laws and principles that had been used to beat me up for so long.

We still lived apart after eight months in Heaven, and she wanted desperately to get out of the MGT House. There were certain benefits to being a married sister that she simply wasn't getting. Being in the MGT House meant being lumped in with the youth or unmarriable Sisters. She saw couples being married and fit into this home and that home and, rightfully so, felt like we were being put on the back burner. She demanded that I do something about this.

I had become accustomed to living in the barracks. I spent so much time at duty that where I slept was not of great importance to me.

Besides, moving out of the barracks meant we would probably be moving in with other families. Other families meant other wives. Other wives to me represented more scenarios. Already I had begun to see the difference between the way Brothers dealt with scenarios and the way Sisters did.

Brothers were charged with getting to the essence and putting solutions to situations. Sisters were encouraged to do so as well, but if there was any shortcoming it would fall back on the Brothers. It was our responsibility to not only solve the scenario but clear up any negative energy that might have been left on the Sisters. This was regardless of whether or not the sister was interested in letting go of the negative energy.

If a group of Brothers had a scenario to deal with, more often than not, they would bring in a third party to resolve it (if necessary) and then move forward. With some of the Sisters you kind of got the feeling that

127

they wouldn't be satisfied until one of Royall's Wives had been called in to deal with the scenario.

Even though I was growing in my knowledge and ability to express it, it didn't take God knowledge to know that Amanda in a house with one or two other Sisters was more than I was ready to handle.

Little did I know that a fate far more challenging for both of us lurked around the corner.

Though I stayed busy with as many extra duties as I could take on, my primary duty remained at the Diner. In my spare time as dish washer, I began to train as a front line cook in order to cover for Brothers who needed to practice for the Allah's Supreme Drill Team. This turned into helping out in the prep room.

Though the Diner was certainly the flagship entity in Heaven, it was still far from a profitable enterprise. On most days we would make less than 50 bucks, which when you add in the amount it cost to feed the youth who ate breakfast at the Diner, the Construction Crew who ate Dinner at the Diner, and the occasional Royall Family meal, the Diner was actually hemorrhaging cash.

The manager at the time was Brother Jay, though it was commonly understood that the problems with the Diner preceded his tenure there. He actually was one of the sharper up-and-coming Brothers in the Nation. Head of the Drill Team, son of the National Secretary, he was coming off of a successful stint as the manager of the Diner in Cincinnati.

But even resume and nepotism were not enough to save him from the cannibalistic nature of the UNOI Laborers. The Laborers represented the heads of the FOI, MGT, the Ministry, the Secretarial Department, and the managers of every business in Heaven. They held their weekly meeting every Saturday in the Diner.

These were the ones charged with coordinating the motion and systems of the Nation as well as resolving any of the issues that existed within the Nation.

The idea was that Laborers would put their collective heads together to make sure things ran smoothly. If something was being missed on your end, though, make no mistake this was a BBQ and you were the main course.

Not only did you have the sharpest minds in Heaven at the table, but you also had some of the biggest egos. That means if you showed up unprepared, they were like sharks that saw blood in the water.

As manager of the Diner there was no easy way to explain or justify why your weekly grocery bill was in excess of 1000 when you only brought in close to $300 gross a week. This lack of results would only serve to make it that much more difficult to get the support needed when you presented a new idea.

In Jay's defense, he was beginning to lay the groundwork for what would be a recipe for success at businesses across the Nation. As the manager in Cincinnati, he understood the importance of getting teams out in the community, especially when you had virtually no walk-in customers.

Slowly but surely he was getting commitments from the few part-time Brothers who could be counted on to give an hour here, a transportation run there. He had begun working with the FOI structure behind the scenes to free some Brothers from duty to go out and sell the sandwiches a couple hours a day.

He was working out a system with Your Bakery in order to get baked goods that would normally just sit on the shelf and mold into the hands of the community teams.

However, to change years of incompetence and mismanagement takes time, especially in a place like Heaven, where every decision had to be reviewed three and four times, for not only in feasibility but also for its political correctness.

For those in positions of responsibility, time was a rather expensive commodity that few could afford. Once the whispers start about you being properly relieved, that fateful FOI class can't be too far behind.

And it wasn't.

Before long, Brother Jay was at the mic in front of the FOI class answering questions that he already knew he didn't have the answers to, but because he was at the mic in FOI Class, he still had to answer.

This, of course, is recipe for disaster and only serves to validate what everyone knew was next.

"Why can't the Brother answer these questions that there are no answers to?"

He couldn't answer that question.

Brother Jay is properly relieved from duties as Manager of the Diner.

When it is asked in class should a Brother or Sister be relived of a particular duty, the will be an endless sea of hands.

When it is asked who will fill in for the person that was so enthusiastically ejected from office, the hands don't go up as fast.

Well, in some cases they do, but never really from ones who you would seriously consider for the position.

Usually you get some combination of that brother can't manage to keep his bunk clean, but wants to constantly tell you how the businesses should be run and that part-time brother who can't be bothered to show up for duty more than once a week, so you really don't know enough about how he works to know if you can trust him or not. Or worse yet, you do.

Still the question had to be asked, so Daniel asked it," So then who is willing to take over the responsibilities of managing the Diner?"

I froze for a moment. Well, I mean it was class so I was already basically sitting still, but still, I began to mull this decision.

My stock was certainly on the rise, and not just with those around me but most importantly with myself. Prior to coming to Heaven I had never worked inside of a restaurant. What the previous six months in the Diner had taught me if nothing else was that the most important thing was a willing spirit and the ability to learn.

Hey, it sounded good at the time.

Besides, I reasoned, they'll probably never pick me. Looking around I saw hands from dozens of Brothers who would be more qualified than I. But the question was who is willing, not who is qualified. I was more than willing, so I raised my hand.

The FOI secretary took note of the Brothers whose hands had been raised, class came to an end, and we began to make our way on to the buses and back to the barracks for the night.

On the ride home, and once we got to the barracks, the Brothers went on and on about who volunteered, who should have kept their hand down, what the new manager would have to do to right the Diner, what Brother Jay did wrong, and all the related topics.

I lay in my bunk that night and pondered the possibilities. I knew certain people had a good impression of me, but still I didn't think it was likely. The Math did not support me, having only been in Heaven less than six months being manager. I lacked the experience not only in the restaurant business, but also in the Nation.

On the other hand, in those months I had earned the reputation as one of the more diligent Brothers in the Nation.

Anytime there was an extra assignment, from security details, to trash runs, the service station, or even special FOI business like chasing Moreen around Missouri or battling with the lost-founds, I was being called. In the Diner itself, I was pretty much a constant. I had gone from the dish room to the front grill to Assistant Manager. Jay had heard about my hustling background, so I had even started to crack the rotation of Brothers that got sent out into the community for fundraiser.

The transformation of my reputation seemed to come over night.

 Literally.

One night, not out of the ordinary, I had stayed in the Diner deep into the midnight hour, cleaning and prepping . The Diner didn't have its own washing machine so we would use the machine next door in the Nation's Colonic Center to wash the Diner laundry.

(Wow, that didn't seem as nasty at the time.)

It was usually the last thing I did before I called it a night. I retrieved the key from the cashier's station, went into the Colonic Center, locked the door behind me and went into the basement to put the clothes in the machine.

And then I woke up. My eyes opened looking at the front door of the Colonic Center. I was lying with my head on the soft carpet at the top of the stairs.

BOOM BOOM BOOM.

I blinked.

BOOM BOOM BOOM.

I had fallen asleep.

BOOM BOOM BOOM.

132

And now, someone was banging on the front door.

BOOM BOOM BOOM.

Hard.

BOOM BOOM BOOM.

Repeatedly.

I sprang to my feet, strode to the door, and swung it open. I was greeted by the sight of Brother Douglas and the staff of the Colonic Center.

I couldn't believe it," What time is it?"

Douglass laughed. "Time for you to get some sleep, Brother."

I did in fact fall asleep in the Colonic Center coming back upstairs from putting the laundry in the wash. If Douglass hadn't arrived to drop off the Sisters, who knows how long I would have slept.

I still haven't forgiven him for waking me up. That carpet was very soft.

When I didn't show up at the barracks last night, and no one saw me in Diner, it was pretty much assumed that I had finally cracked.

The word, which always traveled by light speed in Heaven when it came to gossip as juicy as this, had already begun to circulate that Brother Prostell had finally shown his true colors and jumped ship.

This made it all the more sweet when the truth was quickly discovered. I hadn't run away, I had literally worked until I passed out. This all ran counter to everything that had been said about me prior to my arrival in Heaven.

All of that being what it was, I still had very little expectation of being named the Manager, which was fine because I rather enjoyed the role I operated in. I was below the radar and my duty in the Diner allowed me the flexibility to take on other duties that interested me.

And then the call came in.

I had never really had so much as a conversation with Sister Doctor, Moreen's younger sister, so it was somewhat odd to be getting a call from her at duty.

"Brother Prostell, have you ever worked in a restaurant?"

They had picked me.

Well, me and Amanda.

I was being offered the manager position contingent on the circumstance that my wife would be my co- manager. You talk about a catch 22. I wasn't too bummed.

My hope, and I suspect the hope of the structure, was that this promotion would cause Amanda's perspective of me to change. Surely, if Royall thought enough of me to allow me to manage the Diner, that had to reflect well in her eyes.

In less than six months I had gone from persona non grata in Detroit, then come here to Heaven, made my way quickly through the ranks to be named Manager of the Nation's flagship entity and I couldn't feel more vindicated.

It seemed surreal to think about visiting the Diner on my first trip to Heaven. A human black eye on the Detroit Study Group, I stuck out like a sore thumb-a sore thumb wearing baggy jeans and white tee, too much facial hair, and no knowledge of self.

Now I was the Manager of that same restaurant and as much as I wanted to rub it in the faces of those who doubted me, nothing really needed be said.

There wasn't much time to revel in the moment. I knew we needed to hit the ground running. Like most people, we had many ideas about how to run a restaurant, but none of the experience to make those ideas happen.

Amanda was very sharp mentally and very good about being organized, so we agreed she would be responsible for the inventory, the grocery list, and the overall finances of the Diner. She was also a great chef, so she would also undertake updating the menu.

Under normal circumstances, her assertiveness and honesty would have been perfect in that role, but in the politically charged, twisted chain of command that was the Nation, it was never that simple.

One Royall Family member would tell her to be sure to put EVERYTHING we needed in order to be successful on the grocery list. Then I would get a call asking me to justify a grocery list that was more than $1000, when the normal list was under $400.

Or she would change a recipe to something that would sell like hotcakes in the community, and then we would get a phone call asking who we checked with before we changed the recipe. (This usually meant that the recipe that got replaced had come from one of the Royall Family, which always taken as blatant disrespect).

I would take responsibility for the day-to-day operations and overall logistics of the Diner.

Almost instantly, I began getting compliments on how the overall spirit inside the Diner had changed for the better. Being the neophyte that I was, I took that as a great sign about me as person. Little did I know at the time, Managers in the Nation were treated a lot like new coaches on professional sports teams. They were always the best thing ever when they first came In, If Just by virtue of not being the guy that just got sacked.

Of course, the Brothers in the barracks loved it because the food that The Diner normally toss out, I would send upstairs. Compared to the normal rations of bean soup, three-time warmed up mustard greens and candied carrots were gourmet cuisine.

Those who hadn't been sold on me yet soon became my biggest fans, just by virtue of my tendency to find any excuse to give out food, especially that which was about to go bad. Members had been very reluctant to ask for food at the Diner since its poor finances were well-known. I figured what was the point of holding on to food that if we didn't sell that day we would have to toss out. It's not like we had reason to expect a sudden influx of customers.

All of this good will made the Diner not only a destination for passers thru, but also a duty site. When we took over, the staff had a total of about 10-15 members, which is rather high when you consider that we never had any business and no I didn't realize it at the time. Well, that 10-15 swelled to 20-30 in my tenure at the Diner.

Most of who took my open kitchen policy as a green light policy for them when it came to the groceries in the Diner. Sisters would come traipsing out of the prep room with bowls of macaroni and cheese, salmon sausage, or even dishes that weren't even on the menu.

This was great when it came to improving the overall mood and energy of the Diner, but not so much when it came to maintaining inventory or actually making money.

This was only made worse when the Royall Family children decided to take on duties in the Diner. If I struggled being able to keep 'regular' members in check, I was absolutely clueless when it came balancing proper treatment of the Royall Family with addressing the King's daughters about using the last of the salmon on treats for the youth.

And there lied the crux of my downfall as a Manager. I was fully capable of putting in work myself, staying in the Diner until the break of dawn to make sure that all the stations were clean and business was taken care of.

But that was not my role as a Manager. It was my job to make sure that everyone else did what they were supposed to.

My inability to enforce the law, created an environment where everyone was happy but no one was accountable.

Correction, ALMOST everyone was happy. Because within the 30 or so staff members of the Diner, there was a small group that understood the personal responsibility it took to be successful as a group. The fact that Royall had referred to the Diner as a cursed entity because of its long running failures was something that they took personally and were committed to changing.

The problem was while they were busting their collective butts, the other 20 members were getting away with murder: not doing their prep, coming into duty late, leaving early, not sticking with the systems of the Diner, and stealing food.

And the one person who was responsible to put it in check, me, wasn't doing a thing about it.

It wasn't long before the honeymoon was over with the Laborer's as well.

Laborer's meetings quickly went from asking what measures and changes I was instituting to hour-long Math beatdowns, the likes of which I had never experienced. These interrogations made me long for my Detroit days getting grilled in Math Class.

Among my chief antagonists was Brother Trevor, the Manager of Your Supermarket. Trevor was widely accepted as the best manager the Diner had ever had. In fact he was the only manager in the history of the Diner to ever be Properly Relieved or in other words the only one the not get fired.

At the advice of Kaaba, I began to carry to a notepad to jot down the different suggestions that members would bring to me. This would serve two purposes. One, it would be a good way to catalogue and consider different ideas I might want to try. And on the other hand it would make even those with ridiculous ideas feel included in the management of their Diner.

This, he told me was one of the tactics Trevor employed in his successful run as Manager. He also strongly recommended that I approach Trevor personally about what systems he used to make the Diner a success. Everyone seemed to think this was a great idea. Everyone that is except for Trevor, who admonished me for writing instead of listening to one particular tongue lashing from the Laborers.

Early on in my tenure at the advice of, well, everybody, I had requested a meeting with Trevor to get some recommendations on getting the Diner in order. In our one-on-one meeting, he acted as though he had no idea what I was asking him. Then the following Saturday at Laborer's Meeting he made it his business to tear me to shreds for the very things I had asked him for advice on.

As I got more experienced in my duties and could ask more precise questions, his reply was that he no longer had the manuals that he had written on the management of the Diner and that I needed to take control and institute my own systems.

Oh. Ok.

Of course this wouldn't stop him from filleting me in Laborer's meeting. In my eyes, I was asking for help, and then being taken apart by the very ones who I was asking for help from.

The reality was that being a Manager was not a train-on-the-job position. It was not the job of the Laborer's to help me. It was their job to hold me accountable. No amount of humility or brotherliness on my part was going to change the fact the Diner had become even more inefficient under my watch.

As things began to go downhill, Amanda, tired of sitting in on my weekly lashings at Laborer's meeting began to request duty at another site. She was fighting tooth and nail in her own way to make the Diner a success.

She reasoned that if I would just do things the way she was recommending I do them then none of these things would be an issue.

In some respects she was absolutely right. Unfortunately, that simply was not who I was at the time. Success as a Manager in the Diner required a greater Mathematician and/or Dictator and I was neither.

A couple of shorts months into my post as Manager, the writing was clearly on the wall.

At yet another lambasting of me at Laborer's meeting, Amanda would break down into tears. If I didn't already feel like an asshole, the looks on the faces of the officials said it all as they comforted her like a battered woman.

I was in over my head.

It had just so happened that Independence Day Celebration was rolling around. This was my first Independence Day in Heaven, which meant it would be an entirely different experience.

For the Diner it was exciting because this was the one time of year we would be guaranteed to make a great profit since part-timers rolled in from every corner of the country to enjoy eating their once a yearly righteous cooked meal.

My job was to come up with a grocery list that would cover the expected hundreds of patrons of the Diner. Having no idea how to guesstimate that, I was advised by Royall's wife, Miss White to contact Brother Omar, the Manager of the Diner in Cincinnati. Omar was understood to be the authority of dining in the Nation. He often served as Royall's personal chef and his exquisite meals were the stuff of legend.

It was a welcome change for me, because Omar didn't know me and I didn't know him, and too many of my conferences with the Laborers in Heaven quickly morphed into lectures as to why I needed to do better as Manager, husband, brother, and just better as a man in general.

I spoke to Omar, got a grocery list and submitted it to the Laborers and moved forward in making preparations for Independence Day.

Not so fast.

Next thing I know, I am watching Trevor amble into the Diner with my grocery list in his hand. Turns out the Secretary Department had forwarded the list to Trevor to determine its validity. You know, rather than telling me to run it by him in the first place. No problem, I tell Trevor that I had instructions from Miss White to get the list from Omar and...

Before I get the words out of my mouth Trevor is off to the races.

Omar is a great chef but he doesn't know how to manage a restaurant.

It's not Omar's responsibility. It's mine.

He's not going to do the list for me.

Before I know it, we are on the phone with the Secretarial Department, The National Secretary, Royall's Wives, Two of the Scientists, The FOI Captain, I'm pretty sure WD Fard was on the line somewhere in there, too.

And as the saying went in the Nation, "I was the star of the show."

In the bad sign of all bad signs, by the time we got off of the phone, I was instructed to do absolutely nothing and that the situation would be taken care of.

The next day the call came in. To be honest I don't even recall who it was making the call. All I recall is the words.

"Brother Prostell, you are properly relieved as Manager of the Diner"

And then the only that could make it sting more...

"and Brother Trevor is now the Manager."

Perfect.

It is only now that I am realizing how falls like this built me.

Amanda, who was on the line with me, made sure that the instruction included her as well, and once that was clear, immediately requested duty at a new site. I thought I was already numb, until the words, "I am so embarrassed to be associated with this" came spilling out of her mouth as she dramatically went walking to the back of the Diner, followed by a couple of Sisters trying to console her.

Trevor had to show up minutes later, smiling ear to ear. He carried a manila envelope, and told me to call a meeting for all the Diner staff. Some of the staff members who had grown frustrated with the situation clapped with glee, seeing Trevor, realizing what was taking place.

I did my best not take it personally, understanding that they simply wanted the Diner to run the way that it was supposed to be run.

After all the staff had been assembled in the Dining Area, Trevor broke the news.

"Father has instructed me to take over as Manager of the Diner."

The room erupted in cheers. The smile Trevor had been fighting so hard to suppress now spread across his face. He began to outline his plan for the Diner, beginning with the dramatic reduction in the staff, and the overhaul of the menu.

As he spoke he reached into his manila envelope and pulled out a stack of stapled papers.

"This is the Diner manual."

Riiiiight.

The same one I had asked him to look at, but he said he no longer had, now mysteriously appeared in his hands, moments after being named Manager. Amanda, the only other person in the room that knew I had asked him for it, looked at me incredulously. I had no response either verbal or physical.

My only focus at that moment was to make out of the Diner for the day without having a breakdown.

Trevor dismissed the meeting and the staff began buzzing around to shut things down for the night, some lingering to well wish or speak with Trevor. As I went to break down the front line, Brother Hassan consoled me, telling me that after I got done working with Trevor I would be the best Manager the Nation ever had.

I appreciated his words, and would take them to heart. But right now I just needed to get done and get out of there for the night. This would be one night I would not burn the midnight oil.

Since the transition was not complete, I still ended up being the last member there until the Secretary Department came and picked up the cash for the night. Then I called Trevor to let him know we were done, and I headed up the stairs for the night.

By the time I came down to duty the next morning I was feeling much better. The Brothers in the barracks had spent the better part of the night giving me much needed words of encouragement.

"Once you learn what Trevor knows plus what you already know, you're gonna be on your way."

"Besides, who comes in the Nation and is made Manager that quick? You'll be alright"

"It happens to the best Brothers. Even Bro (insert prominent official here) got properly relieved."

Of course it wouldn't be the barracks if there wasn't a good share of rubbing my nose in the fact that I had crashed and burned so gloriously, but I took it all in the proper spirit.

By the time the night was over I had made my mind up.

The Brothers were right. I had made great deal of progress in a short amount of time because of my capacity to learn. This scenario would be no different. They could take all the titles and play all the politics they wanted. One thing that could never be taken away was my work ethic and my ability to learn.

I would grind. I would hustle.

When I made it to the front door of the Diner it was already open and Brother Trevor was sitting at the front counter. I was impressed.

Even as far back as when Jay was the manager I couldn't recall the last time someone had made it to the Diner before me. I gave the greetings. Trevor returned them and began explaining some more of the steps he would be taking to revive the Diner.

I listened intently as I began preparing the grill for the day.

Before I had ever met him, Brother Trevor was notorious for his ego and short temper with those he was in authority over. But what could not be said about the brother was that he did not take his duty seriously.

The priority with him was always taking care of business and your feelings had very little to do with it. He would act like the person he was talking to was purposefully trying to tear down the Nation, and he had caught them red-handed.

This was fine with me. I wasn't from a place that had made me sensitive. I knew I could take whatever he could possibly dish out. Besides, I reasoned, my priority was the Nation, just like his. No matter what he thought of me before, being around me consistently, he would have to bear witness to who I really was.

Of course he had to try me.

Service was one of the things Trevor harped on the most. He had given us copies of his training manual to study the subject.

Since this was an area of most need in the Diner and I still fancied myself the most able bodied FOI there, I took on the role. It wasn't long before the next Laborer's meeting had come around. Since Trevor was now doing the report for The Diner and the Supermarket, I did my best to deal with the happenings in the Diner so that he would be free to give his reports.

Since I was also serving, this meant staying in eye shot of the Laborers, to make sure nothing was needed as they went over plans for the closely approaching Independence Day celebration. Things seemed to go well. Before long, the Laborers were filing out of the Diner with no major incident.

Trevor had learned that after Laborer's, the Royall Family, including Father himself would be coming into the Diner to eat. It was always a HUGE deal when Allah came out for even a brief appearance. Trevor gathered the staff and let it be known that this was an opportunity for the Diner to make a 'showing'.

This meant everyone needed to be on their very best performance. Trevor let it be known that he would be serving the Family, with me backing him only when necessary. No matter who was the Manager, serving the Royall Family always seemed to invite scenarios that otherwise would never happen.

Spiritually, this would be explained as Satan rearing his head, looking to bring a right idea (Allah enjoying a meal at his own restaurant) back to zero. This is possible, but it also may have had a lot to do with the nerves of a 14 year-old kid, who thinks he is preparing a meal for God himself, and four or five of God's wives.

Of course if you go to any eatery in this country with a decent size party who all have different special requests, chances are there is going to be some imperfection.

The difference is those patrons don't have the authority to get up, come to the grill or kitchen and 'help' the cooks.

In the Diner, if you got the order wrong, then before long, two or three of the wives would be behind the frontline and in the prep room over the shoulder of the staff, explaining to them how a brother, who was no longer even in the Nation, prepared Royall's scrambled eggs three years ago.

Even still, as far as Family trips to the Diner went, this one was pretty much without major incident. Trevor's style was authoritarian and abrasive, but you couldn't say he didn't get results. The only notable hiccup was that Royall had wanted a waffle and the cooks couldn't get the batter just right. Two waffles got sent back to the kitchen before Father decided to go without.

And really that's all Trevor needed. The second we walked back into the restaurant from escorting the Family to their vehicles, he launched into a tirade. Like most of his tirades it started at no one in particular, just a series of rhetorical questions asked to all in earshot. Subliminal stuff about pancake batter, the speed of the food coming or how he wasn't the old manager so none of this was going to fly anymore and if you didn't like it you could get out.
Reading between the lines, I started to respond, and that's when all hell broke loose. Before I could get the words out he cut me off, "If you would do your duty instead of trying to eavesdrop on the Laborer's meeting!"

I felt my temperature go from zero to edge of boiling. Now he was just insulting my manhood, to say nothing of my diligence as a soldier.

I responded, "Wasn't nobody ear hustling yo' damn meeting! YOU said the server needed to be attentive so I'm staying up front to see if you all need anything. I don't care about what's going on in Laborer's meeting... "

He acted like I wasn't even speaking.

"Brother Prostell, YOU are what's wrong with the Diner! YOU! YOU are the problem around here. If you already had it all figured out Father would not have sent me to take over."

So let's do this then.

"Do you think I don't know that!!?!?!? I KNOW that I don't know. I'm trying to learn what YOU know, so that I can do my duty."

By this time he was no longer even talking to me. He turned to Hassan and said, "See, this what I'm talking about right here. Things aint gonna be right around here until we get rid of the right people"

I exploded.

"ARE YOU TALKING ABOUT ME?!?! MAN, I'M STANDING RIGHT HERE IF YOU FEEL LIKE YOU NEED TO SAY SOMETHING TO ME!"

Never one to back down, he screamed, "YOU GON' HAVE TO GO PROSTELL, BECAUSE I'M NOT HAVING IT. YOU ARE OUT OF HERE. I'M REPORTING YOU RIGHT NOW!" He snatched the Diner phone and walked to back of the Diner.

Reporting me? What kind of threat was that? I thought he was from Chicago.

"DO WHAT YOU NEED TO DO, BUT YOU AINT BOUT TO BE YELLING AT ME BRO!" I wasn't even in the Diner anymore. "I'M NOT ONE OF THESE SISTERS OR YOUTH! YOU CAN TAKE THIS SHIT SOMEWHERE ELSE!"

I yelled down the hallway as he disappeared out the back door.

I walked to the front of the Diner and sat down on the first bar stool.

You could have heard a pin drop, as no one in the Diner said a word. Looks of worry came over the faces of the Sisters. Trevor walked back up front.

"Prostell, you can go ahead and go, we don't need you here."

"Pssh, Yes, Sir. Absolutely."

I took off my apron, tossed it in the Diner laundry bin and walked out the back door around to the barracks to avoid crossing paths with Trevor again. I wasn't entirely sure I would be able to keep from putting my hands on him.

I knew I was a valuable asset in the Diner, which is not to say I was irreplaceable, but I knew I more than put in my time, energy and effort. If he felt they would be better off without me, then so be it.

By the time Kaaba came and got me and told me we needed to meet next door in ten minutes, I had already moved on mentally from the Diner.

It hadn't taken long for the report of what happened between Trevor and me to get to Royall. A meeting was immediately called with Kaaba, Brother Emory (the new Lt.) and Brother Daniel.

I was over the discussion, the Diner, Trevor and any thought of reconciliation when we all sat down at the table in the dining room of the Diner. Brother Daniel began.

"Father said to tell you both, 'It is not to where Prostell should not want to have duty in the Diner and it's not to where Brother Trevor should not want Prostell to be in the Diner. Prostell, this is an opportunity for you to learn what you need to get in order to be a proper Manager, and Trevor, Prostell is one of the few Brothers in Heaven that actually has a will to take responsibility. In other words, if things go the way that they are supposed to, he is to be your relief."

As was the way in the Nation, the point was restated 'in other words' a couple of times to hammer it home. We were asked if we understood or if we had any questions, statements or if we thought there would be a problem working together going forward.

We shared we understood, Trevor stated it was his intention to see the things work, I stated it was my intention to learn everything I could in my time around Trevor and that was the end of the meeting.

I extended my hand which apparently was a bit more than Trevor was looking for at the moment. He acted like he didn't see it and simply went back to taking care of the Nation's business.

Whatever. I let it go. I felt like the point had been made. In Heaven, if the wrong report came from the right official then no one was going to be interested in hearing your side of the story.

Trevor, one of Royall's favorite sons, had tried me with the bullying tactics he was famous for, and despite my will to regain my position as Manager, I wasn't having it. My stance had been backed up by Royall. I wasn't going anywhere anytime soon.

Trevor turned out to be every bit the Manager he was advertised as, and though the Diner still wasn't raking in the bucks, he was at least keeping things running smoothly on a shoe string budget and staff.

Though I was his eager understudy, not being the Manager was a welcome change.

After all the smoke had cleared from my being relieved as Manager, public sentiment was still rather high on me. My failures as Manager were offset with the notion that it was unheard of for me to even be in such a position after such a short time in the Nation. Father had made it clear that I was being prepared to take over the Manager post from Trevor when I was ready.

I just wanted to keep working.

None of that positive public sentiment had transferred over into my relationship as Amanda still regarded my relief as a Manager as a complete and utter embarrassment and failure. We had finally been moved into a home of our own, with Sister Brianna, from Detroit, and her husband Carter, a take charge brother from L.A. with whom I would grow close over my time in the UNOI. This helped a little, but not much. As I had anticipated, the living arrangement would often feel like more of a duty.

More and more of our conversations ended up being discussions about how I was falling short of what was expected of me. She would outline how she was used to dealing with more powerful Brothers because of coming up around her Brothers and father (which was at this point as laughable to me, since none of them were even beginning to take steps toward joining the ranks full-time and as such commanded little respect in the Nation outside of their own minds).

No matter what particular angle the conversation started from, it would inevitably end with her expressing her will to no longer deal. By this time I had gone past the point of trying to reason or talk her down from such a decision. If she decided she could do better, then so be it. I knew that she was coveted by more than a few Brothers in the Nation before and after I had come on the scene.

I knew it would hurt my ego to see her with the type of man that she had described to me, this take charge, no nonsense, hard charging brother who could make things happen for her, his Nation, and himself. But I also knew I was doing my best, and it felt like that was not even close to good enough.

Almost a year into living in Heaven she still had not learned to go along in order to get along, like most of the members did. Though she was oftentimes right, her direct, blunt style of communication rubbed wrong those whose help she ultimately needed.

My approach was just the opposite. I would take the path of least resistance, well aware that I had neither the knowledge nor the disposition to go against the structure. I would mostly observe things and ask questions to the select few who I knew would give me straight answers without judging or manipulating me.

We were in complete agreement about this being exactly where we should be in order to guarantee our family's success. Yet we somehow managed to remain on two very different pages even in this new world.

Eleven months ago I had arrived in Heaven worthless as a penny with a hole in it, to others and myself.

I had fought and scraped going from being the Brother no one wanted, to being one of the brightest rising stars of the Nation.

We had gone from "the Sister from the powerful family and her hapless, lost-found husband" to one of the more up-and-coming powerful couples in Heaven.

After close to year of physical separation, we were finally reunited; living under the same roof, sleeping in the same bed and we couldn't have been further apart.

Lesson C-3

Connecticut

And just like that in a flash, it was all different.

Eventually, you learned the only thing that was guaranteed in the Nation was change.

Well, that and the destruction, i.e. Armageddon, or the end of mankind and the eradication of civilization as we know it.

But, yeah, other than that, it was change.

FOI class had been called, as opposed to work detail, which meant we had something big to discuss.

Once the Brothers were assembled and filed into the seats at the University, Brother Daniel laid out the scenario.

The Temple in Connecticut had been calling for assistance.

A bakery had been purchased, in a great location, but the members in Connecticut had been unable as of yet to get it up and running. They had already been blessed with the assistance of two full-time Brothers, but disorganization and personalism had just about brought all progress to a screeching halt.

Reports went in, calls were made, and eventually, Royall himself had been sold on investing full-time Nation resources into Connecticut.

This meant the most valuable resource in the Nation: The Brothers.

He tasked Daniel with putting together a team. And this was why we all had assembled that night late Sept. 2004 for FOI Class.

Our mission should we choose to accept it: Five Brothers were needed to head out to Connecticut and do it.

"IT" meaning EVERYTHING.

Open the bakery. Do the baking. Do the Books. Clean up the Temple. Bake the bean pie. Perfect the bean pie. Sell the bean pie. Rinse. Repeat.

Everything.

It was not known where the Brothers would be sleeping, or how they were be eating. All he wanted to know, was who was coming with him.

And of course being Heaven, before he could get the proposal out of his mouth good, 90 % of the hands in the room went up.

Being dispatched was a Heaven Brother's dream. It was the very reason why we got up and did the same thing, over and over, day after day. All of this motion, all of the scenarios, all the extra duties, all of the classes, all of the studying.

Learning the God meanings of the words we used, learning the spiritual meaning behind every person, place, thing, and idea we encountered, understanding the way that thought worked, reading body language, the unseen, all of it.

This was all practice. These buildings were simply classrooms to practice Mathematical Thinking. But being dispatched, THIS was an opportunity to make something happen.

Putting together a team wasn't as simple as picking the best five Brothers we had and hitting the road. If you were a halfway decent brother, chances are a) you had a major responsibility already in Heaven, and b) you had been around so long that you had a record.

Which was good.

But also could be very bad.

In Heaven not only did your triumphs become the stuff of legend, but so did you failures.

For some Brothers who had been around for ten or more years ,that meant ten plus years of the good, bad and ugly that could pulled out to support or dismiss the brother as a candidate for a particular duty.

The ideal position to be in was to have shown yourself as a trustworthy brother, but not have enough baggage for anyone to make a case against you, because, in the politically charged hierarchy of the UNOI, they WILL make a case against you.

With this in mind, I really liked my chances. I was still new and even my biggest blemish said more about my positives than my negatives. I mean come on…my biggest problem was that I took responsibility for work that wasn't mine. Hell, I had to have shown some type of assertiveness to even be in the position of managing the Nation's flagship business after being in Heaven for such a short amount of time.

Which goes to show how much my opinion carried weight.

Carter, who was definitely one of the more dependable and versatile Brothers in the Nation got the call that he would be going. He, Brother Mason and three youth Brothers were going. As bad as I wanted to go, I took the news in stride. Out of hundreds Brothers in Heaven, only five could go.

Just the Idea of Brothers being dispatched was inspiring. These Brothers' absence presented an opportunity to step up to fill the void that would be left by their departure.

Maybe I wouldn't get to go to Connecticut, but maybe I could step into one of these Brothers shoes and be on the next team sent out.

Even if I stayed in Heaven I was the designated heir as Manager of the Diner, and Kaaba had secretly began preparing me to manage the

Service Station. I could just about write my own ticket as long as I kept working hard. Like the others who weren't picked, I began to prepare myself to continue to sharpen myself, as a brother, father, and FOI.

But then the only thing set in the Nation...change.

I was at the Diner the next day when I got that phone call. Bro Mason was not going to be able to leave. It had been determined that his assistance was indispensable here in Heaven. In his cool, casual way, Brother Daniel asked if I would be interested in heading out to Connecticut with the Brothers.

Now it's been years, so I may be recalling this wrong, but if memory serves I ran a lap around the Earth in quantum light speed to slap myself high five. Also, if I'm not mistaken, I did a back flip over the Hubble telescope. Maybe not, but either way, the point is I was beyond excited.

"Yessir!, I responded incredulously.

Daniel instructed me to head home and begin preparing to hit the road ASAP, as we would be leaving first thing in the a.m.

I don't think my feet touched the ground as I went home and gave Amanda the news. Her response was more disbelief than anything. I don't know if she was afraid I would embarrass myself, or if she felt like I was abandoning her, but it certainly wasn't what I expected. But even that could not put a damper on my mood. I was locked in. This was what FOI dreams were made of.

With all the pageantry and fanfare of soldiers being shipped out to war, we rolled out of Heaven the next morning. We were six deep in a Suburban that had been lent to us by one of the more diligent, and faithful part-time Brothers.

Daniel as a Royall Family member and head of the Brothers in general was the unquestioned leader, followed by Brother Carter, whose natural leadership skills and assertiveness caused him to immediately take the role as a buffer between Daniel and the rest of us.

Then there were three of the more promising youth Brothers, Darren, an apprentice mechanic, Edwin, who was a part of the National Secretary department, and Ramar, who in addition to being an officer in Heaven's FOI, and courting Royall's eldest granddaughter, had a very specific connection to Connecticut.

Ramar was a part of the Davis Family, the Connecticut version of the Hassans Family in Detroit. This is to say they were highly represented in the temple. This is also to say they had been acknowledged by Royall as one of the powerful, powerful families who had a great and divine purpose in the Nation, and summarily had taken that acknowledgement and decided that no further action was needed on their part. Royall had given them several shoutouts in national meetings, so their power needed no further proving.

At least as far as they were concerned.

The patriarch of the Davis family was Edmund Sr., who was a follower of the Honorable Elijah Muhammad. Edmund's brother, Richard, who lived right next door, was the minister of the temple. Both of the elder Davis's had two wives. Richard's children were all estranged from the Nation. He would speak of them and what great things they had done in the Nation, but it meant very little to us. It was far worse to have been a part of the Nation and then turn your back on it than to have never come in at all.

Edmund Sr. had been blessed with six sons and two daughters. His children covered all extremes of participation, from former member, to comfortably part-time, to part-time with full-time aspirations, all the way to his daughter April who was in the secretary department in Heaven and most notably, the wife of King Joseph.

Anytime members would come from Heaven to an outlying Temple for any extended stay, especially for those stays aimed at opening business/temple/study, things would very much take on the feel of a US occupation. We would come under the guise of shoring things up, or providing physical and spiritual support, but just the fact that we were there indicated that someone, or in most cases, a few someones had been falling short of their duty.

Whenever members would gather, you could cut the tension with a knife, as personal feuds, bad blood, and crooked politicians bubbled just below the surface of the "As Salaam Alaikums," hugs and well- wishing.

As members from Heaven, you were automatically sharper on the knowledge of how things were to be done according to Royall, Allah in Person. And EVERYONE knew it. So many of our conversations would be with members who felt victimized, asking some loaded question to round-about-kinda-sorta tell on each other, without actually officially telling on the members they felt had wronged them.

If they were skillful, this would be done by asking some loaded 'hypothetical' question about a situation that you later find out was identical to a scenario that didn't go their way as long ago as five years ago.

If they were less graceful, you would try not to laugh as one member would blurt out some scenario, accusation or ongoing disagreement, completely unrelated to the topic that was currently being discussed.

It was in this environment I quickly begin to discover how much I had learned by being in the controlled environment of Heaven for the last 11 months.

In the Temple, knowledge and ideas that we would have taken for granted in Heaven would create standing ovations in Connecticut. With lost-founds and even some members, you would have to dumb down your subject matter to remedial level to even begin a conversation.

We were so far ahead of the game that we were literally the only ones who could put each other in check.

This would end up having numerous very positive and very negative effects simultaneously raising my stature in the Nation and almost leading me to being kicked out of the Nation: for the first time.

First, the positive.

In Heaven, not only was the knowledge commonplace, but there was also no shortage of members who were willing to state what we considered to be the obvious. This put Brothers like me in the situation of never really feeling the need to speak up in discussion in or out of class.

In Connecticut it was just the opposite. If you didn't involve yourself, not only was the right thing not going to happen, but someone was going to try to pass some bullshit off as knowledge. Or come up with something that they made up in their head and attribute it to you or worse, Father/Royall, which was a great way to get jacked up.

Remember, if some nonsense went down, then the one with highest level of knowledge in the room was the one whose ass was in the ringer, so if nothing else THAT at least had you paying attention.

Once we got into the inner workings of the Temple, it wasn't long before the old regime, (Minister, Secretary, Captain, etc.) was properly relieved of their titles after having been exposed for a laundry list of improprieties (temple money being kept in the sock drawer, full-time Brothers being mistreated\pimped, money mismanaged, etc., the usual).

This only added to the tense, politically-charged atmosphere of the Temple. Those who had been wronged by the outgoing officials often had designs on their position. The outgoing officials themselves hadn't yet fully let go of said position and would take every opportunity to show that perhaps maybe a mistake had been made in relieving them of their title.

As members from Heaven, we had to be cognizant of these dynamics at all times, because in no time flat a member could take something you said in general conversation and go running back to Royall/Daniel or one of the members, or worse, bring it up in class. At any time a small bit of information or a casual offhand comment would be used out of context in some attempt to prop up some erroneous theory or principle they were trying to assert.

A few times of that, and we were less and less willing to carry on casual conversation with all but a few members in the Temple.

As Brothers from Heaven we knew and had been lectured to at length that we were held to a higher standard. If you were set up, then it's your fault for being in a position to allow yourself to BE set up. After all, you were coming from Heaven studying at the foot of the Royall Family. If a part-time member could set you up, it was proof positive that you were not ready.

Brother Daniel and Royall, who stopped through Connecticut shortly after our arrival, did a great job of setting the tone, making it clear that things had been thoroughly screwed up and that these Brothers, us, had been sent to straighten things out and turn things back over to the ones in Connecticut. Royall went so far as to suggest that if the Temple, especially the Davis Family did not get their stuff together, he would just as soon send a tidal wave and take out the entire region rather than to continue to entertain their incompetence.

This had the effect of us being declared the champion before the season even started by the commissioner. After all, we had been selected from all the Brothers in the big leagues (Heaven) to come to the minors (Connecticut).

The Brothers, Sisters, members of the first, youth, even regular visitors, and those mildly familiar with the Nation hung on our every word and treated it like gospel, which when compared to Heaven made it incredibly easy to get things done without a bunch of questions.

The downside to this scenario?

The Brothers, Sisters, members of the first, youth, even regular visitors, and those mildly familiar with the Nation hung on our every word, and treated it like gospel which when compared to Heaven made it incredibly easy to get things done without a bunch of questions.

Yes, you read that right. I'll explain.

Early on in one of the classes in Connecticut, one of the part-time Brothers asked Carter what it was like to be a brother in Heaven. His response: it was just like being in prison. I'm pretty sure I felt my heart stop at that moment.

We were there to show everyone the divinity and benefits of being in the Nation, in particular Heaven. Royall was here to make the Blackman FREE, and this guy says, with authority, across the mic, in FOI class, that Heaven is just like Prison. I almost died on the spot.

In retrospect though, he wasn't that far off.

I had spent 11 months in Heaven, fully immersed, surrounded, 24-7 in the culture of Nation building. It had been a controlled environment where our every move and aspect of life is so closely monitored and calculated, that Brothers were liable to throw you an intervention if you had been eating too many baked goods. Not weed, not crack, alcohol or women, but cinnamon rolls.

You would come home to the barracks to find the Brothers standing in a semi-circle, arms folded, looking grim, around the table with an apple fritter wrapper that had been found under your bunk.

Just like prison, there were Brothers like Carter or Daniel who had been in so long and knew the system well enough that they could matriculate through without much resistance. As a street guy, you could recognize it a mile away, and even if you had similar tastes, you knew enough to not make their spot hot or put your ass on the line by asking about certain things. As the saying goes, what's understood doesn't need to be said. Besides, I had my own connections.

Early on after arriving in Heaven, I had caught a bad case of cabin fever. I had been locked into my duties for a couple of months, and, well, the streets were calling me.

It just so happened that one of my close friends had family in Kansas. I knew his uncle Zig who was a major rap artist in KC.

So I called him. KC was Zig's town, so long story short he showed me a crazy good time that night; in and out of a few live clubs, lots of good looking girls who showed love just because I was from out of town/Detroit. The least of which was not some aggressive young lady who, after some serious sex talk in the club was nice enough to give me a few minutes of fellatio in front of the club.

Great night, right? Well I thought so.

That is until that same young lady was getting off of the city bus, directly in front of the huge picture window in front of the Diner while I stood less than ten feet away on the other side of the glass at the register holding a spatula.

Same young lady, same outfit and everything.

I do not pretend to be a wild life expert but no deer in headlights have ever been as frozen as I was at that moment. There are icebergs and glaciers that would have to get twice as cold to be as frozen as I was at that moment.

To my relief she looked up the street one way and then the other, and then proceeded to walk the opposite direction from the rest of the Nation's businesses. It was at that moment I decided that I would go ahead and end that portion of my KC night life.

So while that part of my psyche did indeed still exist I had tucked it away, and grasped wholeheartedly onto my duties as an upstanding brother in the FOI.

If Heaven was prison, then Connecticut was not only being back on the streets. It was being back on the street having just been named Sheriff. In short, the inmates were running the asylum.

Don't get me wrong, when it came to the Nation's business we were on our duties. The first order of business was to establish law and order in the Temple, and we had done that swiftly and decisively. Carter took responsibility for the Brothers' military. Daniel, though he shied away from titles, was performing all of the duties of a minister, speaking directly to Father, and overall managing the Temple.

Next was the matter of getting the bakery up and running. After a few phone calls around the Nation, we had all the best recipes and advice on how to make what we need to make. I took responsibility for implementing the systems I learned at the Diner (groceries, prep, scheduling, etc.).

Each of the full-time Brothers would volunteer for baking at least two items on the menu. None of us had actually had experience baking or having duty in the bakery, but the way we had been taught, that was a minor detail.

Before the permits had come back to open the doors to the bakery, we had flooded the streets, going door-to-door in residential and business areas with the baked goods. At first we focused on New Haven, but soon we set our sights on bigger cities like Hartford, Bridgeport and New York.

Like most Black people who have never been there, I was surprised to find out that Connecticut had ghettos, projects no less. But even this worked in my favor, as Connecticut's proximity to New York led to its fast paced, quick moving lifestyle. After having spent close to a year in

Kansas City, KS, going out in the community in Connecticut was like being back home in Detroit.

All of the skills I had developed hustling in Detroit came flooding back. Only instead of looking like a common street urchin, I walked and talked like the proper FOI. It was akin to being bilingual. Royall had cleaned me up, taught me, and convinced me that I was God. I was already a pretty quick thinker and talker. The mathematical thinking we had been taught caused me now to analyze everything that was being said and not said, as well as body language and other unseen cues, all without really trying.

After almost a year of talking to members, being taught math, and going to math class, talking to these lost-founds was like shooting fish in a barrel.

In less than three months we had the bakery up and running with clientele in Boston, Hartford, Bridgeport, New York, New Jersey, and just about every place in between. The Temple was running like a well-oiled machine, more and more visitors were coming, AND staying long enough to become members. The entire Nation was buzzing about this handful of Brothers who had come from Heaven and set the East coast on its ear.

We expected nothing less. This was a labor of love. The comradery that had existed in Heaven was multiplied tenfold in Connecticut amongst the Brothers who had come from Heaven. It was essentially us against the world.

The two full-time Brothers who were already in Connecticut when we arrived were another story. Well, two other stories operating at the opposite end of the spectrum.

First there was Brother Robin. Old hoe ass, punk ass snitch ass, cock-blocking ass, smelling like tiger balm ass Brother Robin.

I liked Bro. Robin. Truly.

Brother Robin had been in the Nation longer than most. No one knew for sure what he did before he came to the Nation. Some said he had been in jail, others said he had lived on the streets. But whatever it was it had made him an angry, mean old man. Just mean.

What couldn't be questioned was his work ethic. He was certainly one of the most thorough, hard- working Brothers you could meet and would use that skill to not only make sure his duty was straight, but tell you what you needed to fix with yours, too. He made up for this by being as rude as possible in doing so.

By the time you got done dealing with him, you were too frustrated to talk math and just really wanted to knock him out. He would use this to his advantage to show how you needed to master your emotions, how you were being a tool for Satan. None of those techniques were new, but he had them down to a science.

What made matters worse was Robin had built in his time in the Nation a close relationship with one of Royall's wives, Sis Advisor, the head of the Cincinnati Temple.

His methods were an invaluable tool for the superiors who needed to know all of the facts and wanted to make sure no one was drawing outside the lines. Bro. Robin could be depended on for just that. He used this relationship as a means of going over the heads of Brothers who he couldn't beat down with the Math himself.

He would call with all the dirt and then next thing you know you would be getting a phone call from Father or the National Secretary about a situation he hadn't even mentioned to you or that you all had already discussed and supposedly put a period to.

As you might have picked up, Bro. Robin and I developed a special, special relationship.

The other full-timer was Brother Donald. Donald was the rare case of a brother who was full-time but had never been to Heaven. He was a testament to the need for every Brother to go through the 'filter' that was Heaven before being dispatched.

Donald had a willing spirit, but his general lack of knowledge and experience in the Nation led him to develop a very dependent, victim mentality. A New York native, he had come to the Nation fresh out jail with a will to do whatever was needed.

This will was quickly smothered. Partly by part- timers who were all too happy to have a full-time volunteer to help bake the pies and sell the pies, but weren't so fast to use the money generated from those pie sales to provide for the needs of said volunteer. Before it was all said and done, Brother Donald was living in the basement of the bakery because the members had decided none had room for him in their homes. (The same thing they said to us when we came, so at least they were consistent).

They would then take the money he had earned and send some of it in as charity. What happened to the rest is up for debate...all while turning in very little charity of their own.

As far as Donald, it certainly didn't help that Brother Robin was Donald's first interaction with a full-time brother. By the time we arrived on the scene Robin had Donald so boxed in with the Math that Donald was practically paralyzed.

At its best, Mathematical Thinking could free you from being under the jurisdiction of any person, at its worst you would be so scared of doing something deemed unmathematical that you would hardly blink without checking your thinking on it first.

Where Robin's tactics were too rigid, Donald needed so much attention he took away from another brother doing their duty. In Heaven both of these behaviors could exist, but here they just continued to gum up the works.

Our attitude was that we were responsible for saying what we were going to do and as long as we did that, then we were good. The more we did that, the stronger our bond as Brothers grew. Our word was our individual and collective bond.

Though a room had been made available for Daniel at the former minster's home, the remaining five of us were sleeping on the floor in the room of Brother Edmund's 16 year-old son, Tariq. The first couple of nights, Richard's wives had prepared dinner for us but that didn't last long. None of this fazed us.

We were used to motion so we didn't really think about the sleeping situation until it was time to go to bed. Usually by then we were too tired to really care, and just tried to carve out a corner to pass out in.

Even in our free time we didn't hang around because being at the house meant being around the same people who were responsible for things being out of order. Right or wrong, no one wanted to take phones calls from members who lied to them or tried to manipulate them in scenarios, or disappeared when it came time to do the work of building, and then chill and watch the game on the couch with these same members.

The work, as plentiful as it was, was still far less than what we were used to. A 10-hour day was nothing when you were accustomed to pulling 16-hour days.

Hell, that gave us six extra hours to burn.

These extra hours were spent innocent enough at first.

Sometimes we would go to the mall.

Sometimes, when we had hustled up on some money, we would go grab a bite to eat. One of the members hooked us up with gym passes, so going to work out became an option. And of course we were right outside of New York, so you know I had to go hoop.

One thing was for certain; no matter where we went, we stood out. Here we were this group of young men walking into a room, clean, confident, well-groomed, sharply dressed, witted and all on one accord. In most cases it was something they had never encountered before. Hell, it was even a new phenomenon to me.

They say that confidence is an attractive quality in a man. Well, what about three or four men who knew that that they are the God of the Universe, Cream of the Planet Earth?

As I said earlier, I had become a keen Mathematical Thinker, yet balanced that knowledge with a lifetime of knowing how to handle myself in the street. A year in Heaven had done well to drill these ideas into my mind, and though the environment kept my more street tendencies at bay, there were no such buffers in Connecticut. In fact, one could argue that the more street elements that existed in Heaven had come along to Connecticut with me. Me and Carter had never really spent time together outside the house, but I knew enough about the Brothers he liked to hang with to know he was a party boy, himself. He had a very serious cocky, pretty boy swagger, so much so one of the Sisters in the Diner had commented that he looked like a righteous pimp. It fit. It stuck.

In Heaven where EVERYTHING was under a microscope, he had managed to not only get a personal vehicle and cell phone from God knows where, but he had also evaded any questioning as it relates to the source of said car and cell phone. As far back as the Moreen episodes on Farrakhanfactor.com, Daniel's wild side had been well documented. In Heaven, he would drop little hints anytime we spoke to let me know that he was into things, but I could recognize all the symptoms without him ever saying anything.

His car always smelled like anti-weed spray anytime we went to hoop. The dudes he was always 'recruiting' into the Nation just happened to be some of KC's biggest dope boys, the nondescript phone calls where he wouldn't give the greetings. I mean they didn't sound guilty, but they certainly didn't sound innocent either.

Growing up in the Nation had made him very calculated in who he allowed to get close to him, so him exposing me to those things gave me the feeling that he was testing the water to see how much I could be trusted.

I did my best to just let it be known I peeped game, but not seem too eager to sign on as one of his entourage. As much as I respected Morris, a lot of the guys that hung around Daniel acted a little too much like yes men, just happy to be along for the ride. I understood that he was Royall Family and I respected and admired the brother and everything, but I definitely didn't want any parts of that (dick-riding is what we called it back home).

We would talk openly about weed, women, and street stuff, making sure to keep it in the context of general conversation or the past or finding some way to find the divinity in the elements of common thuggery. Being in Connecticut provided the first opportunity to test the waters to see exactly how far we were willing to go with this thing.

Coming in and cleaning up Connecticut against all odds was all the comradery needed to take things to the next level (up or down is anyone's guess).

As calculating as Daniel was, his natural way was to be generous. So even though he had snuck out a couple times solo, he eventually brought Carter and then me in on some of the perks he had established in his past visits to Connecticut.

The first of which was a ritzy little bar at the top of the Omni Hotel in downtown New Haven. It was the perfect spot where we would never run into any of the members of the Temple. This became our primary chill spot, or launching pad for any night exploits we might get into.

What made it even more perfect was the bartender. Dave was the brother of one of the full-time Brothers back in Heaven. He was one of those people who had come to class, decided that the idea was not for him, but remained friendly with a member or two, in this case, Daniel.

This was a classy place...top shelf everything, designer peanuts, even the French fries ran $8 a pop. We would sit at the bar, Dave would keep the drinks coming, and we would make sure that he left that night with a very healthy tip. He was real good people and aside from that he was local and could put us up on where to hang out or get what we needed in the hood.

Now, what we needed depended on just how comfortable we were with each other at that point. The bar setup was cool and while neither of us were really drinkers we were all taking baby steps to see who could hold water.

I knew that when it came time to really kick it, Daniel majored in the herbal arts. Actually, I should say he majored and I minored. I mean we both smoked together, but once Dave put us on the best place to score some weed, I soon learned Daniel's knowledge of weed was on par with his God knowledge.

The stresses that came with being placed in charge of the Nation's military at age 11, subsequently kicked in and out of the Nation twice before the age of 15, hustling on the street, in and out of jail, seeing yourself marked for death by your Grandfather, Allah himself, being given a chance at redemption, being forced to wage war against your Mother all the way up to her death as she tries to leave the Nation. . . . can do a number on a guy's nerves. Let just say somewhere in all of that, he developed the appreciation for a good grade of THC.

He could explain everything from the strain of weed, what those little crystals meant, what the way the weed was bagged said about the guy who sold it.

Being a casual smoker, I had only really smoked the basic stuff, but Daniel was putting me on to all types of exotic weed. I was used to lighting a blunt, hitting it and passing that boy around until it was gone. Not with this. We would hit this stuff once, twice, maybe three times, and then we would sit.

And sit.

And sit.

This was around the time Kayne West's College dropout album came out, so picture two Muslims sitting a truck smoking weed listening to Jesus walks. Yeah.

There were times we would roll up to go to a club or visit someone we had met. We would pull up in the car, roll a blunt, light a blunt, hit it and just never go inside. Sitting in the car and talking about Royall, the Nation, Moreen, family, life, love, the hood.

Of course if weed was Daniel's drug of choice, he, we, not even you at home reading this should have to guess what mine was.

My relationship with Amanda had been deteriorating by the day. At this point we hardly spoke and when we did it was always some disagreement about something that had happened a long time ago. She had heard through the Nation grapevine that we had been hanging out which she didn't like one bit.

One of the things I had heard repeatedly from the Brothers about me being dispatched was that, 'absence makes the heart grow fonder'. Well in our marriage it had the opposite effect. An already affectionless situation grew colder from the distance and by the time I got off the phone both of us could do without talking for a while.

169

The attention that came from being an FOI was pretty much a constant. You knew that if you walked into a place you were largely going to be the center of attention. If the weed and liquor in my system made this a risky proposition, being with Carter most of the time made the end result inevitable.

Carter was exactly the type of guy you needed to have if you wanted to break the ice, in ANY situation, out in the community or at the bar later. He is to this day one of the absolute most aggressive people I have ever met. But he smooth tho.

He was raised in Napa, CA, and I used tell him that was a protection for him (and the hood), because if he had been in South Central, he would have leading somebody's gang or behind bars with a hell of a body count. His accent and mannerisms said 'Valley' but whether it be in a confrontation with lost-founds or talking to women, his entire attitude said projects.

During one of my first interactions with him in Heaven, we had been playing ball with some lost-founds. Daniel and I were on the court, Carter was on the side chatting with some Sisters or youth. Things started to cross the line between a good physical game and guys playing dirty. Pretty soon warnings turned to threats, which turned to pushing then shoving, next thing you know the ball is rolling off of the court forgotten about, as we are standing chest to chest with a few knuckleheads from the neighborhood ready to get it in. I'm sizing my guy up, when a body smashes itself between us. It's Carter. To this day I don't know if he put himself in the middle to break up the scrum or line up the first shot.

I have gotten to know him well over the years. I suspect his mind was doing the former and his heart the latter.

He was just about the polar opposite of me in many ways, which likely explains why we got along so famously. Where I would sit back and try to calculate how I would approach a person or situation, he walk across the floor confidently and tap a young lady on the shoulder, "Um excuse me, How are you doing?" and just like that we were off to the races.

Our personalities played off of each other perfectly, he applying pressure, me being the comic relief keeping things light.

Before long we each had a regular rotation of lady 'friends' from New York all the way to Hartford. Daniel being the pretty boy would get more than his fair share of attention from the locals. Nothing too serious at first, just a few pretty faces to keep us entertained in between being at duty, class, and avoiding the part-timers.

I would get up early every day and walk the few miles to the bakery, do my baking, manage the schedule and grocery list, put together the fund raiser teams, and everything else that duty entailed. Right around closing time, Daniel and Carter would come to check on the progress of the bakery and scoop me and we would head downtown for a few drinks to get our evening started.

Sometimes that would simply mean inviting a few ladies up to the bar for some company or hitting a club that we had heard would be particularly live. Sometimes we would just head home to catch the game (the Pistons won the Championship that year).

This was always fun because it meant trying to avoid smelling, acting, or looking high to the members who were in the house with us.

We would shoot each other bemused looks as Bro. Edmund would invariably catch one of us in the kitchen with a story from the First that he couldn't dare tell us without being an inch from our face.

You haven't experienced awkward until you are standing face to face with a person you came to teach about righteousness, with nice buzz from a few too many long islands, and marijuana smoke floating around in your system.

Though we tried to never take anything for granted, it was a clear indication that our infallibility was well intact.

With almost everyone.

Yeah, almost.

While our balancing act did not arouse any notable suspicions of any of the members, Bro. Robin was sitting back skeptically watching the whole scene unfold.

He had been a full-time member for a very long time, so our ripping and running stood out to him like a sore thumb and he was not in harmony at all. While he had a very good and begrudgingly respectful relationship with Daniel and Carter, respectively, I was an entirely different case.

Robin had been trying without much success to do what we were sent to do. Though he was an incredibly hard worker, his people skills sat in direct contrast to his work ethic.

He would work hours on hours through the night perfecting the bean pie which was the most popular and important product that the bakery produced. To add to that, he would tirelessly travel up and down the east coast selling said pies.

He held in contempt anyone who he felt was not matching his level of dedication, which is to say everyone. He had a raspy voice that sounded like he was doing a bad 'Dirty Harry' impression, which only added to his confrontational aura.

He would go to war with the Minister about an incorrect quote or teaching in class. He would disassemble one of the Brothers in FOI class for not keeping his word. And my favorite, he would go on and on about the Sisters' 'naaaaasty' thinking, being the reason that they were producing 'naaaaasty' baked goods.

Brothers like Robin had spent years in the Nation learning the proper way to conduct themselves like an FOI. While I was an enthusiastic and friendly brother, none of that made up for what I lacked in polish and discipline.

It didn't help our relationship that Robin had made it clear that he had designs on being the Manager of the bakery once we got it open, a position that went to me shortly after our arrival. After all, he had been there long before us fighting and scrapping to get things going. Then here comes this sloppy, goofy, rough around the edges, poorly spoken, excuse for an FOI...

The thing about being at odds with an experienced Brother like Robin was that I never saw him coming until it was too late.

The first salvo was fired at a short FOI class that had been called at the bakery.

"Brother Prostell, I was told you had the truck last night, and on my way to the bakery at 3am the truck wasn't there. I even circled the block to see if it was parked up the street and I still didn't see it. Where were you Brother?"

My blood instantly started to boil.

Did this MF just say he circled the block?

So much for a shot across the bow, this was a full-fledged Pearl Harbor, midnight air raid. I nonchalantly looked up at the class, including Daniel and Carter. If I was out at 3am, surely they had been with me, but Robin made no mention of them, leaving me in the position to not only tell on myself but if I was extra clumsy incriminate them as well.

That was not even remotely an option.

More than anything I was incensed at his conduct. It was a rule of the FOI that if you saw your brother slipping then you were duty-bound to pull him to the side, or at least bring it to his attention when you saw it. Certainly you didn't call them onto the carpet in class with an issue you had never so much as brought up in conversation.

The fact that he did it this way not only an open challenge, but far more immoral than anything I could have been doing at 3a.m. with the truck. It said loud and clear that we were not Brothers, and that he had nothing but the worst intentions.

I didn't try to hide my anger, but I easily answered the question. "I got hungry; there was nothing to eat so I went out to get something before duty. But you're right; I should have called and let someone know where I was."

Polished or not I knew enough to handle that situation. Robin asked the same question a different way in an attempt to trip me up but to no avail. Daniel wrapped it, giving me the obligatory tongue lashing, emphasizing the fact that we had not come out here to become scenarios ourselves, and that I had to do better or someone would be replacing me.

I said I understood and sat hoping someone would ask the million dollar question.

Why hadn't Brother Robin come to his Brother to address the issue before trying to bring it out in class? Why hadn't he at least called and reported it to the local structure?

No one did. But for those that knew better the questions were right there hanging in the air.

Technically it could be argued he didn't have to. This was after all FOI class.

If he suspected accurately that I was in cahoots with Daniel/Carter it wouldn't have made sense to report it to them. Either way the writing was on the wall.

I exploded once we got in the car on the way back to the house.

"What the fuck is wrong with that nigga?"

Daniel immediately turned it back on me.

"Ah man, I aint tryna hear that. This is what you signed up for. We already told you it was gonna be like this. You can't expect every Brother to do what you would do. Robin is not here because he brotherly, he here for the same reason we here. Cause they wouldn't do the work."

I understood everything that Daniel was saying but it didn't cause me to have any less dislike for Robin.

Either way it was clear that we or more specifically, *I* was going to have to be a lot more strategic in how I handled my business. Or in this case, pleasure.

Though his thinly veiled accusation didn't stick, Robin's statement had opened a door. Now my movements would be subject to a little closer inspection.

Up to this point, we had not only been above the law-we had *been* the law.

Even though I had escaped any substantial damage, we all had an unspoken understanding that we would cool our jets at least for any major collective undertakings for the foreseeable future.

Daniel would just slip back into his regular routine. It was a part of his M.O. to disappear regularly so no one was ever going to question the ranking Royall Family member as to his movements and whereabouts. But by having me with him, it would bring unwanted scrutiny and attention, so he simply went into his default activity of distancing himself when it came to extracurricular activity. We would hoop, and work out, maybe hoop but after that it was don't ask, don't tell.

After the nonsense Robin had tried to pull I preferred it that way. After spending time with Daniel, I learned that he was a loyal brother who would have your back as much as he could. But he had been burned in the past by vouching for Brothers who had crashed and burned spectacularly. As good as his heart was, the Nation he had been raised in was a political environment so when he had to, he could be as coldly calculating as the best/worst politician.

He had his share of run-ins with the authority, including all the fallout from the Moreen Scenario that had just about ripped the Nation in half. The last thing he was trying to do was to come out here and blow it.

The reason he had identified so readily with me was that he saw a lot of himself in my situation. Though he would never come out and say it, a lot of the recognition I had received in the Nation came from having someone so close to Royall who was willing to go to bat for me.

The last thing I wanted was for my actions to implicate or put a black cloud over any of my Brothers, but especially those who had looked out for me.

The same went for Carter, although I know he was a little less tolerant of my fuck ups. He and I had grown just as close in working shoulder to shoulder, and going on Fundraiser in Hartford on the weekends.

For the foreseeable future, everything was going to have to be done solo. This worked just as well for me since Connecticut reminded me so much of home. My life became a hybrid of my Detroit and Heaven existences.
I would get up early, spend most of my day busying myself at the bakery, attending classes, and going out the community on the weekends. Then after duty, I would go home and change from my Nation uniform into my street uniform, some jeans and a usually a button-up shirt.

Then I would find any reason to walk to the store or the park, knowing I would pass plenty of what I was looking for.

And I did. The corner store, the ball courts, the girls, the library, the barber shop... I was in my comfort zone more than ever now.

We stayed in a part of New Haven known as the Trey. I used to regularly walk around the corner to play ball in the park where the locals gathered. One my first days there a couple of guys starting clearing people off the ball court so that 2-3 of cats could settle an argument.

Not a fight, but these cats had gotten into an argument about who could clear a fence the fastest. So, with the whole hood surrounding, cats betting hundreds over who was gonna win, they lined up, with the whole park starting to buzz for the Hood Olympics. At the OG's signal, they were off, scaling the 15 foot fence in seconds with world class athleticism. Only after a best-out-of-five contest was the crowd was satisfied that Boonie was now the undisputed fence jumping champ of the Trey. (It is worth noting that the champion secured his crown with a cigarette hanging from his lip the entire time).

Anyway my point is: I was home.
Not only did the people at the ball courts, street corners, corner stores, etc. provide me with a welcome break from the atmosphere of the Nation, but they served as a reminder of who and what I was fighting for.

Ironically, though, we had come to assist the 'Righteous' Family in the Connecticut Temple. It was this immersion into the local culture that sustained me during my time there.

Despite my hopes, my absence had not served to cause Amanda's relationship with me to become any fonder.

My selection for this important mission hadn't seemed to improve my stature in her eyes much, despite my best efforts. Part of the duty in Connecticut required that I go on the Nation's Local cable access program channel. These programs were then aired in front of the entire body in Heaven for class, which only served to increase our UNOI celebrity.

In addition to the personal thanks he was constantly sending through Daniel, Royall began giving us shout outs at National meetings and when speaking to the body in Heaven. And if getting name dropped by Allah wasn't enough, Royall's wives had actually come to our home in Kansas, picked up Amanda and taken her shopping for items she had long requested but never received.

This ended up being both a blessing and a curse.

While most members considered it an honor to even be in the company of the Royall Family, Amanda was not so impressed. She respected Royall as Allah and the Nation as the only place of peace for the Original Family.

While most took this as a reason to overlook inconsistencies, improprieties, and disrespect at the hands of Royall's wives, she took it as all the more reason to call out such behavior.

After all, she reasoned, isn't that how Moreen was able to get away with what she was doing to the members? According to Royall he had no idea about his daughter and second in command's bad behavior because the members had never spoken up about it.

Fair enough.

Amanda Hassan, meet Miss White.

Debra White was recognized as the 'wife' amongst the wives. In other words, while the other wives were said to be there for the purpose of serving the Nation or Royall's children or even the other wives, her sole duty was to perform as Royall's wife. This was all well and good, except that she served as a Supreme headache for much of the rest of the Nation.

There were horror stories from every corner of the Nation about her reign of terror. If most members bowed in the presence of the Royall

Family, Miss White's only question was why their forehead was so far off of the ground.

She fully reveled in the power that her position afforded her. And to complicate matters, she had little respect or regard for the structure. For example, if you had instruction from the Captain to stay by the front door on post, she would press you as to how that didn't make sense and that you should hold your post from another position.

If you didn't move she could cause problems for you by mentioning it to right/wrong officer, who would make a huge deal about because it was Miss White.

If you did move and she decided to conveniently forget your conversation when that same officer asked you about it later, then you were left hanging out to dry.

There were a handful of officials deft enough to handle her confrontational ways without getting tied up or crumbling under the pressure. But for even the most skilled members this was a gamble so, usually most members just avoided her as much as possible.

She developed such a reputation that if you mentioned her name, you could usually get a pass, because most officials had been burned by her, and knew pursuing things further would be a much bigger headache.

In Amanda, Miss White had finally run into a member who was not hardly interested in backing down.

It was a grocery list that had brought about the inevitable. Miss White had instructed Amanda to go ahead and order item A on the grocery list.

When the item was questioned, Amanda said that Miss White had told her to order it. Miss White of course said she did no such thing. Never one to mince words, Amanda said Miss White was lying.

Not mistaken.

Not misremembering.

Not an error in communication.

Lying.

Which was true. But still. It was no small thing to refer to the wife of Allah as" liar." Amanda didn't see it any other way; either she was lying or Miss White was lying. And of all the things she was, Amanda was no liar.

She was no diplomat either. She was right in the scenario, and those close to her in the structure told her as much. But in the UNOI there was a such thing as being 'Dead right'. The way she was going about things, trying to fight Miss White's fire with her fire, was the opposite of wise. It essentially cut off anyone's ability to speak up on her behalf, lest they align themselves with the statement of Miss White being a liar.

Her force and aggression and unwillingness to concede even the smallest amount of ground in the scenario culminated in the phone call I received one day after duty.

"Well, I got myself kicked out the Nation."

She had gotten an instruction that because of her conduct it was being shared with her that she had 3 weeks to get herself together and get out of Nation's care.

I was silent with shock.

"Are you serious?""

She tried to lighten the mood and joked,

"So what'd you do today?"

The conversation went nowhere fast.

I told her this was no time to joke. She took umbrage that I would 'attack' her when she was simply trying to keep things light and have the proper spirit about the situation.

I didn't see how there could be a proper spirit in being asked to leave the Nation.

We were destined to never be on the same page.

A little over a year ago I had my mind made up that I wanted no part of the UNOI and she was determined to be full-time in Heaven. Now she seemed to set on making her way out of Nation's care, and I couldn't fathom what was wrong with her.

I was the constant comedian, yet failed to find any humor as she made light of such a serious situation.

I immediately put in a request to return to Heaven for a week. Without telling her, I purchased a plane ticket and flew into Kansas City Friday night while Amanda was at Math Class. I sat in the bedroom waiting on her and the children to get home. The initial surprise and excitement of my return was short lived. The heaviness of the issues we had to deal with hung over us like a black cloud.

I wasn't particularly interested in the events of the scenario as much as I was taking the proper steps to correct it. As bad as Amanda's relationship was with the wives, I had built up plenty of credit with Royall.

I could just as easily speak to Royall on her behalf once she and I got on the same page.

We were never even in the same Library.

Fed up with over a year of being a full-time member and the squalor that came with it, being out of Nation's care began to look less and less like a punishment to Amanda.

181

Her only question for me was what was I going to do?

I didn't understand the question.

I had a duty to Allah. We were building a Nation. Coming back to Kansas to join her out of Nation's care was not even remotely an option.

If she was not willing to reconsider her position, then we had nothing to talk about. In all this time, her constant requests for a divorce had been received but never answered by Royall due my lack of commitment on the issue.

Now I was washing my hands.

Royall had told me to call him if I made no progress with Amanda, so on my final night in Kansas I did. Our marriage was no stranger to conferences with Royall and his wives. This one was notable because it was the first one in which I was not being taken to task. Amanda mentioned that she was unwilling to deal and reiterated her request for a divorce. Finding this laughable, I finally consented. If she couldn't submit to me in this of all situations it was NEVER going to work.

I flew out of Kansas feeling like I had ended a major chapter in my life. I thought back to when we first arrived in Heaven, Sister Etenia remarked that sometimes a person's divine duty is to bring you to the Nation, and after that happens then you often find that person no longer around. At the time I silently took great offense because she was telling this to Amanda about me. Now that the shoe was on the other foot, I could see it.

I missed Tammy and PJ greatly, but I had been counseled that the best thing I could do for them was to continue to labor in order to prepare a place for him in the future. Ray and Allen were still full-time, going to class and duty every day, living with the Brothers in the barracks.

I returned to Connecticut feeling fully justified in moving on. I had done my due diligence in trying to guide Amanda. My efforts had been rejected so it was out of sight out of mind.

Back in Connecticut things were looking up. Business was booming at the bakery, our opening was featured on the City of Hamden's website, including a write-up I had done myself. The demand for our products was increasing in all areas. We had begun shipping products to the other temples in the Nation. It had gotten to where we had begun sending funds back to Heaven, the ultimate goal of any Temple.

And then really good news came. There was a call out for a brother at Your Diner Cincinnati: a very specifically skilled brother. The Brothers in Cincinnati had long ago developed a reputation for being soft. Someone was needed to come and change the laid back atmosphere of the temple.

Someone disciplined. Someone hard. A Drill Instructor of sorts. Well, in Connecticut we just so happened to have such a brother.

Brother Robin. His abrasive, dictatorial style was the perfect remedy for the problems in Cincinnati. He already had a relationship with Sister Advisor Yvette who was the head of the Cincinnati Temple.

For our part, you wouldn't find any objections about Brother Robin leaving.

As unliked as Robin was, it could not be argued that the brother did not pull his weight. If we were willing to part with such a significant part of our workforce, then of course we would need to get something in return. This was my first experience with the inner workings of the process that could send members of the Nation back and forth across the country at a moment's notice. This aspect of the Nation resembled a professional sports league with one temple negotiating with another to make a deal that worked for both. If one temple didn't have something that the other temple needed/wanted in return, often that meant involving a third or sometimes even a fourth temple.

Cincinnati needed our baker, but had no Brothers that we were interested in having. But Heaven did have plenty of Brothers who we knew could not only bake, but would also not stir up trouble. We also happened to need a Minister, and since we were the one's doing the favor and had a ton of Royall and the Nation's favor, we had the leverage to demand a little extra.

Just like a sports league, all trades had to be approved by the Commissioner's office (Royall). When the smoke cleared, we had had pulled off an executive of the year type transaction.

We got rid of Robin and got Brother KC from Heaven. Now, KC was from New Orleans, but had been in Heaven so long he had acquired the nickname KC. Only Allah and Moses (you know, from the Bible) knew his real name. He was the premiere bread baker the Nation had, working long nights in Heaven to fill bread orders for most of the Nation.

Long hours in the bakery had made him an expert on everything to do with baking. Many years in Heaven had made him an expert doing his duty diligently and not making waves.

He had been in Heaven so long that he looked forward to the freedom and flexibility that being dispatched provided, far too much to go to war over anything political, certainly not as it related to a Royall Family member.

In addition to KC, and more notably, the long standing void of Minister was to be filled by Bro. Asst. Minister Yunus.

This was huge.

Son of one of the architects of the UNOI, Abass Rassoull and Yunus were as close to Royall Family as one could get without actually being that. He had grown up in and around the Royall Family. Like true family, he and Daniel had had their share of falling outs but still considered each other cousins. He was also in a courtship with the second oldest of Daniel's Sisters.

He was barely 20, but the "Assistant" in his title was less an indication of his body of knowledge or talents as a Minister, but of the fact that there had been a Minister there when he arrived in MD.

In reality, Yunus had not only a deep body of knowledge, but the unique talent of being able to relate that knowledge in numerous, vivid ways. I repeat: numerous. As in, "more than one." Like way more than one.

To say he was a talker is to say Earth is big. It is. He was.

His mind was like a bear trap and he was well-studied on most subjects, Nation and otherwise. He and I became fast friends. I was eager to hear his many experiences growing up in the Nation. He seemed just as eager to talk about the different aspects of life OUTSIDE the Nation.

Having grown up in the Nation, he never claimed to be a street guy. But like everything else that mattered to him, he knew a lot about what he knew about. Besides, the lines of street life and life in the Nation were often so blurred that much of it related. So many gangsters were either in or had a relationship with the Nation dating all the way back to the time of Messenger that much of it related. For instance, even though Royall had clearly outlawed all things rap, it was Hip-Hop that first introduced Islam to me.

In addition to a love for our Nation, Hip-Hop, hooping and all things hood, Yunus and I shared one interest that much of our activity together centered around: Women. The young fella definitely had some game. The same skill he used to captivate a Temple class, he employed pushing up on the mixed girl who worked in the dollar store.

His experience in the Nation made him my elder in many respects as he schooled me on everything from Royall, his father's exploits in the first, to how have your fun at night without attracting the attention of the structure.

A lot of which was a moot point since Robin, our chief antagonist was on his way to Cincinnati. By this time we had received a couple of extra vehicles from the corners of the Nation in order to meet the increased demands of business. This pretty much meant we (Daniel, Carter, Yunus, and I) all had our own vehicles.

It was all just too easy.

And isn't that around the time it always spins out of control?

It's crazy to think that many of the vices I had before I joined the Nation, where all intensified.AFTER I became an FOI. As wild as my life was in Detroit, I never smoked more weed, went to more clubs, drank as much, went harder than we went in Connecticut.

Our entire operation depended on everyone holding down their end, which we all did masterfully (said the guy who would end up blowing it all).

We still maintained the individual routines that we had developed on our own, but without the fun police around studying our every move, hanging out together became less problematic.

Carter and I began spending the night in Hartford on our weekly trip up there. We had a regular rotation of women there who would gladly entertain, feed, and lodge us. If one of us wanted to come back to New Haven early, it was nothing to have a lady friend offer to simply bring us back to New Haven in time for Temple Sunday morning.

Hartford was not only a bigger city than new Haven, but no one knew us from the Nation there so we never had to look over our shoulder thinking we might run into someone who knew the Davis's or someone who had seen us on the TV program.

We really felt like we hit the jackpot when we met a couple of biological Sisters who were from Jamaica. We would drive up, knock out our route and then head to their house for cards, home cooking, and whatever else our imaginations could come up with.

On the weekends when we made plans with our other friends, they would play at being mad at us, but only until the next time we came through. On one occasion, my Jamaican Buddy was blowing up my phone the whole weekend because I had told her I wasn't coming thru. I politely told her to pretend that she lost my number, which she assured me she had no problem doing, as I was easily replaced.

That was until my plan B fell through and I called her back a few hours later to tell her I was on my way to her house. Not bothering to apologize since I already knew what her answer would be, I parked my car and made my way up to her apartment, just in time to see the befuddled look on the face of the young man she was rushing out the door just as I was walking in.

It really was all so unfair. They say that women love a man with confidence; well, we represented the very best of a class of Brothers that were being taught that they were God.

Everything we had experienced over the course the past months had done nothing to convince us of anything different.

We had come to a distant, strange city and set it on its ear. Not only getting a business open, but one that we had zero experience in up, running and thriving.

If the members of the temple weren't in the same ball park with us when it came to the math, lost-founds weren't even in the same solar system. They didn't even realize they were playing the game.

We had adopted the strategy that would eventually become standard operating procedure in the UNOI: we would present the bakery as a business we had started with no affiliation or mention of the UNOI or religion of any kind.

This meant when they saw us, they saw a group of clean-cut, business owning, fast moving, quick thinking, self-assured black men, which is attractive in itself, but then if all that was not enough, we would open our mouths and/or worse yet they would open theirs.

Collective years of practicing mathematical thinking 24/7 left them effectively playing checkers with world class chess players. We knew that the person who asks questions is the one who controls the conversation, so we would ask questions until they were suggesting to us what was in OUR mind.

"Sure we can go back to your place...I mean if you insist..."

We were so skilled at paying attention to the language that we could tell them what they were thinking just based on what they weren't saying or even their body language. And if for whatever reason they disagreed with our assertion, we could gather and present enough facts to have them second guessing themselves.

Though we usually rolled alone, anytime two or more of us gathered it was guaranteed to be entertaining.

Carter was the designated ice breaker, who didn't mind approaching any woman under any circumstances. Yunus would make great efforts to make it appear that he was making no effort to impress. Like Daniel he always seemed to have a surplus of cash that he didn't mind pulling out in the company of females. It was a need of his for all to know he was in charge.

Carter and I took to teasing him because anytime he walked into a room, he was prone to start doling out orders to whomever was in ear shot, like he was Royall himself.

Competitive to his core, he was never to be outdone, or outshined, either by us or by some poor lost-found souls who happened to talking to a female he had his eye on.

The first time I rode with him out to the mall in New Haven, he casually greeted a couple of females he had met on a prior visit.

As soon as he noticed those same females a little later talking a group of New Haven's scruffiest thugs in the food court, he couldn't be social enough, interjecting himself into the group and then carrying on a conversation with the young lady like her company didn't exist.

I hovered close enough to let them know I was there in case they felt some kind of way about it and wanted to do something about it. To my surprise, they kinda of just stood there waiting for Yunus to finish his conversation with THEIR company. Eventually, they all drifted off one by one. They didn't mind but, Hell, I definitely felt some kind of way.

We didn't know these guys or their relationship to these girls. Picture me in the mall fighting over some chicks that ain't neither one of ours. When I pointed this out to Yunus, his only response was, "If they had a problem, they were free to jump..."

Amazing how the smartest people say the dumbest shit. Then again that's probably the pot calling the kettle black. Read on.

Though we would all hoop together, work out together and of course have duty and class together, the four of us moved more and more independently. When we did connect, our talks turned to the idea of maintaining balance. In the Nation, just about anything could be justified, but we knew that if we let things get too far away from us, it could blow the lid off of our whole operation.

So who you were kicking it with, whether or not you had a drink or smoke, whether or not you even came home the previous night, were all immaterial as long as you a) showed up for duty, b) didn't have a negative impact on the Nation or its members.

One rule of the Nation was that if what you were doing had the appearance of being wrong, then it was wrong. Though we could make sense of our activities amongst each other, none of us wanted any parts of presenting our case before the body or Father.

Quite often there was a thin line between math and bullshit, and your ability to pass either one off depended greatly on who bought into your story. Our policy was akin to the CIA; if you got caught out there, don't expect any back up. We disavow all knowledge of you and any mission.

One day, Daniel and I had been riding around Connecticut and decided to stop and get an alcoholic beverage to get our evening started a little early. The problem was that this particular day, there were a couple of teams of part-timers out selling baked goods.

New Haven is only so big, so in order to escape detection, we decided to park around the corner from the Liquor Store and one of us would walk into the store.

Rank meant everything even when you were doing wrong. So I hopped out of the car, dipped into the store and dipped out without incident. Pardon me, without immediate incident.

Sure enough, that following weekend, I'm in the back of the class after temple chatting with Carter, when Daniel walks up with his arm around Bro. Aaron, one of the teen Brothers in the temple. His face is serious and he is speaking to Aaron in a stern tone.

"If you have a question about what Bro. Prostell was doing, you should pose that to Brother Prostell"

Aaron and I were relatively close, so he looked like it pained him to even say anything. He looked at me, "When me and Brother Donald were on the support raiser, we saw you go into the liquor store and I just wanted to know what you were doing."

I didn't even blink. Actually I chuckled, "That's funny. No, I just ran in there to grab a pop. They the only ones I know of out here that carry Cherry Cokes."

I laughed again. "Oh, so you thought I went to...oh naw, I buy all my malt liquor from Walmart, man."

Everyone laughed. Thin line, indeed.

Unfortunately for me, the more that you toe it, the more that line becomes obscured. If you're not careful, your bullshit starts to sound a lot like your math and vice versa.

If you don't know me by now, let's just say being careful was never my strong suit.

With Yunus securely in the Minister's role, Carter presiding over the FOI, and I managing the bakery, things were running so smoothly we began to come to the realization of New Haven as an ideal long term duty site as opposed to a temporary tour of duty. As long as the dollars continued to roll in, that in itself would continue to justify the wide berth of freedom we had.

This made incidents like the liquor store all the more troubling. Too many slip-ups like that and the whole operation would be shot to hell.

If anything, the acceptance of the bullshit and the relative ease with which I could do what I wanted to do probably made me a little too comfortable. And while I was enjoying all the exotic strains of weed Daniel was getting his hands on, hooping and working out with the Brothers, my vice hadn't changed. Neither had my sloppiness.

For their part the women on the East Coast were even more assertive than I was used to at home. A whole bunch of smooth talk was not required. Once the nature of our relationship was understood, we needn't bother ourselves with pomp or circumstance.

191

Between being out on the community on support raiser, my walks in the neighborhood, hanging with the Brothers, and even being online, I had no shortage of opportunity to meet the opposite sex.

This resulted in me having plenty of options from New Haven, to New York, to Hamden, all the way up to Boston. No matter where I was in the state or what my plans were, if I felt like going out, or staying in, if I wanted to smoke, if I wanted to bring the Brothers with me, hell, if I needed a little extra dough, no matter the circumstances I had a female suitor that fit the need.

Not that my dealing with females would require much finance at all. There was no romancing or beating around the bush; if I was coming over, it was not for a date. We were not going out for a slice of pizza and a movie. There were enough females that although I did have favorites, I didn't have to spend so much time with anyone who would take my presence for granted. They just seemed to be excited to be dealing with a guy that looked different from the typical New Haven guy, had a half way decent personality, and was good in bed.

Certain times I would be talking to as many as four or five chicks, in the span of a few weeks. After a few months, the novelty and ego stroke having the attention these different women would begin to fade, and I would have the urge to start a 'relationship' with one in particular.

These were marriages of convenience more than any real connection between me and any female.

I would grow tired of trying to line something up when I wanted affection, and I missed the security of knowing there was someone waiting at home for me. I enjoyed the variety, but ultimately, I have always been wired for married life. Though my marriage had been rocky, I missed the experience of co- habitation.

The problem was that I was still largely inexperienced when it came to love. I wanted a wife, but I had no idea what I was looking. Like most people I framed what my wife should be in perspective of my cultural group.

I was in the Nation so of course that meant, she would have to be submissive.ast. What I hadn't realized at the time is just because you know how to get a woman to submit, doesn't mean you should accept every submission.

I would invariably end up posting up at the home of whatever female showed me the most attention and was the most convenient for me, consciously or otherwise. I would even be faithful for the most part. I would clear out my inventory of females, deleting numbers out of my phone, committing for the time being to this one particular female.

I know how this being stated makes it sound horrible, but that is genuinely how we looked at it at that time. We knew that we provided the stability and consistent manhood that is lacking from many women's lives (Black women in particular), so our company was coveted even if we didn't bring money, a car or anything else to the table. Just having someone who was able to give you peace of mind and understanding was priceless.

I would wild out and meet a group of chicks, then settle down with one of that batch for weeks, maybe even a month, then get tired of that act and get back into the streets. Then I would get tired of that and shack up again. Rinse. Repeat.

First there was the former stripper that stayed just a few blocks from the Davis's. She worked midnights which meant she was home all during the day, so on days when I didn't have to go in, I would literally manage the bakery from her living room, while she um, entertained me. It was within walking distance, so I could go to or from her house without ever moving the car or arousing unnecessary suspicion. Two weeks.

Next there was the insurance woman who stayed in Hartford. She was ideal because she smoked and had a connect on some really good weed. This also gave us a place to crash on the weekend when Carter and I were in Hartford and wanted to stay and party. She was your stereotypical garden variety 30- something woman who was just hitting her sexual peak and wasn't looking to keep tabs on me as long as when I came, she did too. That was about a three and a half weeks.

And then there was Jessica. Fitting name. She was built every bit like a Black Jessica Rabbit. We had met while I was out with the Brothers doing some shopping for Ray and Allen, just before a trip back to Heaven. The running joke was that Yunus and I both suffered from severe color struckedness (medical term not mine), just at opposite ends of the spectrum.

I had always had a thing for dark girls, excuse me dark, dark girls, while Yunus wouldn't look at a girl unless she was lighter than a light-skinned paper bag.

Well, Jessica was right up my alley. I got her number before I left town and told her I would get at her when I got back to New Haven.

I had gotten in the habit of asking, "So how do I get to your house again?" the first time I met a female. It was a good ice breaker. A shot in the dark, but surprisingly at least half the time, they would start giving directions without any hesitation.

On the phone and even once we got there, there was something about her I couldn't figure. (Now picturing the scene I am screaming at the younger me to Run!)

Don't get me wrong... from the moment we set foot in the door, she was an incredible hostess. She offered us food, fruit, drink, made sure we had everything we needed in order to be comfortable. She was nice enough but I hadn't come over there to talk.

After a couple of hours and all the pushing up in the world wasn't getting me anywhere, Carter had went on a mission of his own and told me to call when I ready. Resigned to this being a dry run, I fell asleep on the couch watching something or other.

194

Next thing I know, I wake up and this girl who was waiting on me hand and foot all night, but playing clueless when it came to the affection, was laying with that amazing body pressed up against me. Needless to say Carter never got that call.

Three nights in a row.

This girl was a beautiful, sexy enigma. An Aquarian like myself, she was kind of a weirdo, who would in turns seem distant, in her own world, and then in the next moment, humble and submissive.

She would take pains to include us in her shopping, stocking the fridge and cabinets with food that she knew we could eat. She lived in neighboring West Haven, so if transportation was ever an issue, she would gladly give me the keys to her car, just to be sure I would return at the end of the day.

All this served by this docile, quiet woman who looked like she could have been anyone's video vixen. I wasn't all the way sold, but this type of loyalty and service was a far cry from what I was accustomed to. The MGT were being taught how to be the proper wife, but Jessica was proof that either you had it or you didn't. After a long day at duty, if I could just come home to that sort of peace, I wouldn't need much else.

After months of sleeping on the floor of the Davis's and the beds of strange women, I was burnt out.

Yunus had taken to calling me a sloppy pimp, because while I was good at meeting and getting with the females, I was exceedingly horrible at hiding my Lifestyle-literally. Brother Robert's wives had taken the initiative to wash some of my clothes I had hiding in their basement and found a pack of condoms. Not the worst thing ever, but certainly yet another blow to the aura of divinity that once covered us.

Duty was still inspiring, but I was beginning to get the same feeling I had in my last days in Detroit.

Days and nights blurred together in a mix of weed, drinks, sex and more weed. I recognize it now as imbalance, but at the time I was simply in a fog.

Jessica was the cure for that. Her home was a sanctuary away from everything. Just an accommodating, peaceful, sexy, submissive woman, and the tiny two-bedroom apartment that she opened up for my comfort. And comfort is exactly what I felt.

To the point of bringing her up to the bakery with me on occasion. To the point of beginning to teach her about how to be a suitable mate for me. To point of even calling and introducing her to my mother via telephone. I broke every major rule of how to be a player, aka how not to have the lost-found chick that you're boning blow up your spot.

Then once I got done breaking all of those I broke the most basic rule. The one even the lost-founds knew.

I.

Took.

The.

Condom.

Off.

Well I didn't so much take it off as much as I didn't put it on one (or two or three or ten) nights.

Talk about being caught up in emotions.

Or just being a dumbass.

At the time the whole situation seemed so right (famous last words if I ever spoke em). If nothing else, I knew that I had put my thing down and this woman was completely submissive and devoted to me. I had but to say "jump" and she would jump a hundred times at all different heights in order to not bother me with asking how high. The more we were together the more I was convinced that we would be together.

I had come home, like any other day in the long two months we had been together. I didn't hear anything so I walked to the bathroom door; it's locked and she isn't responding.

This is nothing new for her, so I go to the bedroom and lie across the bed and wait for her to get out. The next thing I hear is her calling me into the bathroom, saying she has something to show me. Sure enough I turn the corner and she is holding a home pregnancy test, smiling. Positive.

Even then I wasn't too shook. Not that I knew what I was going to do, but I knew what my options were and I knew that she would go right along with me. If I played my cards right, no one that mattered would ever know a thing.

I just needed a couple of days to figure out how I was going to handle this. Those couple of days never came.

Carter called. Before I could even give the greetings, he blasted off on me.

"Man please tell me you didn't get this bitch pregnant!"

I was silent. Carter had talked to Jessica's cousin.

"Man please tell me that shit."

"I can't even do that man."

"Aw shit, Man! DAMN!" Carter was going into full blown panic mode. Before he could get going good I raised my voice.

"Look man I am on top it. I'm going to take care of it."

He didn't even acknowledge my statement, "I gotta call you back I need to call Daniel. This is ALL fucked up!"

He was instantly trying to create space between himself and my epic masterpiece of a fuck up, rightfully so.

I told Jessica she needed to stop talking to people about a pregnancy until we decided what we were going to do. I had already told her that the possibility existed that we may not want to keep this baby. Since we were going to be together it was important that we start things off right foot and this was not that.

I did want to bring her to class but, there was no right way of introducing her to the class carrying a baby that looked exactly like me. Everything in my life centered on how it would affect my relationship with the Nation. How this could be explained in a way that represented divinity?

Now that Carter, and conversely, Daniel knew, a definite needed to be shared ASAP.

As I locked up the bakery the next evening, Daniel called saying he was on his way to come and get me. Knowing that in Nation speak that could mean everything from a ride home to a FOI beatdown, to coming to escort me off the property. He pulled up and I jumped into the car.

His demeanor didn't betray any sense of agitation. He had the uncanny tendency to be his most calm in the most fucked up situations. I spoke first.

"So I know you heard..."

"Right. So what's gonna happen?"

"We spoke about it and she agrees that we should get an abortion."

"How much we need?"

I took a moment to digest his words.

We.

Maybe I was grasping for straws, but I was taken aback. This was clearly a shit storm I created. I don't even think he was in the State, but he definitely wasn't in the room when I must have knocked the girl up. But he still looked at it as a 'we' situation.

I thanked him but told him I had some money on the way and the 'situation' would be resolved in a matter of days.

He shared that he would pass the information on to the Father and further information would be forthcoming.

In the meantime, it was highly recommended that I buckle down and lock in to my duty. I needed to effective immediately, come from over her house and immerse myself back into the Nation fully. With all the turmoil of this recent fiasco, I needed make sure that I reminded everyone exactly how and why I was valuable to Connecticut.

This scenario was not known outside of the top two or three members in New Haven and Royall and as long I kept things together it could stay that way.

And then all hell broke loose.

"Dude, where the fuck have you been?"

It was Carter. I had just walked in from doing the weekly bakery shopping and he was calling me, spastic once again.

"I was shopping what's up?"

"What the fuck is wrong with your girl, Man? She has been calling the bakery and blowing up my phone all day going off, looking for you."

Nooooooooooooooooooooo.

I looked up. KC, looked at me like he knew exactly what Carter was saying. This was hugely bad. I hung up with him and called Jessica.

"What's going on?"

"Don't ask me what the fuck is going on! Where the hell you been? You tryna to play me like I'm stupid, Nigga!"

I stared at the receiver. There was NO WAY this was the same person.

"Baby?"

"Oh you wanna talk that Baby shit now, you haven't even called me. . ."

I needed to end this conversation now. It's bad enough that she called saying God knows what earlier, but now I was on the phone dealing with real life, baby mama drama in front of the Bakery staff.

"Look I'm on my way, just unlock the door."

I hung up the phone, shouted out a few instructions in a feeble attempt to seem in control of something but clearly this was coming apart at the seams, but fast.

By the time I pulled up to Jessica's house, the dragon on the other end of the phone was nowhere in sight. I asked what had come over her but all I got was that she missing me and she didn't know what to do.

I tried to measure my words, thoughts and actions. We would be going to the clinic the next day. I couldn't let her out of my sight until this situation was stabilized. I don't know where this crazy person came from but there was no way on Earth I was gonna let her hold my seed ransom.

I made a call to Carter. I knew he would be willing to cover for me if for no other reason but to ensure that he didn't get any more of those calls.

Shocking now how cavalier I viewed the termination of my unborn child, or how small a gesture it seemed in relation to keeping my duty to Royall, or making sure we avoided any appearance of impropriety. We had come here to be Saviors for our people, and when I had gone off the path, the primary concern from those in the know all the way up to Royall, was that this child would be 'taken care of' so that I could get back to the business of Nation building. You know saving the souls of black folks. Disgusting.

The divine explanation was that this child was Satan's way of taking me off of my path, and a million more lives would be saved.

I spent the rest of the day comforting her, painting pictures of the future we could have together if we could just take care of this little business and keep things cool for the time being.

We woke the next morning and made the drive to Hartford to the clinic. And that's when I met the person who had been on the other side of the phone, in person.

In my eyes we were still together at this point, so we were there as husband and wife, but the moment we set foot in the clinic she was another animal altogether.

My first instinct told me it was the emotions of the situation getting to her, as she almost instantly got into a verbal confrontation with the Clinic secretary.

I began to speak up to bring calm to the situation, when Jessica continued her nasty tone loudly right over me, and then the Clinic secretary dropped a bomb.

"Look, we told you last month you couldn't come back here anymore! Do we need to call the police again?!"

MY jaw fell off.

Last month?

Anymore?

Police?

Again?

I felt like I was falling down a bottomless pit. What in the entire fuck did all of that mean? MY head was officially out of the clouds and into the fog. After she was done going back and forth with the staff in her most loud confrontation ghetto tone, we walked back to the car silently.

Who was this woman, and what was I doing here with her?

Where had I planted my seed?

How could I be so damn stupid?

Everything that I had worked for, that the Brothers had worked for, that we had worked for so diligently, was teetering like a car on the edge of a cliff. And this mad woman was jumping up and down on the hood of said car.

And I had helped her up onto the car. This was very, very bad.

This time the angry woman stuck around even after we arrived back in West Haven. Taking the hint I went back to the bakery and told her we would discuss plan be later.

In my head, the only thing to be figured out was how to get my seed and then me away from this womb.

As if things weren't fishy enough, she called the next afternoon, telling me she already had it taken care of everything. At this point taking no chances, I went to her house and asked her to show me the paperwork.

She produced a stack of forms dated for the previous date and a prescription for pain medication.

I crawled up in the bed with her, wrapped my arms around her and breathed a silent mental sigh of relief.

That would be the end of that. I would go to duty the next day and just not see Jessica for a little while. It's always after tearing their ass does a young fool become an advocate for conservatism and piety. I didn't want to see another female any time soon. This would my time to refocus myself on duty, on serving Royall, and being the best FOI and Laborer I could.

If only it weren't too late.

Once the resolution of the scenario had been reported to Father it was decided I needed to go somewhere and be 'refreshed'.

I couldn't agree more. Mentally, I was exhausted after all that I had put myself through. I requested the opportunity to go to Heaven for 2-4 weeks. I wanted to make it back to being the Brother who had come to Connecticut, submissive, humble, diligent, focused, and with clean piss.

However, there was opening in Cincinnati and Daniel advised I go there. It was still a fast- paced place where my skill set would be of good use. But far more regimented, so that I would be able to get back in the rhythm of what I was supposed to be doing as a proper representative of Royall.

2-4 weeks.

It sounded great in my head, but I knew how the Nation worked. Hell, we had been commissioned to come out to Connecticut for six weeks and here we had been here more than 10 months. Daniel let me know that what I did in Cincinnati would have a lot to do with how quickly I would return to Connecticut. Keep making rookie mistakes and being sloppy, then how could one justify me being shipped out anywhere when I was the one that needed help? Stick to the script and do what I had learned and I would be back in no time.

For the record, I requested that he let Father know words could never express how terrible I felt about letting him down. We had been sent to perform a job, and I had almost single-handedly torn down the whole thing.

Daniel let me know that what Father valued was the Brothers. It wasn't about any business or building or even a temple. We were doing the work and that was what Father valued. I told him that I was impressed that Father even knew who I was, and to let Father know that I will be back and I will be better.

Jessica had a couple other blow-ups, making it clear that she was not going to gracefully fade into the background, so I had made it a point to talk with her, just to let her know she wasn't forgotten about. Yeah, classy, I know.

I let her know I would be leaving but that I would stay in touch while I was gone. I still had feelings for her despite it all. She would blow up Carter's phone a couple more times, but once she was in my presence she was as gentle and docile as a lamb. I told her that if we were to have any future at all, I needed her to be good while I was gone, so that when I got back, we could work on us.

I left plans and a written schedule for the interim Manager, packed all my clothes, which was less than two weeks' worth, and let all the members know that I would be gone but I would be back.

Daniel and I would spend my final night in Connecticut like we had spent so many nights, sitting in a parking lot, watching the cars roll by, passing an excellent blunt back and forth, discussing life in and out of the Nation, and what the future would hold for us. The next morning we pulled out for Cincinnati.

C-4

Cincy

I almost killed us.

Swear to God,

I almost killed us.

I can only imagine the reaction once Heaven would have gotten word that Brother Prostell fell asleep at the wheel of the Royall Family vehicle and crashed into a median somewhere between New Haven and Cincinnati, killing himself and Brother Daniel.

What most in Heaven would likely never get wind of was the $20000 worth of weed found in the wreckage. Somewhere in the midst of my drama and preparing to get deported to Cincinnati we got the notion to buy some exotic weed and transport it to Kansas where it would fetch top dollar.

It was many a Brother's aspiration to hit a quick lick that would bring a significant amount of money to the UNOI.

It was also many a Brother's aspiration to bring national attention to the work we were doing in the UNOI. Well, we would have all the publicity we could handle once the cops and the media found out about what would surely be labeled a Muslim extremist drug smuggling ring.

Luckily the moment I passed out just happened to be along a stretch of highway where there was no median, wall, or rail to crash into as I veered off the road. Another half mile or so and we would have been killed on impact, if we were fortunate.

I woke up with both hands on the wheel and the car bumping along in a shallow ditch at about 70 mph. I'd like to think it was my natural cool that allowed me to remain calm, but I am sure our last smoke session helped.

Of course chances are that same session greatly contributed to the relaxed state that allowed me to doze in the first place.

Nevertheless, I slowed down gradually, bringing the car to a rest along the shoulder of the road.

We both got out of the car to check for damage. Everything looked in order so we stepped back inside the car. I sighed deeply, waiting for him to cuss me out and tell to get my punk ass out of the driver seat.

He didn't even look at me.

"I guess you should be woke now, right?"

I chuckled nervously, and started the car, pulling back out onto the highway.

Classic Daniel. It would have been expected, in fact it would have been standard operating procedure for him to admonish, strip me of all driving privileges, and make sure I had the shittiest duty in Cincinnati as punishment for almost taking the life of a Royall Family member.

But that wasn't his way. For all his quirks, if he messed with you, he messed with you all the way.

The rest of the trip went without much incident.

He actually gave me a great deal of credit for not panicking once I woke up and was driving on the side of the road. He told me about similar incidents that had happened in the Nation, and the thing that made a bad situation worse was always when Brothers started to panic.

As we pulled up to Cincinnati he reemphasized what had been his main talking points since I got the word that I would be coming here; do what I know how to do as far as Nation building, keep my nose clean, oh and don't worry about this weed money.

I'll take care of that.

It'll be a donation once we get it all sold.

Truth be told, I wasn't worried about it.

I had managed to save up a few thousand bucks to cover most of what it would cost to make the buy.

This wasn't the first time I had done business legal or otherwise, but under normal circumstances there was NO WAY I was putting thousands of dollars in someone's hand and then watch them drive off no guarantees in hand, and trust that they would do the right thing.

But that was my Brother.

In my eyes we had been in the foxhole together, he had given me the opportunity to go to Connecticut, had supported and promoted me in doing the work that I did, didn't toss me into the flames when I had the ultimate ass tearing in the Jessica situation.

Only now am I even thinking twice about it.

Besides, it was never about the money. The thing that had made us Brothers, our ultimate common ground was the Nation. Even this illicit activity had at the base of it Nation Building. It was just another way of bringing in finances only Instead of a bunch of baking and spending weeks out in the community we just had to drive a package from one end of the country to the other.

Maybe a couple of bucks in our pockets for our families, but anonymous thousands being dropped off at the Secretarial Department in Heaven.

Ultimately did it ever happen that way?

I don't know.

A few months after I got to Cincinnati, he called me and told me it was done and he was sending me a few hundred bucks, and that was the last time we ever talked business.

I was received in Cincinnati with the respect of a returned war hero. The wives told me to be sure that if I needed anything that I contacted them personally. The Lieutenant Bro Leon, gave me a brief tour of the place, led me to my room and told me to go ahead and get some rest as my help wasn't needed.

Despite my messiness in Connecticut, what we had done as a whole was what most full-time Brothers in the Nation dreamed of.

Daniel made sure that credit was given to the Brothers at every turn, to the extent that sometimes it was almost embarrassing to hear him brag on us to Father, the Family, or even the whole FOI on a National conference. A good word from Father or Daniel, you were essentially a Nation Legend.

Of course, the Brothers in Cincinnati had become legendary themselves, albeit for an entirely different reason.

Not at all a good one.

The most contentious relationship in the Nation was the one between Brothers and Royall's Wives. The Brothers in Cincinnati had earned a well-documented reputation for consistently being on the losing end of that equation.

208

It was the often repeated mission of Father, the Royall Family and the Nation to uplift the Blackman and bring him back to his proper standing as God of the Universe. The unspoken implication of such a statement was that the Blackman, specifically the Brothers in the FOI were definitely not currently God.

In places like Cincinnati, they would be reminded of this at just about every turn.

On the other hand, Royall's family, in particular his 10 wives, were learning and being prepared by Allah himself, as emphasized by the section of the FOI book entitled " Proper Treatment of the Royall Family." To put it mildly you had to be very tactful in how you conducted yourself with the wives. Many a brother had had his ass handed to him for disrespects, real, perceived and otherwise.

Cincinnati, like Connecticut, had the advantage over Heaven of having a great deal of activity and opportunity for Brothers to make things happen. Your Diner, Cincinnati, was at the time the UNOI's most successful business venture.

It was also its busiest.

More activity meant more responsibility, more opportunity for Brothers to make a name for themselves, more ways to have an impact in and the Nation, and of course more scenarios.

More scenarios wasn't a negative in and of itself, but in Cincinnati the FOI had the nasty habit of using scenarios as means of reporting each other to the wives. Sometimes this was done out of ignorance, but oftentimes it was done as means to get in good with the Royall Family at the expense of your brother.

What was lost on the brother engaging in such cowardly behavior was that this consistent running to the wives was not only an admission of the individual's inability to resolve issues, but also an indictment on the entire military structure in Cincinnati.

Imagine the embarrassment of the Lt, Captain, or Secretary when they get a phone call from the wives about a scenario between the Brothers that they have heard NOTHING about. How many times does that happen before it is just decided that the Wives will be in charge of everything, from the day-to-day operations of the Diner, all the way to what topics would be gone over in FOI class? How long before the wives are teaching the FOI class itself?

This was the greatest slap in the face. Though it was rationalized that the Wives were an extension of Father, so there was nothing wrong with them teaching the Brothers, the very mention of such things caused any FOI worth his bowtie to scowl his face and silently shake his head in disgust.

While most of the members couldn't see past the aura that came with the title "Royall Family" member, the reality was that the wives were often fighting hard to make a name for themselves as well. Inside the confines of the Royall Family there were agendas as well. Those who got close enough to any given Family member could quickly sense the undercurrent of politics that existed. It was often stated that Royall held his Family to a higher standard, and for the most part, this was true.

Of the four or so wives who regularly inhabited the Family apartment that sat across the street from the Diner, only one, Sister Advisor Yvette was considered to be a 'major' wife. Sister Advisor was the designated "mother" of all of Royall's children. This meant she was the authority when it came to the growth and nurturing of Royall Family children, even those birthed by the other wives.

As far as the Brothers were concerned, she was one of the cool wives. She did her best to encourage the Brothers to handle their own business, only stepping in when her level of responsibility required that she do something.

I recall shortly after my arrival in Cincinnati, one of the Brothers reported me to her for having a stack of condoms in my overnight bag. Sister Advisor replied that the brother should be glad that his brother was protecting himself, and don't worry about the rest.

She was the person in charge in Cincinnati, but was having health issues, and the word was that Royall was looking to free her up from that position.

Dawn was the wife next in line for that job. Officially one of Royall's concubines (that line was often blurred), she was very young, inexperienced and not particularly good with handling people, but she made up for all of that by being very sharp mentally, dedicated and assertive. She was still very new to the Royall Family and was looking to establish herself, so she had no problem getting elbow deep into the many scenarios that Brothers twice her age would continuously bring to her.

She developed a cut throat reputation for quickly tearing into the Brothers when she saw them slipping, once even going so far as putting nearly the entire FOI in Cincinnati on class A (not being permitted to speak unless spoken to) at one time.

All of this was compounded by the fact that the Brothers would rarely speak up for themselves, much less each other. Things had gotten so bad in Cincinnati that even the phrase, "the Brothers" had developed a nasty ring to it.

"'The Brothers somehow forgot to lock the Diner up last night'."

"The Brothers haven't been keeping up with the detailed cleaning in the Diner"

"I guess The Brothers are just going to let the lost-founds loiter in front of the Diner."

This abusive relationship was easily apparent to most full-time Brothers who would come through Cincinnati. The Sisters would see something, point it out, and the Brothers would hop to it. As an isolated incident there was nothing wrong with this, but in Cincinnati this was an overall pattern of thinking.

This was one of the reasons that Brother Robin had been sent here. He had an amazing eye for detail and knew the law, which allowed him to nit-pick even the most disciplined soldier.

Unfortunately, he lacked the humane qualities that would have allowed him to be an effective leader. He could point out to you what you missed but only as a means of telling you what to do. Every correction was about punishing the offending Brother. Because of this, the Brothers had equal portions of both fear and resentment toward him.

This added to more of the same turmoil and nationally, the FOI in Cincinnati was looking more and more like a collection of lightweights who toiled under the thumb of the wives.

Then, finally someone had decided to bring in the big guns.

Shortly before I arrived, Brothers Morris and Emory were sent from Heaven to Cincinnati to help bring about change.

Brother Emory was a former follower of Farrakhan and lifelong student of the Messenger's teachings.

Upon his arrival in Heaven, he had taken the Nation by storm.

He was literally the poster child for the Blackman being God.

He was 6-2 and built like a God; chiseled, charismatic, energetic, and knew the lessons like the back of his hand.

Most of all he was about getting shit done.

Sisters would swoon when he walked into a room, but he was still a soldier's soldier always. You could always find him right in the middle of every work detail.

Even though he had studied for years, he was humble enough to listen. He was a reformed street guy and as dedicated to Nation Building as anyone I have ever met, even today.

He had arrived in Heaven shortly after I did, and in less than a month he had been named the head of the FOI.

Which, of course, ended up making him more than a couple enemies. The least of which was not Kaaba.

Shortly thereafter, he was dispatched to Atlanta to help get things going there. His unwillingness to play politics ended up biting him in the butt, as his assertive style clashed with those he was working with in Heaven and Atlanta.

After returning to Heaven for a few months, he was sent to Cincinnati with a chance at redemption.

Morris's situation was not much different from Emory's.

Morris was Daniel's closest friend in the Nation, which was very much a double-edged sword.

He was a very poised and sharp brother. Hard-working and diligent to his core, he was the type of Brother you could see holding and mastering whatever post you needed him in. The other side of that same coin, he was a street guy, one of the few people Daniel trusted to run the streets with.

The problem with that, of course, was that Daniel avoided a lot of scrutiny by being a Family member. And while Morris could dodge the spotlights riding shotgun with Daniel, once Daniel left with us to Connecticut, it was open season on those who were seen as part of his "clique".

Less than a month after being in Connecticut, we got word that Morris had got caught sneaking off the hang with some unsavory lost-founds.

By the time the lynch party got through with him, he had been placed on 90 day away from us status. Father's instructions were that he was to get a job and turn in his paycheck to the Nation. He was to stay in the Nation home and be a model soldier.

True to his character, he came through his punishment with flying colors and Cincinnati was to be the crowning achievement on his comeback tour. Years as best friend to Daniel had given him just the insight needed to wrest control away from the wives and at least gain some measure of respect for the FOI in Cincinnati.

At best, it was conceivable that he had the skill to ascend to the seat of authority in Cincinnati.

Outside of having a mutual friend in Daniel, Morris and I became fast friends while having duty together at the Diner. I learned a lot from him in the line of duty about how the Brothers should conduct themselves. He was one of the first examples to me that you didn't have to be a square in order to be a good FOI.

It also helped that our wives got along famously, eventually becoming very close friends in and out of the Nation. His eldest daughter was the same age as PJ and they were good friends as well.

Though he was from South Central L.A. and I was from Detroit, our perspectives were close enough that it never needed stating. Above all he was a Brother I could count on to give it to me straight and not have to worry about his hidden agenda.

Though we had never had duty at the same site, Emory and I had an equally strong rapport. Any thoughts or apprehensions about being shipped to Cincinnati were quickly buffered by the thought being able to soldier with two of the very best Brothers in the Nation.

I was still a little worried about fitting back into the rhythm of full-time life. For most of my first week there I still felt the fog of that good Connecticut Kush over me.

Cincinnati had much of the structure of Heaven, but was much smaller, which meant there was less chance to slip between the cracks. WIth the Royall Family a stone's throw away, justice was much swifter, and in most cases, harsher. There were inspections on an almost daily basis of the restaurant, homes, and the members.

In Connecticut, we had managed to stockpile a vehicle for every driving brother that was there. In Cincinnati there were three vehicles between about 25 members and all the keys, including the keys to the Diner, were kept at the Royall Family home. If anyone went anywhere it would need to be justified with the Wives.

In most cases the cars were parked right outside their apartment so if you even cranked the engine it would wake someone. Every day's schedule was so tightly packed that nary a moment of time for any member was unaccounted for.

So someone always knew where you were supposed to be and what you were supposed to be doing. If you were at the prescribed location at the prescribed time, there would questions to answer.

This was pretty much the standard as far as how things were dealt with in the Nation, but coming from the willy nilly atmosphere we had established in Connecticut it was a major adjustment. But that was the purpose for me being there. I had gotten out of the rhythm of how Father would have things to be done and needed reestablishing.

Unlike my arrival in Heaven there would be no sneaking in under the radar. In the first case, Cincinnati was too small; there was nowhere to hide. Secondly, because of the notoriety that had come with the work we had done in Connecticut, members would be looking for great things from me.

The problem with this was part of what had made it easy for me to thrive in Connecticut was the lack of structure. I was not then, nor was I ever going to be the sharpest and cleanest cut brother in the Nation. I had been rough around the edges when I got there, and sure, I tucked my shirt in when I got there, but it still always seemed to find its way out.

Carter used to laugh at me because I paid so little attention to things like a smudge on my shirt, a tear in my pants or even keeping a fresh haircut. He said I was so wrapped up in the spiritual and mental I would completely miss the physical, which was pretty accurate. Being the Aquarian I am, I took it as a complete compliment.

There was a certain discipline that an FOI developed over the years of scrutiny that made certain behaviors second nature. When you saw a group of Brothers clean cut, suited and booted, it was because they had been made that way.

They could have come from the roughest corners of the country, single or no parent homes, raised by or in some cases not raised by some of the oddest characters you can think of, in and out of jail, but life in Heaven was an extended boot camp, meant to clean up even the scruffiest amongst us.

Because I had been shipped out to Connecticut so soon after being in Heaven, many of those things I had never internalized. Now here I was in Cincinnati and things most would assume I had mastered stood out like a sore thumb.

After all, I had been shipped out across the country to help correct another temple. SURELY, I must be the proper representation of Allah.

Well, shouldn't I?

The truth was, yes and no. There was one thing that couldn't be taught, and that was work ethic. I had that. There was hardly anything you could ask in the way of duty that I wasn't able to do or learn rather quickly. I would work and stay until the work was done without so much as a complaint. I would strive to treat all I came in contact with right and brotherly.

Be that as it may, in Cincinnati, my appearance was one of the first things that set off red flags.

I was on security at the Diner one Monday morning when we were closed. My duty was to just be there in case of emergency so that the Sisters could collectively complete their required prep for the restaurant. At most, I would run a couple of errands back and forth between the apartments and the Diner, but my duty was just to be helpful and stay out of the way. In my mind, the day went well. I chatted casually with the Sisters, played with some of the Royall Family children, and basically just hung out in the lobby of Diner.

After escorting the Family and the Sisters home, I go to my room to crash. Before I can close my eyes I get a knock on my door and it's Brother Captain Leon. He was there to read me the riot act for having shown up to this duty in work dress less than befitting of an FOI.

It was one thing to do it, an entirely different thing altogether to do so in a room full of Sisters, which was just plain stupid.

Situations like the one at the Diner were especially frustrating to me. After all, we were all sitting right there. If my appearance was offensive, was it so hard for one of the Sisters to pull me aside and say, "Hey Brother P, you need to go change"? After all we were family, and families communicate.

Unlike the Brothers, the Sisters were not responsible nor expected to deal with a scenario when it happened. If a Brother missed it or failed to put a definite to it, then the Sister would simply report it to the MGT structure.

In the case of Cincinnati, that meant directly to the Wives. The more scenarios that went to the Wives, the more poorly it reflected on the Brothers as a whole. All of this, of course, fueling the tense relationship that already existed between the FOI and the Wives. Eventually, it began to even challenge the relationships between husbands and their wives.

For example, you might have a disagreement, big or small, with your wife, you leave from duty before you can resolve it. When you arrive home that night (unless it couldn't wait until then in which case you are getting called at duty) you are now in a conversation with your wife, one of Royall's wives, and a spineless FOI official who is already on the side of the wives.

Before you know it, there are no disagreements that you and your wife work through naturally and even the most intimate of rifts are discussions between the two of you and Royall's wives.

For his part, Leon was actually a pretty cool brother. He had only been in the Nation a little longer than me, and had already had a tremendous impact. He had not long ago been one of the more successful hustlers in Cincinnati when a rival had got the drop on him. He got shot.

As he lied in the Hospital recovering, his mind floated back and forth between thoughts of bloody revenge and changing his life.

A visit from some of the Brothers of the UNOI, whom he had recently met, convinced him that both he and the boy that had shot him were victims of the same system of genocide set up by the Devil. Soon he saw the course for him was to join the Nation, which he did with the same vigor that he had applied to his own business.

This, of course, was a boon for the Nation. Not only did Leon bring a fair amount of money with him, but his most valuable asset was his standing in the community. Usually, if you go to someone's town, it doesn't take too long before you find someone that doesn't like them. Everywhere we went, and we went everywhere, they LOVED this guy. I mean they would actually verbalize, repeatedly, "Where Leon at? Hey we love Lee. Ah, Man We LOVE that Dude, that's our dude."

And it was those relationships that in effect powered and financially supported the Diner. As opposed to most cities where we would stick to hitting the Salons and stores, in Cincy half of our business would be with the clusters of young hustlers or cats posted on the corners. They knew Leon was down with us, so they would always buy SOMETHING.

Once we stopped to check with a group of about 6-7 of them to see if they wanted to buy any sandwiches from us. A quick scan of the crowd reveals no takers.

No big deal, we move back toward the car to keep it moving. It's not like they OWE us buying a sandwich. Hell, they buy all the time so no hard feelings right? Wrong.

Out of nowhere one of these little dudes just starts going OFF!

"Man that's some bullshit! Y'all niggas got something! How we out here making all this money but can't support the Brothers? Y'all niggas always running up here to the lil Korean sto' buying they shit, but then Leon and them come here y'all act brand new....."

This goes on for like five minutes. Before we leave we get back in the car with no less than 40 bucks. And they still didn't want a sandwich. To say we had the support of the streets was an understatement.

One of my most touching experiences with this dynamic happened when Emory and I were out in the community together. As usual, we are having a good time and stop in a food store to see a sister who is one of our best customers. Despite the fact they sold food there, If we went into that shop three times a week she was buying at least one sandwich each time, oftentimes more than one.

We come in and small talk for a moment, then ask if she would like anything. This time she says no. Maybe it was a slow day for us, maybe we were going for a record that day, but for whatever reason we start to pick with her a little bit.

"Aw man, Sis, you sure you don't want nothing?"

"What you gonna eat? I know you not going get some of that fast food?"

She suddenly gets a somewhat serious look on her and tells us to come here, as she walks into the cooler in the back of the store. Not sure of what to expect we follow her.

She opens the cooler and we are staring at rows and rows of the white bags that our sandwiches come in. This woman has no less than three weeks' worth of our food in there.

She goes on to tell us she doesn't like our food. She doesn't even eat fish (which was the main thing that we sold). She just buys the sandwiches because she loves the Brothers, what they represent and she wants to support what we are doing.

We often talked in class and amongst each other about how the community was behind us, but it was in moments like theses I understand what that meant.

For all the politics of being in the Nation, for all the complex theology and ideology, this was where I so often saw divinity. We would regularly set up shop in the worst inner city areas, go out "suited and booted" offering everything from fish sandwiches to cookies and cakes to invitations to an upcoming meeting.

If we did our job properly, the people in those neighborhoods didn't just see a bunch of well-dressed handsome Brothers, but a piece of themselves in us.

For many, we were a welcome break from the realities of living in the hood, the constant barrage of the same sights, sounds, smells and stimuli.

For others we provided a sense of pride that we were not the dregs of society that the school, the justice and socioeconomic systems had tried to convince us that we were.

For still others we represented hope. Society had taught them that you had two choices: you could be a part/victim of this system or you could be a criminal. There was no escaping the long arm of the law/Whiteman/government or whatever you called the powers that be.

Yet here we stood, outside and above it all.

Powerful, self-determined men who ran businesses, raised families, owned farm land, built homes, drove trucks full of produce across the country to said businesses, didn't answer to some White man or punch some clock, didn't drink or smoke (at least not to their knowledge).

What most of them didn't realize was that for many of us, they were just as much a welcome refuge from the inner workings of the temple.

Especially in a place like Cincinnati, the community was a welcome break from the structure, politics and the hidden agendas of the Nation.

With a temple full of Brothers who seemed to delight in nothing more than turning each other in for every little infraction, the Wives right across the street only so ready to deal with FOI business, and my lack of refinement constantly landing me in hot water with the Sisters, I began to find most of my peace in the community.

The Diner did its fair share of business, but the lion's share of revenue came from Brothers going out in the community. On any given day there were at least two teams out on the street.

Like all the other Brothers I would be expected to pick up a second duty, as well as take responsibility for my share of prep items. But by this time in my career in the Nation, it was understood, I earned my keep by going out amongst the people.

Morris was the acting Manager of the Diner, which meant he had input into and eventually would take full responsibility for the schedule. Not only did he make sure that I was consistently in the community, but that I went with him or Emory in most cases.

Although I tended to defer to the Brothers on Spiritual conversations in class or in the businesses, I was just the opposite when it came to dealing with the lost-founds. In most cases I was the designated spokesperson.

The relationship between some of the Brothers and the community was often a microcosm of the relationship between some of the Brothers and their Brothers IN the Nation.

For some it was a necessary evil. We needed money to run the Nation, these drugs dealers and vagrants bought the sandwiches, so we would just have to deal with them on some level until they all burned up in the destruction.

The other group, which I saw myself as part of, saw these lost-founds as the very motivation and reason for what we were doing. The food, the fund raiser, The Diner, including and especially the money itself was just an excuse to talk to them.

Your Diner was located in one of the major intersections for drugs and prostitution in the Bond Hill section of Cincinnati.

These locations were ideal since many of these dealers, prostitutes, etc. were the lost-found Black man and woman in the wilderness of North America that we had come to save.

At the same time, we were running a business that was supposed to be a beacon of peace, hope and civilization. Therein lay a great juxtaposition that existed on the intersection.

On one side of the street, you had the Muslims at Your Diner and directly across the street you had a flea market of every criminal enterprise you can think of going on in the parking lot of the Quickie Mart.

It had all the geographic quandary of Midwestern American Israel.

Their focal point of activity, including but not limited to, drugs sold, tricks turned, shots fired was smack dab in between the Royall Family apartment and the Diner. This meant when we escorted the Family or the Sisters to and from home, most times we had to walk them through the heart of the action.

From their perspective, no one had asked us to come and open a "beacon of peace, hope and civilization" in the middle of their hood.

If this was supposed to be for and about them why hadn't anyone come and spoken to them? Why did the Brothers and Sisters walk by with their nose in the air on the way to the Diner? Why did the Brothers come out The Diner like Gang Squad anytime somebody sat on the stupid bench in front of The Diner?

In truth, the only thing we did ask was that they did not post up in front of the Diner.

Some of the Brothers could have been a lot more cordial when it came to making that "request" clear. This contributed to an adversarial relationship with the guys on the corner, which is ironic when you consider that we were treated like royalty in most other hoods in Cincinnati, but right outside our own doorstep, things were as tense as ever.

This was another benefit of having Morris, Emory, and me on the squad. Leon could only do so much, and between the three of us, we understood and related to many of the lost-founds better than we did some of the Brothers.

So instead of crossing the street to avoid the lost-founds, we began to go out of our way to speak to them, even if it was just a passing, "What up." Conversations started, rapports developed, and you would come to find that the lost-found brothers actually had a great respect for what we were doing. They only had an issue with the one or two overzealous assholes, usually the same Brothers most of us didn't like. An asshole was an asshole whether he had on a bow tie or not.

Before long, they started to police themselves, keeping the space in front of Diner clear, coming in to buy something to eat, even coming to class a couple of times.

But eventually, I would always have to come home.

Unlike Heaven or Connecticut, my strong work ethic and brotherly reputation could not mask my overall lack of polish and discipline; or attention to detail; or lack of understanding of the Nation politics.

Slowly, the image members had of Prostell the razor sharp, upstanding Brother who had helped to get Connecticut cracking began to get replaced with an altogether different version.

Some might call it the truth.

In addition to constantly being addressed about my appearance, I began making absent-minded mistakes. Not big enough to get me kicked out of the Nation, but big enough that they would have to go to the Wives. And if they went to the Wives, you can be certain they were going to Father.

First, I lost a money bag.

On what would be a routine delivery, I took an order across town and then when I arrived back at the Diner and it just wasn't there.

I searched the car, the delivery bag, went back to the location of the delivery...nothing.

I had the money to run and go get another bag and replace the money, but our relationship with the Community was so good, I was legitimately concerned about someone finding it and bringing it back to us.

The cover-up they say is always worse than the crime, so I just called Morris and reported myself.

By the time it got to Royall it was no big deal. It was asked what I was going to do about it.

I was experienced enough to know the real answer that was being sought was not how I was going to replace the 25 bucks and the money bag, but correcting the thinking that had allowed me to lose the bag in the first place.

Knowing all the answers in the world wasn't going to change the fact that I was slipping in a major way. And I wasn't in Kansas anymore, or around a group of Brothers who would pull me to the side and tell me to tuck my shirt in. With all the Sisters around and the Royall Family, hell they could hardly afford to.

This meant I kept chugging along, doing my thing in the community and providing positive energy, while at the same time consistently missing the small things, and keeping my name in the ears of the Wives for some blunder or another.

Finally, it was rationalized that I needed balancing. The proper wife and helpmate would be just the thing to help me get my bearings.

Not coincidentally, shortly after my arrival, the entire Nation was abuzz of a meeting in Heaven wherein, Royall addressed Amanda.

She had come to the mic with concerns about PJ, and her recent request to come full-time again. Long story short, Father told her that she needed to go back to her husband.

This led to a chorus of back pats, and wish wishes for me. Of course, at no point had anyone asked ME or HER if we were interested in reconciliation.

I wasn't. I was still licking my wounds from the Jessica situation in Connecticut.

To my knowledge, neither was she. We spoke often enough about the children and the subject of her and I never came up.

Nonetheless, when Allah spoke you listened.

Even if you hadn't considered an idea feasible, you would at least mull it over in your head. One thing was for certain, the shoe was certainly on the other foot. Amanda was out of Nation's care looking for a way back into the Nation. I was struggling in some respects, but I was certainly a valuable asset in the Nation. To put it plainly I was a ticket back in AND, probably more importantly, out of Heaven which she hated so much.

Long story short I had leverage and no one could take that away from me.

Except, of course, me.

Which I did.

Before long, because of Royall's comments and the subsequent chatter, we had put in a request to begin speaking. Up until that point, our conversations were relegated to the children and ideas concerning them and we had largely stuck to that. Now we began slowly to undertake the idea of being a family unit again.

This meant questions about the previous year or so we had been apart.

I had grown a lot in that year but there was no way in Hell I was going to divulge to her the gory details of my hedonistic existence in Connecticut. The situation with Jessica was still hovering above my head and I definitely wasn't eager to have that discussion with her. I still had feelings for Jessica, and felt like it was possible for us to rebuild if I could make it back out to Connecticut.

At the very least I kept tabs on her, to prevent her from going kamikaze on one of the Nation's out there. Shortly after I had arrived in Cincinnati, she hadn't talked to me for a few days and ended up calling the Davis's home, going off about how she was gonna have me arrested for rape, and the murder of our child.

What can I say, I can sure pick 'em.

With my sloppiness, and both of these women's combined proven ability to hack into voicemail and email accounts, I should have known it wouldn't be too long before they would track each other's existence down.

And just like that-advantage gone.

Jessica divulged to Amanda some the more torrid details of our relationship, including things she figured would burn her up.

She was right.

Amanda immediately reported this incident which got me a firm reprimand from the military in addition to the dressing down I got from Sister Advisor.

Because it was a private matter my lynching wasn't public, but I knew enough to know my chances of a swift return to Connecticut were looking slimmer and slimmer by the scenario. Whatever dreams I had of starting a family with Jessica were quickly dashed by her erratic behavior.

If I had to choose between the two, having my children with me was surely worth working on my marriage. Even with all the foolishness I had allowed to pass between us, Amanda and I were still very good friends. Whatever our struggles were intimately, on paper we made a powerful, powerful team when it came to taking care of business.

Her sharp mind for law and order complemented my energy and spirituality. To further stress the point, Cincinnati was in need of a secretary for the MGT. Amanda had been the secretary in Heaven for a time, which made her an ideal candidate for the job.

Royall was our example and constantly spoke of the idea that several of his wives he had not because he liked them, but because of the duty they performed for the Nation.

Whatever dysfunction we had as a couple, one could not ignore her acumen as a wife, mother, and MGT. Even though I had gotten off to a rough start, I had grown exponentially in this knowledge. With assurances from Amanda (and I) that things would be different this time, backed by Royall's ringing endorsement, the request went in for us to get back together, and before you knew it Amanda and PJ were on the next thing smoking to Cincinnati.

Ray and Alan were still in the FOI apartment under the care of the Brothers. Amanda still filled the maternal role for them albeit from afar. Because of the duty I was doing, the FOI in general made it their business to look out for them and they had begun to make men of themselves.

Ray was studying under the construction crew and Alan was aggressively pursuing any responsibility he take. All involved thought it best to allow them to continue to develop in this capacity.

Tammy took the opportunity to move into the MGT house and branch out on her own.

At the time there was a huge youth movement in the Nation. Royall had made it clear that the youth were responsible to bring in the new, so while it was our duty to branch out and take over the cities, it was imperative that the youth be developed in his thinking, without being infected by the baggage of ours. (In other words, you Negros are crazy and we can't have y'all infecting the kids).

Though at the time it made perfect sense to me, if I came to regret anything it would be taking this hands-off approach to their growth and development.

Nonetheless, I was happy as ever to see my family, Amanda included. Even with all of our doubts, Royall had said she needed to come back to me, so how could this be wrong? Amanda was well received by the MGT. Jan and Shemelle, Morris and Emory's wives, were as excited to see her and the children as I was. As expected, it was not long before she was asserting herself within the MGT structure. Between Morris, Emory, me, and our families, a significant amount of power had been added to Cincinnati.

The FOI began to operate more cohesively. Not only did we have things cranking in the community and Diner, but we were making progress as Brothers. If we saw a brother behaving out of order, then we would address it on the spot and put a definite/solution to it so that by the time the Wives heard of a scenario, the math had already been applied to it.

Robin had been shipped to Heaven not long after my arrival and Leon not too long after him. In return we got Brother Douglass and his wife, Lashawn. While losing Leon hurt, this was yet another huge win for us. Douglass was another vet of the Nation who was especially skilled in the politics of the UNOI.

This was ironic because he was so much like me. This is to say he was a very happy spirited Brother and a hard worker who was usually dressed rather shabbily.

Somehow, he managed to deal with the Wives without much of a problem, alternating between covering for the Brothers and drilling Brothers who didn't hold up their end. His abilities as a go between for FOI and the Wives would prove invaluable. Lashawn was no less valuable. She was what most Brothers considered one of the good Sisters. Single-handedly taking charge of the prep for the Diner, she would constantly cover the Brothers' prep, freeing us up to divert more attention to what we did best. Make money.

Amongst Morris, Emory, and me, going out in the community was the focal point of our duty. Sure, the opportunity to teach class was great, but in essence, you were preaching to the choir. Duty in the Diner was good, but if we wanted mindless manual labor we could have stayed in Heaven.

And if Carter and I had been a formidable duo in Connecticut, the three of us were outright illegal. In more ways than one.

We would walk into a shop and literally hold it hostage until we walked out of it. These weren't the modest, soft spoken Brothers that they were used to seeing from the Diner.

All eyes would turn quickly to us and we walked in like we owned the place, one of us addressing the room in general, letting it be known who we were, where we were from and what we had for sale. The other would sidle up to potential customers one by one, making eye contact, charming their socks off and the dollars out of their purse. If one of us didn't connect, there was no way they all could say no to both of us.

I learned in my hustling days that sales were all about relationships. People weren't buying what you had; they could get fish sandwiches anywhere. They were paying for the experience of being around us. Sounds egotistical, I know, but never was this more evident than Cincinnati.

We would come into a shop and check with the stylists and customers to see if anyone wanted food. Even if they all said no we would stay, talk, joke, and kick it another 15-20 minutes minimum. Once we felt we were wasting time and started saying our goodbyes, they would start buying, keeping us there another 20 minutes. This cycle could repeat itself a couple of times before we made it out the door. It was nothing to look up and realize we had burned as much as an hour in a single shop, which was ok as long as you sold an hour's worth of sandwiches.

What made us equally potent was that we had a full restaurant behind us, so if we couldn't sell you on a $5 sandwich now, we would book you for a $12 Salmon Dinner later. All the more excuse (for us and them) to come back and kick it again.

Previous records for earning in the Diner began to fall one after the other. Of course, in the process of building relationships with these shops, regular customers started developing favorites amongst the Brothers (and vice versa). A sister who might never buy anything, ever, would dig to the bottom of her purse if her"Muslim boyfriend" came into the shop.

We noticed this and accepted it as part of the duty that we were just gonna have to deal with.

Hard, I know, but hey, we were soldiers.

If things were slow, I knew I could go to Keisha at Diverse Styles or Tonya at Hair Action and they would spend with me. In exchange, we became the sounding board for whatever rumors or legends they had heard about Islam.

You haven't truly had a discussion until you have discussed the idea of polygamy with a shop full of Black women. And you haven't truly won until you have said shop full of Black woman open to idea that it might not be the worst idea in the world. Maybe it's not for them and THEIR man, but they could at least agree that it was possible with a strong man.

In class I would struggle to articulate ideas to the members and would often find myself being addressed for using language that was inappropriate. In a shop full of "lost-founds", I would find no limit of ways to explain the divinity in our way of life.

Of course there were Sisters who had plenty of interest in us but not in our divinity or our way of life. They may or may not foster the illusion of being a Muslim wife, but wouldn't allow that minor detail to stop them from pursuing a Muslim man.

It was a familiar test for all of us. Some Brothers would play it by the book, cutting them off immediately. Others would play the middle, being social, never quite telling the sister no, but never letting them in enough to incriminate themselves. After all, there were plenty of examples of Brothers bringing another brother's wife into the Nation. She might not be for you, but there were plenty of good men in the FOI looking for a wife (or two).

Still another group adopted the 85% rule that ruled so much of our activity in Connecticut.

It had been stated by Royall that 85% of Black women would never accept the idea, and thus burn up in the hell fire. Now, when, I don't know, and never really bothered to ask the context of the comment, but like so many religious zealots before us, our interpretation of our God's word had more to do with our agenda than his.

If the sister wanted something physical then who were they to deny them a taste of divinity?

Getting away was simple enough. You just had to be out with a brother who didn't mind a) dropping you off and b) working the community to sell the food solo, giving you a couple of hours for whatever you might do with two spare hours.

I didn't have a problem doing the dropping and selling. I was retired, but I still respected the game. Though there were a couple of sisters I had connected with in the physical before Amanda came to Cincinnati, I had decided the last thing I needed was another scenario with a female.

Nope.

No thanks.

Not the kid.

Yeah.

So.

Her name was Tasha and I promise...I promise I tried. From the first moments of our interaction I knew there was something there. So much so that I made a conscious decision I wasn't gonna say anything else to her. Wasn't even gonna open my mouth, I would for once let the other Brother in the shop do all the talking.

My luck was so rotten, I was sure I would be found out one way or the other. The Brother I was with was a pretty serious sister magnet so I figured he would try to holler at her, and at best I could live vicariously through his experience. He cooperated with my plan. She didn't.

Fair enough. I walked out of the shop, sure that would be the end of that.

Until I saw her again.

And again. Each time the conversation picking up where it had left off last time. Somewhere in there finding out she was a Gemini.

Did I mention I was an Aquarius? (Still am)

Sigh. I'm such a victim in all of this.

Ok, I decided, I'll just see where this goes. I got her number and we began talking. And talking. And talking.

Eventually, I was the one getting dropped off to spend a couple hours at her house. She was banker, doing pretty well, and her place was huge. The more I talked to her; I could tell she was looking for so much more than that.

Finally, on one visit I told her as much. I told her that I could see how much she dreaded going to her job, how much she hated the emptiness that came with it. How there was so much more inside of her than what that place allowed her to be. When she broke down crying I knew we both were in trouble.

The Brothers in the community's methods would eventually backfire when unbeknownst to us the daughter of one of the elder Sisters was audience to one of our impromptu teaching sessions in the shops. The elder decided MGT class, in front of all the Sisters, was the place to report this scenario. Which meant in no time we were in a joint FOI-MGT class and the Sisters' account of "the Brothers' blatant flirtation" was being relayed for the entertainment of the whole class.

"So, then the sister says, 'Well what would we wear if we came to class' and then Brother Prostell said 'Well you couldn't wear that skirt!"

Cue gasps and pearl grasping. I knew exactly which shop and sister was being referred to. I even recalled the conversation, and knew it didn't happen exactly like that, but understood with my reputation I wasn't about to get the benefit of the doubt.

Never mind that we had lost-founds actually considering coming to class, never mind the numbers we made in said shop more than justified the attention we showed them, never mind even that this was a third-hand, inaccurate depiction of events that had happened more than a month ago. One thing we had learned was that you had to pick your battles. We had been garnering some respect for the FOI and control from the Wives, but this was Nation politics and someone had to pay.

That would be me.

I was promptly busted down to the dish room and suspended from the fundraiser until further notice, which was just as fine with me. I had come into the Nation and made a name for myself in the dish room, and I would do it again.

Sure enough, a few weeks later I was being addressed as to why I hadn't put in a request to get back on community fundraiser. Not only did I get my flying wings back, but I was named Inspector shortly after that.

Well yeah, that shocked me too. It was really more of a project. The Laborers reasoned that I was certainly sharp enough to do inspections, and that being in the position of checking others would require me to make sure I had my stuff together first. I figured out what they meant quickly.

The first thing any Brother did when you told them they had a mark on their shirt was to look at your shirt. On the plus side, this would include me in Laborers' meeting, which was another significant step back in the right direction. It would give me access to the Wives and another important FOI voice at the Laborers' meeting.

This was a dramatic improvement from when we had arrived and the Wives conducted business autonomously. Make no mistake, they still had the final say, but we were certainly in the conversation. Ultimately, with all of the hidden agendas and power struggles, success for The Diner was in everyone's best interest.

Just like the Brothers, the Wives just needed to know that they could trust the person they were working with to do what they said they were going to do, but success reflected well on everyone.

With Emory, Morris, and I holding down the community, Douglass balancing things in the Diner, and Jan, Amanda and the MGT supporting the whole operation, the numbers started to go up.

A lot.

Before long, Cincinnati was once again the toast of the Nation. Don't get me wrong, we still had minor disturbances, but one thing that bought patience in those areas was the number$.

Outside of the usual FOI and Laborers' meeting, Emory, Morris, Douglass and I would hold impromptu pow wows to make sure that the Brothers were all on the same page. We would coordinate everything from what ideals we would present to Royall's Wives to who would present them, when and where they would bring them up, etc.

If we wanted to be especially calculated, we would hit them from all sides. I would plant a seed with my wife so that she would bring it up to one of Royall's wives. Then Morris would mention to another one of Royall's wives knowing they would discuss it with the first wife. And then when they brought it up at Laborers' meeting, Douglass would present the missing pieces of the puzzle to make it all work.

Finally, the FOI was of one accord, we had the respect of the Wives, the attention of the Nation and most important, the appreciation of our Father, Royall.

With all the activity we had begun to expand.

We had been covering Cincinnati so thoroughly that Emory had gotten the go ahead to accompany one of the part-timers to Dayton for fundraiser.

At the time, a good team was doing $300-400 on a Saturday. The first time Emory hit Dayton they came back with $600. That would be the lowest a Dayton team would come back with.

Funds continued to pour in.

Plans were made to go to Columbus and Indianapolis.

We had begun to focus on bringing in visitors.

Like most other things in the FOI we made it into a competition.

Luckily for me, talking to lost-founds was my thing.

I would have at least one guest at each class, even if I had to pick them up myself.

Even though I was successful in this effort, I still hadn't managed to bring the one guest I hoped to bring.

Tasha.

We began meeting every chance we got. Often I would volunteer for a late grocery run and meet her at a midpoint as she raced from across town, all for ten stolen minutes of passionate kissing and making out. I have never met, and to this day have yet to meet anyone like her. To this point, though, kissing and cuddling had become our routine. We had not yet consummated our illegal relationship.

I would speak to her about the Nation and what it would mean to be a part of it. She wasn't sold on being full-time but saw herself being part-time, still working, bringing in money and Amanda and I moving into her home. I thought it would actually work for Amanda, who still hadn't adjusted to the squalid conditions of full-time living. Just the fact that she was exploring how to make the idea work meant the world to me.

Amanda was a different story. The idea of having more than one wife was something that was gone over consistently by the Sisters, but in my house it was still a long divide from principle to practice.

Just mentioning the idea was grounds for an all-day fight.

Our relationship had stabilized, but one false move would send it tumbling backwards.

Amanda was ready to expand our family in other ways.
We discussed the idea of having another child, which both agreed would be a great idea. We checked with the structure, it came back approved and we began working on it at once. If nothing else, it restored some much needed romance to our relationship.

There are few things I have experienced as divine as laying down for the express purpose of creating a life together. Like all other things in our life, this was framed against the backdrop of Nation building. Not only would this baby be an expression of the love you had for your spouse, but also ideally a valuable asset to the Nation. Everything was to be taken into consideration, in particular the sign of the expected baby and how this would mesh with the existing personalities in your family and even the long term needs of the Nation.

Coming into the Nation, we all agreed to give "all that I have and all that is within my power". This act was an extension of that. Men like me viewed our families as the "all that was within my power". In addition to the duty I was physically doing myself, I had a powerful and productive wife who held a major role in the MGT, three children back in Heaven who were making names for themselves, and a small son who was already captivating everyone who he encountered and begged daily to go to duty with me.

Another young soldier or soldierette would be another feather in my cap.

Before long, we were successful and consumed with preparations to receive our expectant seed. The excitement of procreation had carried over to doctor's appointments and visits with the midwife who would be assisting in our delivery. Those appointments that I couldn't make, Amanda would schedule simultaneously with Jan, who conveniently was expecting a baby as well.

The anticipation did not put out of my mind my ongoing relationship with Tasha. I had done my best to slow things down to a platonic level, but the love we had for each other was obvious.

I was at an absolute loss as to how to introduce the idea to Amanda, but I couldn't' walk away. I had never felt anything like what I was feeling with her. We still hadn't become sexually active and I didn't have a problem with that. Our connection was so much deeper than that. We would sit and talk about the future and what it could be. I knew I would have to eventually introduce her to the MGT, but I was biding my time with that.

Ironically, many of the Brothers had vowed that their second wife would be a lost-found that they brought in and taught about the idea, because too many of the MGT were loyal to the MGT structure, or the Nation or even Royall above their husband. This meant being very strategic in how you introduced a potential Sister to the Nation.

Tasha seemed to understand. She was in love with me as much as I was with her. She appreciated the idea of the Nation, but when we spoke, it was of how she could assist me as part of my family. I would continue to prepare her, and at the right time bring her in.

They say if you wanna make God laugh, make plans.

One day in class...the phone rang. Class was going on and as the Inspector I was on post and paid no real attention to it, knowing whoever was standing in the rear of the Diner would answer it. Probably just for Dawn.

Brother Steve came from the kitchen, "Brother Prostell, Sister Advisor is on the phone for you..."

Instantly, I started going over in my mind what I might have missed in my duty to be receiving a phone call from Sister Advisor who wasn't even in town at the moment. She had been out of town as of late, so most messages and directives from her came through Dawn or even Morris, who was getting closer and closer to the "throne."

I picked up the phone.

"As Salaam Alaikum"

"Y Laikum Salaam, Brother Prostell," Sister Advisor began, "Father is on the line!"

"As Salaam Alaikum Father!"

Being in Royall's presence or even on the phone still had a great effect on me. Like most members who considered this man to be Allah, you thought three times about every word you said, how you said it, why you said it, almost to the point of sounding like an idiot. Oftentimes to the point of sounding like an idiot. My times around those who spent a great deal of time Father's presence (Daniel, Morris, Yunus, etc.) had taught me that it was better to be yourself and err than try to be perfect and sound even crazier.

Father returned the greetings, "Brother Prostell, what would you think about the idea of going back to Detroit to help your Father-in-law get things going there?"

I couldn't believe my ears. I hesitated for a moment. I was heavily invested in what we had going on in Cincinnati, but from the very first

240

moment I set foot in Heaven my plan had always been to bring whatever I had gained in the way of knowledge back to Detroit.

"Father that would be a dream come true. Detroit is a city with a lot of potential. A lot of our people and no one is doing anything close to what you are teaching, Father."

"Well, what do you think about being the Assistant Minister there?"

I wasn't so sure about that, but I had learned a proper FOI never turned down and opportunity to do what was needed, "Absolutely, Father, that's something I can do!"

"What do you think, Yvette?"

"I don't know about that, Father."

"Prostell what makes you think you could be a good Minister?"

"Father, I am very good at expressing ideas in more than one way so that people can understand it."

Sister Advisor repeated, "I don't know about that, Father."

Pretending not to hear her, I continued. "Plus, Father, I am from there. I know the people in and out of the temple so I can relate ideas to them..."

Father cut me off.

"Well, Brother Prostell, we want to make this happen as soon as possible. You need to speak to your Father-in-law and make arrangements immediately. Is your wife there?"

"I will go get her right now, Father"

I walked back to the front of the Diner, got Amanda's attention and waved her to come back. She looked concerned when I handed her the phone and told her who it was.

As I watched her on the phone, the entire thing seemed surreal. I recalled speaking to Kaaba years ago about it being my dream to learn what I needed to know about Nation building and then return home to Detroit to employ it. He laughed at the thought. That would never happen, he surmised, because home is the number one place for any person to get caught up in some foolishness.

Now here I was waiting as Royall explained to my wife that we would be going back to Detroit.

"Thank you so much Father and Sister Advisor, As Salaam Alaikum."

Amanda extended the phone back towards me, "Father wants to talk back to you."

"Yes Sir, Father."

"One more thing, Brother Prostell. If you do this and do it right, the blessing that will come to you will be more than you can imagine...but if you mess this up or get caught up in some scenario with a female, then the punishment will be equal to that, but in the other direction."

My brain flashed a picture of Tasha.

"Yes Sir, Father. That won't happen!"

"Ok, well I expect you to keep your word. Get with Brother Joe and get this done immediately."

"Yes, Sir. I am on it."

We exchanged the greetings and that was it.

When I hung up the phone, Amanda and I sat there staring at each other.

I tried not to act as surprised as I was at my selection for such an important assignment.

"Ok, we will have to call your Dad after class to see what they already have set up and see how long before they can receive us. Then we are also going to need to make arrangements to find a new midwife and OB-Gyn for the baby. Also... "

While I sat there rattling off a to do list what I was really thinking was, "

"Oh my God! Oh my God! Oh my God! Oh my God! What am I gonna do? What am I gonna do? What am I gonna do? Oh my God! Oh my God! Oh my God!"

I knew I had been making progress in my growth and development as an FOI, but I could have never seen this coming. I was just happy to be holding down the Inspector post, be going out in the community consistently, and having significant input into the happenings of Cincinnati.

I was excited about the things that we were doing in Cincinnati; the increasing prospects of a restaurant opening in Dayton, other outings to cities in the area, more and more members processing and coming into the Nation through Cincinnati. On the fundraiser alone, we were setting and breaking National records weekly, which was inspiring other Temples, including Heaven, to step up. Every Saturday would end with a round of calls from the top Temples to compare bank rolls.

Inevitably, we were our only real competition, but it was an exciting time to be in the Nation. Connecticut was continuing to flourish, Kaaba had taken over the fundraiser in Heaven and they had finally begun to make some noise. Atlanta and New Jersey were beginning the very first baby steps in getting their names on the map.

Being dispatched to my hometown trumped all of that.

I knew enough about what was and wasn't happening in Detroit to know that the opportunity for growth was limitless. I could barely wait to tell Morris.

By this time, he was so immersed in responsibility in Cincinnati that he was sad to lose a good soldier, but we both saw the big picture for what it was. Many nights we stayed late cleaning the Diner and prepping for the next day, plotting on how we would take over the city.

With me in Detroit and him in Cincinnati, it wouldn't be long before we had the whole Midwest covered. We chatted it up well into the night, even calling Daniel on three-way. I was shocked when I realized how surprised he was at the news.

I had just assumed that with Sister Advisor's skepticism that Daniel MUST have put in a good word for me with Father. In fact, he was dealing with issues of his own at the time and had no idea that Detroit was even being discussed.

This made the decision mean even more to me. This meant Father had decided to make a phone call to me and invest in me based on what HE saw in me. Once again, I felt vindicated against even my own self-doubt.

I couldn't fail.

We all agreed on this and on the importance of us all holding down our respective ends and how what we were doing fit into prophecy. Eventually, I bid the Brothers good night as I needed to make phone calls to arrange transportation for the long road home.

C-5

Detroit

Ever since I was a little boy, there was always something euphoric about returning to Detroit; passing the giant Michelin Tire, seeing the skyline as you roll past downtown, hitting that first pothole that rips your axle clean off your car.

What made this return even sweeter was I had long ago accepted that I would never again set foot in this town. I was a full-time soldier for Allah, and with no Nation's business or Temple in Detroit, there was nothing in Detroit for me.

Granted, I still had plenty of family and friends in the D, but if they wanted to see me, they knew where I was. I was about the business of Nation building. It was taught and understood that if you really loved your family, then what you should really be doing is helping to build the Nation so that when this system (America) fell, they would have someplace to go. If they were mad at you now, they would eventually understand.

That's not to say the idea was totally absent from my mind. I knew that Detroit would be ideal for what we were doing.

It was a major metropolitan area that was at least 90% black. That included much of the police force and most of the elected city officials. It was also full of disenfranchised people. After tours in cities where I knew no one before moving there, it would be a cakewalk getting things rolling in my hometown.

There always seemed to be things happening to bring Detroit to my mind: a song on the radio, a street with the same name as one I grew up on, someone who looked or acted like someone I used to know...

Sometimes it would get downright spooky.

Shortly after I had come to Cincinnati we had been exploring the idea of opening a bakery. Since I had the experience of opening the bakery in Connecticut, I was commissioned to contact restaurant equipment suppliers to price shop. This included one warehouse that had a number of used mixers and other equipment. As I am walking around this dark warehouse in the middle of the industrial district in Cincinnati, I turn a corner and am stopped cold in my tracks.

In front of me is a giant framed mural. It shows a man kneeling playing with who appears to be his son, a couple walking in a park, a basketball player, number 44, with a jersey that reads Highland Park. Now if you grew up near or around Highland Park, MI (a small peaceful municipality that rests smack dab in the middle of Detroit), this might sound familiar to you. This picture used to hang in the Pizza Hut that sat in the plaza at Woodward and Manchester during the 90s.

I remembered it from sitting and staring at it the 247 million or so times we went to get a Personal Pan after or while skipping school. Fast forward eleven years and here I am standing in another city more than 200 miles away in a dark corner of some obscure warehouse and this artifact from my childhood is staring me in the face. In the UNOI, one thing we were taught to pay attention to was signs/the unseen. This was clearly a sign, both literally and figuratively.

But even a sign is useless if you don't know what it means. The mural had gotten my attention, but I still saw no plausible way I would end up back in Detroit. Fast forward and here I was pulling back into town having just been named Assistant Minister.

Considering the circumstances of my departure, it was a dramatic difference indeed. When I had left for Heaven years ago, I was a laughing stock. Bets were literally being made about how long it would take for me to get thrown out of Heaven. Most people's money was going on not long at all. If I had been betting, I would have too.

Now I was returning home, being called personally by Allah himself to come and straighten out the Study Group.

It had been years since I had been home, but the Detroit Study Group had made little progress in that time. I didn't know what motion was going on in Detroit, which was telling in and of itself. They hadn't made as much as bleep on the National radar.

Bro. Minister and his oldest son, Bilal were still pretty much the focal point of anything Nation-based in Detroit. They had successfully gotten their Trucking Company off the ground and were very significant financial supporters of the Nation. This allowed them significant access to Royall and those in the upper echelon of the Nation. To the members who rarely got a look at the books, this didn't mean a whole lot of anything. It was known that they donated more than most members across the Nation, everything from money, to vehicles, to flights and hotel rooms, and even business connections.

Father mentioning their names across the rostrum did garner a bit more consideration and/or patience, but ultimately, we viewed all part-timers the same way: as bull-shitters, Brothers who were afraid or too weak or just didn't have it in them to commit to this idea fully.

While theirs was an important role in the Nation, it served to make them feel justified in still being out in the world while the rest us had committed fully.

The way we viewed things, Allah was here and he was calling your name, in order to make you God, and provide a better future for you family-what else did you need? If you know the world out there is going to fall, then why are you working and building a future out there instead of in YOUR OWN NATION?!?!? If you could make things happen for yourself out on your own in the world, how much more effective would you be if you had the powers of the Nation at your disposal?

Like Connecticut, I was coming to a temple that was largely run by one family.

Unlike Connecticut, I wasn't coming with a team of six Brothers. I was coming with my wife, who was a very capable person, but also happened to be the daughter of said family. These were my in-laws and despite all the personalism I had encountered when I had first been introduced to the Nation, I didn't consciously harbor any ill will toward them.

Like most who knew them in the Nation, I saw the immense potential they carried if they would just lose the one foot in, one foot out mentality. Much like the Davis's, this was a proud family, a strong patriarch and four tall, strong, able-bodied, sharp-minded young men.

For all their faults and shortcomings, they had almost single-handedly kept the idea alive in Detroit with not only their finance but their energy. They may have been part-timers, but they were amongst the very best part-timers the Nation had.

But I also knew that there was a wide difference between the way they did things and the way Royall did them. It would be my job to bridge that divide. My loyalty without question was to Royall, the FOI and the Nation. That being understood, I knew there was no way I was going to get anything done if I just came in pointing fingers and tearing anything down.

I figured my best bet was to lead by example. We were often taught the way we knew we were being like Royall, the ultimate goal, was that we were inspiring the God in our brother or sister. This would be my mantra.

I was pleasantly surprised to see that the study group had grown in size adding about six members who came to class regularly. Like Connecticut, this influx of personalities had fostered an undercurrent of animosity and politics that would bubble to the surface in and out of class.

With no real motion to speak of, most of the scenarios were minor in nature, some disagreement of the God meaning of a word, or if a

Brother was right or wrong in his opinion or what they might have said to someone.

In most cases, scenarios could be resolved by pointing out to either party the importance of looking for the solution and showing them what they could have done to make the scenario go the way that it was supposed to. Like Connecticut, in the most simple math principles like these, common knowledge, to most full-timers, amounted to deep science in a part-time temple. By this time, the practice of conference calling officials from other parts of the country to deal with scenarios was at an all-time high.

An unsuspecting Brother or Sister would get a call from an official.

"Salaam Brother Bilal, you got a moment?"

The conversation would start out innocent enough, and then you would hear those words to let you know you were basically doomed:

"I got Brother National Lt on the line... "

This usually meant that the caller and Bro. National Lt. had already spoken and were on the same page long before they called you. They could either play good cop-bad cop, bad cop-worse cop, or one of the Brothers could simply be on the line in order to make sure that there was a third party record of the conversation.

This was extremely helpful to me because it allowed me to address scenarios without members taking it AS personally with me.

I could simply conference in Kaaba, Yunus, Daniel, Carter, or any of the Brothers across the Nation that delighted in being in such conversations. In most cases, they were the same people I ran the scenarios by, and were all too eager to play the bad cop and address the party in question.

Just the ability to resolve scenarios and feuds that had been going on for years elevated me in the eyes of the members. It was a living testament not only to me, but even more so to the power of Royall. After all, when I had left here I was a complete and total fuck up and had returned one of the most heavy- hitting Brothers in the Nation.

If that wasn't motivation for the Brothers to go full-time, I don't know what else would have been.

My duties included conducting Math class with Brother Minister on Friday, managing the weekly motion of the study group, and making weekly reports to Royall or one of his wives. Oftentimes, we would tap into spiritual class on Sundays. On occasions when we did not, Royall would give topics to cover and then we would give the spiritual teaching.

Though he had great access to Royall, and a library of knowledge about the Messenger, what Royall was teaching was new to Joe. He was from the First Resurrection and the teachings of the Honorable Elijah Muhammad in their purest form. I had been developed in Royall's thinking, which had some roots in the Messenger, but was all new.

It was my job to ensure that Father was the base of whatever we were doing.

So in class when he would answer a question in a way that didn't quite represent Royall's teaching, it would be my job to reel things back in.

Sometimes it was as simple as correcting a word or phrase or restating something he said and changing one thing slightly. Other times when he was more adamant or passionate about what he was saying, it would require some tact. Usually, even if I knew that I knew I was right, I would feign ignorance but insist that we check with Father or one of the other Ministers in the Nation and get back to the class.

It was in these moments Amanda told me that I surprised her the most. In truth, I surprised myself.

Although I was very adept at expressing myself in casual settings and out in the community with the lost-founds, I had never been terribly articulate in class settings.

In fact it was just the opposite. I would get very nervous to the point of having shortness of breath, which would in turn make me feel and sound like I was having an emotional breakdown.

I knew this is what Sister Advisor had meant when she said she was unsure about my ability to express myself.

Perhaps it was the comfort in knowing no one here could touch me in terms of knowledge, or maybe just the comfort of being back home, but I was drastically different in Detroit.

There was no stuttering, stammering or shortness of breath, the only hesitation coming when trying to guide a class that had run off the rails back onto the prescribed subject.

I did my best to give correction in the most humble way, as I had great deal of respect and admiration for Brother Minister. In addition to being my Father-in-Law, he was a member of the First and the very person responsible for introducing me to this idea that was now MY LIFE.

Anytime we reached an impasse about what should or shouldn't be covered in class, which meant getting a third party, one of the ministers or one of my advisors.

To his credit, Brother Minister would come to recognize the pattern and began simply deferring to me on certain matters, allowing me to conduct the classes, while taking care to make certain key points he thought should be brought out were covered. He began to use most of his energy and focus on matters of finance and business, his area of expertise.

Brother Minister clearly loved the Nation first and above all else. He was truly about giving all that he had and all that was within his power.

Which was a challenge because Brother Minster was an old school hustler; wherein a lot of part-timers didn't really give a damn, he did.

He just always had an angle. It was just the way he was wired.

He was a property owner, which was a major point of contention in his relationship with the temple. Each of the homes that the temple rented for my family we rented from him, which is fair. I mean a man's got to make a living, and why not support those who support you? The problem came in when three out of four times we had to renovate, decorate, restore and repair them. This, of course, with money from the Nation, all while still paying rent.

It was a deal we would never accept from a lost-found.

Even the bakery we were supposed to be opening was an issue. Brother Minster had purchased a building with his sons after we had moved to Heaven.

Shortly after, they opened a family store and the building had a major fire. So, now it was a burned out shell, that, SURPRISE, he was willing rent out to the Nation for a bakery, if we would just send the construction crew to come and restore the building.

Oh, ok.

After seeing the building at a FOI detail to clean the building, it seemed to me it would take nothing less than a miracle. Which was still doable in my mind, because I had seen the construction crew and the FOI in general pull off a few miracles.

Even though to most of us, all of this seemed like a questionable deal at best, Royall green lighted the project, sending construction crew members from Heaven and Maryland to get work started on the project.

A hammer never hit a nail in the building.

They took one look at the building and declared that it would be best served being torn down.

Of course, they came all that way, so they decided to build and make improvements to the home we were renting from Brother Minister, including eventually turning the basement into a makeshift bakery.

In the meantime, the wheels were beginning to turn in Detroit. We had begun making progress across the city. Detroit was still a hustler's paradise, with what seemed like a hair salon every half mile apart on every major road.

Before we got there, the support raiser ran one day a week and covered a very small strip in a city full of potential supporters.

To say we were going to have to do better was a huge understatement. Not only did we have rent and cost of living expenses, but Amanda was six months pregnant with our second child. Above and beyond that, I was not willing to accept coming here and not being able to send money to Heaven.

This, after all, was the overall goal of any Brother or group of Brothers being dispatched to outlying temples. At the time, there was an announcement every week of a different Brother or Brothers being dispatched to a Temple to get the ball rolling. Despite all of the drama that followed our time in Connecticut, we seemed to have opened the flood gates for Brothers going out and magnifying the idea.

Kaaba and Daniel were in Atlanta, and were doing everything from selling t-shirts, to garage sales, to fish sandwiches and sending thousands to Heaven weekly. Trevor was in Alabama working getting a restaurant there. North Carolina, Wichita, and New Jersey all had members dispatched for the purpose of either opening a new business or improving a substandard business that was there in the first place.

This created an ultra-competitive culture across the Nation. Weekly calls circulated around the Nation as the heads of the various groups debated over who would send in the most money to Heaven that week. My family accounted for the only full-time members in Detroit, but I was not interested in allowing that to eliminate us from contention.

I began making my rounds Tuesday through Saturday with the cookies that we were baking, and increased our production tenfold. This still wasn't much considering how low it was at first but it was progress.

I had gotten word that there was a double convection oven that was just sitting in the warehouse that had been donated to the Nation and made the necessary calls to get it to Detroit. The very next truck that came from Heaven to the Midwest delivered it, and our production went through the roof overnight.

Before long, a support raiser that was bringing in a little under 200 dollars a week was hovering around 1000 dollars. I was fine with that, as we hadn't even pulled out the big guns yet. Cookie sales were one thing, but I knew once we started the dinners it was a wrap.

The benefit of being able to speak directly with Royall on a weekly basis made it so ideas were much easier to bring it into fruition. It was simply a matter of saying we wanted to do a thing and we could get the ball rolling. Royall would simply say what a good idea it was or ask if we thought it could work, to which we of course would respond in the affirmative, and then that was that. As Ministers, it was our duty to see that the plan was executed and report back the result.

At first, this was a welcome change from being subjected to the politics and prejudices of a temple head, be it a wife or Minister. I would soon learn that local politics were nothing in comparison to the games that were played at the National Level.

More on that later.

We began the Fish Dinners and would quickly see our weekly totals exceed $1500 on average. Though we were still regarded as a study group, we greatly outclassed any study group and/or temple made up of mostly part-timers. In fact, these numbers put us on par with much larger temples that had a roster of full-timers to send out and, in some cases, a restaurant.

But, of course, Mo Money, Mo Problems, or in this case, Mo Money, Mo Money Management. Being the Business-minded man that he was, Bro. Minister's thought was to send a hundred or so to Heaven like Detroit always had and start stockpiling money for a bakery.

My thought was the same as it had always been; we were here simply for the purpose of magnifying Heaven. I thought we should keep enough for bills and groceries and send all the rest to Heaven. In my experience, this would justify help coming back to us once we found a project worth investing in, be it a bakery or a diner.

This was usually resolved weekly depending on the circumstances of not only the study group and what we had brought in, but also what call outs there were for funds in Heaven. And were there ever call outs. Invariably, a bus or some major vehicle would break down in Heaven, or a boiler would go out, or someone had forgotten to pay the taxes on ALL the properties for like three years, and a huge emergency call would go out for whatever funds were needed immediately.

Even though we were doing great for a part-time study group, the vision I sought to give the members was of constantly being able to do better.

This was, after all, Detroit, aka "Temple No. 1." The first place where Master Fard Muhammad had introduced Islam to the Blackman in America. This is where the Messenger was raised up. What did we look like coming in behind North Carolina or Mobile or Wichita? Did they even have Muslims in Wichita?

I was pushing, but in reality we couldn't possibly do much better than we were doing. The Hassans, in particular Bilal, were committed to not being outworked. So even though he was still running the family trucking business and other business endeavors and contributing large amounts financially, Bilal began having other drivers cover his routes in order to free himself up for shopping, baking, or whatever else needed to be done. He had a level of commitment that often defied the label "part-time member" that had become such a scarlet letter in the UNOI.

More than anyone else in his family, possibly even Amanda, he understood what type of commitment it would take for Detroit to get the respect it deserved. His involvement set the tone for everyone else in the Temple, including those not in his family. As he stepped up, so did they.

He was the FOI Lt. for Detroit and more importantly, a natural leader. His influence was such that he could get most of the members to take on responsibility that they might not normally take.

I knew before I arrived back in Detroit, his assistance would be integral if we were going to make any real progress. He didn't disappoint.

I made it a point in my weekly report to let Royall know that this is what we are doing now, but with a few more full-time Brothers there is so much more we could be doing. We had teams going out on the east and west sides, and I was going out during the week, but that was still only scratching the surface of what we were doing. But we were hardly alone.

With all of the motion going across the Nation, there was a constant battle between temples and study groups vying for the limited resources; the construction crew, finances and the most valuable resource of in the Nation: manpower.

You could have a bustling metropolitan area but it meant absolutely nothing if you didn't have enough bodies to produce enough and then get out and work that area.

In addition to that, you needed to RIGHT bodies. There were Brothers falling over themselves trying to get dispatched and make names for themselves in the next business to open.

After getting things started in Atlanta, Kaaba and Daniel had moved on to Wichita to clean up the Temple there. It was the unstated plan of the Nation that they would go around from temple to temple to help shore things up, and get things jump started.

Most importantly to me, they would be bringing more than themselves. Kaaba and Daniel were great leaders, motivators, and organizers, but if they were coming they weren't coming alone. Brothers with that level of responsibility weren't to be tied do a duty, so they would definitely be coming with Brothers.

Despite what we had going in Detroit, I still didn't have the pull to get members dispatched there. We were making consistent progress but my reputation still hung over me like a black cloud. In the Nation, your reputation was everything. It was the currency with which you could purchase needed energy and power to support your ideas.

With many of those in power, it was just accepted that I was womanizer. This in itself wasn't the end of the world; there were plenty of Brothers and Sisters who had records that were less than pristine.

Royall even had taught that it was not in any powerful man's nature to be with just one woman. My biggest problem lied in the fact that I was still a "sloppy pimp' as Yunus used to call me.

My marriage was extremely productive in terms of Nation Building.

Amanda's passion about the Nation knew no bounds. She had taken full responsibility of the MGT and the Temple Secretary position. She had fine-tuned the baking and dinner recipes which had such respect that Temples from around the Nation called in to get our recipes. Other than that she was a de facto inspector, never shy about pointing things out that simply were not up to par with her understanding of Father's teaching. Hers may have been a reputation for being abrasive or overly assertive, but along with that she was absolutely known as a sister who would stand up with the truth until the very end. Even that abrasiveness was born of a will to see this idea be successful by any and every means.

For all of our collective productivity, our relationship with each other was not any more improved. We were far from enemies but still a million miles apart when it came to just us. The things that did unify us- our Nation, our children, the opportunity to do something wonderful for the city and the people of Detroit-kept us going.

But at the end of the day, after kids were in bed and there was no duty until the next day, none of that Nation building or smiling little faces had built up enough good will to bridge those finals few inches that always lie between us in our bed at night. That little space may as well have been a million miles.

We were often at odds about how to do things, but usually that was because she thought I was doing more than my share of the work, and that someone else needed to step up.

None of this was ever enough to erase in her mind the misdeeds of the past. I'm sure in her eyes the past was never really the past when every so often I could be counted on to leave some number in my pocket, or have some random female text my phone in the middle of the night. Most of it would be innocuous, but you could never tell that to a woman who was a victim of serial lying and cheating. There was no way to tell the difference between women who were trying to sleep with your man versus the one who actually genuinely interested in the Nation.

By this time, she wasn't sitting back waiting to find out. She was doing her research.

Ladies, you know what I'm talking about.

Years of improprieties had left her paranoid to my every move. Shortly after arriving in Detroit, she had hacked into my phone and found text messages I had exchanged with Tasha.

Sigh.

I still had strong feelings for Tasha, but our future had been put on the back burner with my deployment to Detroit. We still kept in touch through email and text every so often, talking mostly about the Nation, my motion, and the ever fading possibility of us having a future. We had a song called "Must be Nice" by Lyfe Jennings that we would text each other every time it came on.

After the expected blow up towards me, Amanda made the report to Royall, whose response to me was simply, "Fix it."

I called Tasha with Amanda listening on the phone and gave her the run down; I had enjoyed our time together, but if we were ever to be anything at all, it would have to be done through the structure of the Nation. She handled it with the calmness and intelligence of a person who had been practicing mathematical thinking for years.

She said she understood, thanked me for the knowledge and the time I had shared with her, and said she loved me and that was the end of that. Well, it should have been, but Amanda hacked into my email. After reading a couple of my more mushy emails to Tasha, the emotions of seeing her husband exchange sweet nothings to some random female was more than she could handle and she sent a series of emails to her that were, shall we say, not so friendly.

True to her character, Tasha deflected them deftly, saying that she had nothing but positive experiences with me, and that if I was the horrible person Amanda described me as, then that was Amanda's problem since she was the one who married me. She repeated that her time talking with me about the idea was nothing but a blessing, and wished Amanda nothing but the best.

Tasha had a sharp mind and tongue of her own, so I wouldn't have blamed her if she snapped back at Amanda, but the way that she handled herself only endeared her to me even more.

In any case, it was a moot point. As much as I truly loved this girl, I had a lot more on my plate than my own happiness. More to consider than just breaking up my immediate family, but also the fate of an entire Temple, and ultimately, the entire city rested on my shoulders.

Knowing I needed to clean up my act didn't change the reality of who I was. I was still a man, and a very affectionate and sexual being. I could rationalize to no end that I didn't need affection or that I would one day have what I needed, but eventually, the reality of my nature would rear its head. It was one big, ugly, vicious cycle.

I would come off of getting caught with improper contact with a female. I would consider what was at stake and rededicate myself to the idea, understanding that the salvation of an entire city was in my hands. My bedroom, still reeling from the last violation would remain cold much longer than my loins, but okay, I would simply take care of my own business like any self-respecting undersexed teenager, at first with my imagination. After I ran out of images, then I would find myself at the computer desk in the middle of the night. Then that would get old.

Each level of artificial stimulus would fade in its effectiveness, until finally I found myself sitting in a car in front of some female's house agonizing over my next move. Sometimes I would drive off, sometimes I would go inside.

Whether I went in or not, I would always leave the same-cursing myself. Sick with grief and guilt, I would begin to wonder if what had been whispered about me for years was true.

How could it not be?

How could I continuously be so weak?

Maybe the things that were said about me back in the beginning of my coming to the Nation were true; maybe I wasn't cut out for righteousness. Maybe I was destined for the hell fire.

Maybe I did have a sexual addiction. I began to research the condition and so many things matched; I was lying or hiding my sexual behavior even to myself; I would rationalize or justify what I knew was otherwise unacceptable sexual practices; I would compromise my safety and ultimately the safety of others to satiate this feeling.

I MUST be an addict!

But even coming to that "revelation" was something I wasn't about to share. It had been said about me even by Royall's wives, but to agree with it publicly was to jeopardize the position I had worked so hard to put myself in.

It was a long time before I would understand my behavior and needs. In the meantime, I followed the same pattern, eventually finding a system that worked for me. I would develop hideaways for myself to satisfy not only my sexual needs but also just to get away from the emotional, political grind of being in the role of Minister. I finally began to fully grasp Daniel's distancing himself faithfully from the members.

Because of people's preconceived notions of what righteousness looked, acted and smelled like, you could never really let your guard down. You could be 100% innocent, or heaven forbid just have a human moment, but the mere appearance of impropriety would cause so much trouble that you may as well be guilty. It wasn't like I was going to get the benefit of the doubt.

Detroit was my hometown, so knowing a few good places to disappear where I would never run into the members was no problem. It was in these spaces where I would catch my breath and not have to worry about speaking or being perfect for the time being. Ironically enough, it was also in these spaces where I found the most support for what we were doing.

Where else was the need to hear a gospel of Black Love, Divinity, and Superiority most needed but in the most hopeless and down trodden corners of society, and Detroit had plenty of those. I might have connected with that single mother for the purpose of coital activities, but before long I found myself on the couch talking, or more importantly, listening to her talk about her troubled youth and helping her pick through and find the redeemable factors in it.

I might have stopped by the trap to kick it, but maybe that was the first time the young Nino Brown on the block ever saw someone from the North End in shirt and slacks who walked and talked and used the same slang as him. One who wasn't working for a White man, but still had some sort of freedom and manhood about himself.

This is not to make myself out to be a savior because again, they had as much of what I needed as I did of what they needed.

These escapes were few and far between as we continued to keep things rolling. Before long, we had an opportunity to make a great showing. Royall was coming to Detroit on one of his regular tours. This would be his first visit since sending me to Detroit.

Needless to say, we all wanted to show progress and justify more aid being sent our way.

We secured a room in the Charles H. Wright Museum of African American History, a world class facility in the heart of the Cultural District. This was a quantum leap up from the shabby rooms that had been previously secured for Royall's Detroit meetings, and certainly meetings across the country. As nice as the facility was, my major concern was getting people there.

We figured that a high profile venue like The Museum would attract a certain number of people in itself. But in addition to that we set up daily details in every major intersection to pass out flyers, which we called invitations.

In class we went over "Proper Treatment of the Royall Family" over and over so as to avoid any embarrassments. Detroit members were not immune to the usual coonery that would rear its head whenever those in power would come around. We formally invited the Cincinnati members to the meeting since they were the closest Temple. I knew that if we had a respectable turnout we would need experienced Brothers and Sisters holding security posts.

I also talked Carter into coming into town to assist specifically with Royall Family security. Despite our falling outs, I knew that he and I made a formidable team. I knew he could take care of the Royall Family, and I wouldn't have to worry about it for a second.

After intense preparation, finally the weekend of the meeting came and the family rolled into town. Friday there was the usual joint FOI/MGT meeting conducted by the wives, in which members try to tell on each other but end up getting admonished for their own shortcomings. Then Saturday, there was an MGT outing with the wives, and finally, Sunday morning, the day I had been both dreading and waiting on came.

As usual, I was the first to arrive at the museum to prepare the building. Slowly, the local members and those from Cincinnati started showing up and being assigned posts. Having been to more than our share of Royall's meetings with very low attendance, we decided it best to remove a few rows of chairs so that it did not look emptier than it needed to.

And then finally, a few people trickled in. And then a few more. And then some more. And then more still. We ended up having to not only replace the rows we had taken out, but also scramble to find chairs from other parts of the building to accommodate the audience.

By the time the Brother on the door post announced, "All Rise" and Royall made his entrance in the room, it was standing room only. Even during the meeting, there were countless ideas to attend to, so I couldn't really stop and take it all in, but I knew right off we had done our job.

Even those factors we couldn't control went in our favor.

Royall's meetings could more than occasionally turn adversarial, but this one had gone smoothly with plenty of questions from the audience. Even those who didn't necessarily agree with what they heard, managed to disagree respectfully.

In a city with the varied conscious community that Detroit had, this was also an accomplishment. I recalled on the East Coast there being numerous verbal sparring matches and flat-out wars at the mic.

On that tour, Royall had hit cities like New York, Boston, New Haven, and Washington, DC. None of those meetings had more than a few dozen visitors. Even in those meetings in areas with relatively large populations of Nation members, they still hadn't come close to the turnout we had. What made our turnout most notable is that it consisted mostly of visitors, people who had never heard of the UNOI.

I didn't grasp how well we had done until I got a phone call that next day from Kaaba, congratulating me. We had shattered the previous attendance record for Royall's meetings, not to mention the all-important totals of Nation's goods that were sold in the back of the room after the meeting.

Of course, there was always politics to be considered. Not 24 hours after the congratulatory call, I was getting a call also from Kaaba to find out why I hadn't gone out to dinner with the Royall Family that evening. What had been an act of humility on my part and wanting to give the Family its space had been twisted around and was now being viewed as a shunning.

In truth, I was so turned off by the buck and shuffling that would go in the company of the family, I didn't even want to be associated with it. I knew how phony people behaved around me and I was a lowly Assistant

Minister. People who couldn't be bothered to show up for duty, or show respect to the Brother who labored next to them every day would put on the perfect soldier stance, with their chests puffed all the way out when Father and the family were around. I had heard and seen more than enough ass kissing that went on during face time with the family and I wanted no part of it. Now I was being called up on charges of the very thing I was looking to avoid-not having the proper respect for the Royall Family.

Fine. I submitted and shared that I would personally apologize while making my report that coming Sunday. I apologized and explained my reasoning for not attending dinner with the Family. It was shared with me that Father had wanted to thank me for the job I was doing. The meeting and the numbers leading up to the meeting had been a clear indication of the job that was being done.

I scoffed at the possibility of Father thanking me. I knew anything I was doing was made possible entirely because of what Royall was teaching, and that my only will was that we could have more assistance to continue to magnify his idea here in Detroit. In particular, it would be great and a further example of the work Royall was doing with the Blackman if Ray and Alan could come so the Detroit members could have a firsthand example of what Royall was producing in us.

Though we hadn't talked much on the phone, maybe once or twice a year, and only actually saw each other once or twice a year, Ray and Alan were never far from my thoughts. I knew they had some idea of what I was doing, and I did my best to keep tabs on their growth and development. We never were the type to sit on the phone and talk. I knew that performing my duty well would create plenty of favor and good will for them. I also knew it would inspire them to follow in my example more than any words I could share with them.

About a week later I got the call.

All the blood, sweat and tears had paid off. Kaaba, and Daniel were slated to come to Detroit next. And they were bringing Ray and Alan with them. All of this was the ultimate reward to me. I had pretty good relationships with Kaaba and Daniel, who were generally regarded as the two very best Brothers in the UNOI.

What was only slightly less known was how much they didn't get along. When I first arrived in Heaven, Kaaba made it no secret that he had little respect or regard for Daniel. He essentially saw him as a slacker and underachiever who used his position as a Royall Family member to avoid any real work.

Though Moreen was long gone, Kaaba saw Daniel as an extension of her infamous reign in the Nation. While he wasn't entirely wrong, Daniel had a slightly less antagonistic view of Kaaba.

Like many of the Brothers, Daniel recognized Kaaba as a power hungry brother, who might step on his brother's face if it might get him more authority. But he also saw in Kaaba a powerful brother whose sharp intellect and tireless work ethic was an incredible asset to the Nation. He knew Kaaba didn't like him much, but he didn't have any real fear of Kaaba's ability to do him any harm politically. After all, he had been raised in this idea, there was no way Kaaba or anyone was going to out-FOI him.

Once I found out that they were touring together, I figured they must have at least buried the hatchet to some degree, if for nothing other than the sake of the Nation.

I had long wondered how two of the cooler, yet honorable Brothers in the Nation could be so dead set against each other. To me it was like having Michael Jordan and Scottie Pippen on the same team but not on speaking terms. Your team might be good, but it could be so much more.

Though Kaaba had the cleaner reputation, he still did his thing in between the lines, he was just way more covert about it. I had ridden with him many nights in Heaven when we were supposed to be on Rover Patrol for security and made stops at Walmart, spending money we weren't supposed to have on food we weren't supposed to eat. One night I happened to see him steal off into the wee hours of the morning on a bike. The next day, I made the mistake of teasing him in front of other people about sneaking off on a midnight rendezvous and he just about ripped my head off.

On another occasion, he got irate with me for calling him on a phone I wasn't supposed to have. Not because I wasn't supposed to have the phone, but because I did it in front of Emory, whom he considered a major rival. He didn't want HIM knowing he knew that I had a phone, since it could be used as political leverage later.

It must have been different at some point in the past. I had heard from both of them how they got in trouble for going on a mission to Florida years ago and ending up in the clubs. In conversations when Kaaba's treachery would come up, Daniel would almost always remark incredulously, " Man Kaaba used to be so cool".

Either way, all of that appeared to be in the rear view mirror as Kaaba and Daniel were on their way here, which worked for me because they were also two of my most trusted advisors. I still hadn't totally settled into the Minister's role. I knew more than the members in Detroit, but there was still so much that I did not know and at any time I could call them or Yunus and get an answer that made perfect sense.

They would also serve as a valuable buffer between me and the Hassans. At this point, I had avoided fighting any major battles in house for the sake of making progress. But there were improprieties all over the place.

Bilal's wife, Asia, who had been the acting MGT official before Amanda's return was still being permitted to have the rights and privileges of a member without actually being a member.

In fact, she had gone on record numerous times as not believing Royall was Allah, not agreeing to a Brother being able to have more than one wife, and definitely having no interest in pursuing getting her X. She made it no secret that she only interacted with the Nation to please her husband. That might be considered a noble gesture in the regular world, but in the UNOI it was blatant disrespect.

She was, in effect, enjoying all of the privileges of being with one of the Gods that Allah was preparing, while simultaneously having no regard or interest for the source that had made him into such a good husband and father.

The fact that Bilal was in the Lt. position completely compounded the situation. He was responsible for teaching the men in the temple. How could anyone respect him as a representative of Allah if he couldn't enforce the law in his own household?

Father and the Wives had questioned Brother Minister and me about it on more than one occasion. Brother Minister agreed to be the one to talk to him about it. I figured he wouldn't put any real pressure on Bilal, but never bothered to follow up on the subject. He was still the main source of help I had, and without any help coming I had no interest in creating a more awkward situation.

Kaaba, of course, never entertained any such apprehensions. He was the poster child and engine behind the anti-part-time movement in the Nation. It would be his greatest pleasure to root out part-time thinking, and ultimately, part-timers in general. He had long ago told me his opinion that the Nation would take off like a rocket if Father would just let us get rid of all part-timers.

I appreciated the sentiment, having been frustrated by part-timers before, but wasn't quite so militant about it. We had plenty of Brothers who were full-time that didn't work as half as hard to magnify the idea as Bilal did.

Be that as it may, the argument still stood that however effective he could be as a part-timer, he could be doubly so full-time. Like many of us, Kaaba couldn't for the life of him understand why a brother with so much power and potential would settle for little from not only his relationship but also himself.

He really didn't care to understand.

He hadn't come to understand Detroit, Detroit needed to understand him.

True to his nature, Bilal didn't run from it. It was universally understood and accepted that Bilal was operating at a fraction of his capacity for effectiveness in the Nation. When it came to this idea he was the standard bearer for a very long time in Detroit. In a private conference shortly after their arrival, Kaaba and Daniel let Bilal know that they would be putting pressure on him. He was no longer going to be allowed to just be the best of the part-timers.

They were here to clean house so they had to start at the top.

Well, at least close to it.

For all the potential Kaaba saw in Bilal, he quickly came to realize Bilal was just the tip of the iceberg. He was the oldest Hassan brother and a natural leader, but all of the Hassans were uniquely talented and had the potential to do great things.

Something was holding them all back.

Kaaba quickly decided that "something" was Brother Minister.

In his estimation, Joe was incompetent and unqualified as Minister, and if it was up to him, should be properly relieved at the first opportunity. In short, he saw him a bullshitter and rarely missed the opportunity to say so. He even bragged to me often how he had told Royall as much.

Luckily, it was not up to him. Joe still had a very good relationship with Royall and a relatively good one with Daniel.

For all of his shortcomings, Royall saw him as a passionate supporter and patriot of the Nation. He also knew Joe was an astute businessman, not only with a successful trucking company but with dealings in several countries overseas- just the type of activity the Nation needed to be involved in.

Kaaba also had another reason for being a little terse with Joe, one I could easily relate to.

Hassan Family Pride.

Ironically, Kaaba happened to be married to Joe's other daughter, Rebecca. In fact, Joe and Kaaba's father had been friends since their children were very small. By the time Royall and the UNOI came on the scene, the families had known each for decades.

That blood lines would eventually cross was only logical as few things were as important as marrying the "proper" righteous man or woman.

One thing about being married to a Hassan daughter or the daughter of any strong Muslim family is the difficulty one may find replacing the Father as the symbol of authority in her life.

Rebecca and Amanda had been thoroughly indoctrinated with the wisdom of their father their whole lives. They had carried this image of Joe as a man of insurmountable knowledge and wisdom from the age of a small child. They saw their brothers as younger, slightly less omnipotent versions of the father, but the only person their father had ever acknowledged as being greater than himself was Royall.

What made this frustrating for us, their husbands, was that in this idea (that their father had pointed out to them) we were among the very cream of the crop. I knew that I had done well considering my short time in the Nation, and Kaaba had been in 3x as long and produced seemingly 10x as much, yet none of that seemed to impress Joe's girls.

We could hardly make a point to our wives without them bringing up something their father had done or said on the subject. It was one thing for a Sister to try to use something Royall taught against you in conversation. That happened all the time. It was your job as a Brother to be able to give them greater understanding of Royall's teachings. But it was another, greatly insulting thing to be sent to assist a family because they haven't made any real progress, and then constantly hear from your wife what that family thinks about you and what you are doing. If it irritated me, it would make a man with Kaaba's ego insane. er.

He would never miss an opportunity to go out of his way to correct the Minister or show that he had superior knowledge and authority.

Bro Minister was just happy to see progress being made. I find it hard to imagine he was unaware of Kaaba's dislike for him, but he held a begrudging respect for him.

He had invested many dollars and much energy in trying to get something, ANYTHING going here in Detroit, and now it was paying off. He knew by this time that there was no way he was going to compete with any of the younger Brothers in this new knowledge that Royall was teaching, but he could take the Nation places where no one else could. In particular, overseas, as he began introducing the Nation's business department to his connections in Africa, China and the Middle East.

With Kaaba in town to deal with the motion including baking, that freed me up to focus exclusively on the community sales and my duties as a minister. This included public relations, securing donations, setting up accounts, etc.

Ray and Alan would arrive in Detroit shortly after Kaaba and assist with the baking and sales, giving us double the teams going out into the community on a daily basis. This put us in corners of the city that we hadn't yet been able to reach. With the full-timers on staff we weren't at the whims of part-timers, which meant our numbers were more consistent and higher.

Kaaba finished off the bakery that had been started in the basement of our house so we no longer even had to bake at the members' homes. It was either step your game up or get left in the dust.

For the most part, those riding the fence actually start to step up. Unlike Connecticut, where members took the arrival of help as a sign to relax, Brothers and Sisters who had been undependable began showing up and showing out.

Those who couldn't commit to an actual duty time found other more creative ways of contributing. Many of the Brothers still hustled, so the optimal times for cookie sales was the same time that they would be getting their money.

They may not have time to go out and sell $100 worth of cookies, but maybe they knew someone who could fill up all of the Nation's vehicles for free. They might not be available for a transportation run, but maybe they could donate a few cases of diapers. Maybe they couldn't give charity, but perhaps the Study group could use some gift cards with a few hundred dollars on them.

Detroit was, after all, still the hustle capital of the world.

Ironically enough, Kaaba loved it. I say ironic because it was through Joe that all of this creative enterprise had been taught. He was tearing down the man out one side of his mouth, and basking in the benefits of his tutelage on the other. If nothing else, saving hundreds of dollars a week on groceries, fuel and other amenities was having a wonderful effect on our bottom line.

Be that as it may, I knew from hustling myself that ALL hustles are temporary, especially the lucrative ones. The inevitable conclusion was that things were gonna dry up, and if you were lucky no one would get pinched in the process. The last thing we needed to be doing was encouraging Brothers who were already one foot in, one foot out, to engage in illegal activity for the sake of the Nation. What if things went bad and they get locked up doing something on our behalf?

If they wanted to make a monetary donation, we weren't about to conduct an audit to see where the funds came from, but we couldn't sit and watch a Brother, for a completely random and unrelated to anything that ever really happened example, steal gas then pull up and have him fill us up, then screech off as the Feds pull into the gas station.

Kaaba reluctantly agreed, but not before he got the number of a Brother that could get him a couple of flat screens for half off.

Not that I was about to knock the hustle. All of this help had allowed me to build up my comfort zone even more. Ray and Alan being home went a long way towards making me comfortable in my own home. I knew that seeing them was not only good for the members of the Nation but for our blood relatives, so many of whom had given me HELL when and after I decided to take them to Kansas.

Now here they stood, two clean cut, handsome, responsible, well-spoken young men. The children they used to play with not so long ago now walked up and down the street, looking half dead, pants sagging, smelling of weed smoke. Maybe this UNOI thing wasn't such a horrible idea after all.

I was amazed how much they had come into their own, yet still were very much the two little boys I used to play with in front of my Mom's house on Courville.

Ray was still pretty quiet and to himself. He didn't mind doing the work of the Nation but he was the strong silent type just like his Dad. He wasn't interested in a bunch of talking and debating, he just wanted to

273

do his duty and be left alone. Beyond that he just wanted to be around his family.

He looked like his dad and just happened to have inherited his mercurial temper. He wasn't fast to anger, but pester him the way Brothers in the Nation often did, and he couldn't hide his rage. This often got him into trouble and deepened his reluctance to engage in Nation's politics. He was a soldier, but he was never going to be a politician.

Alan was the more ambitious of the two. He was very image conscious, never leaving the house wrinkled or with a hair out of place. He needed to have responsibility and he needed you to know he had it. He would never turn down an opportunity for duty or to show that he could be counted on to handle responsibility. He was also naive to the intricacies of UNOI politics, where one's ambitions could be used to fuel another's agenda.

He studied faithfully and had fallen in with a group of youth Brothers who were pegged for success in the Nation. All of the youth were of optimum importance to Royall. They had been given permission to call the Wives directly with whatever issues they had. He would often quote the Bible, "Suffer unto me the little children, for within them lie the kingdom of Heaven."

Even the older Brothers recognized that we had come to the idea with all our own baggage. For some of us it was women, for others it was drugs or alcohol, for others still it was that thirst for power.

The youth were often referred to as "the New", alluding to their responsibility of being the ones who would build the New World.

The premise being that they had none of the baggage of the old world, and could be developed ENTIRELY in Royall's thinking.

This, of course, ignored the fact that youth like Ray and Alan had already seen more by the age of 5 than most adults would see in a lifetime.

Nonetheless, the "the New" had its own structure unto itself, run exclusively by the Royall Family. In the hierarchy of the UNOI, this structure superseded the Temple structure, FOI and MGT structure, even the natural family structure. We were often reminded that we were damaged goods and that the children belonged to Royall. It would be a damnable thing for ANYONE to interfere with that relationship.

Even though I was glad to have them home, our relationship, by this time had gone from parental to more big brother. Unless they had specific questions or concerns for me, I would allow them to be dealt with through the structure, whether it be FOI, MGT or The Youth. After all, I hadn't really operated in that role with them since leaving Heaven.

Yes, I kept tabs on them, but more than anything, I let them develop in Royall's teaching without too much influence from me. I was fully on board with not saddling them with any of the negative from my mind, and certainly none from my activity.

Speaking of my activity, Daniel was in town. Though I knew it could never be like it was in Connecticut, I figured it would be good to have one of the REAL Bruhs around. Daniel had taken a largely advisory role in Detroit, even more than usual. The idea that Kaaba and Daniel were now best buds was not quite the reality.

Though their mutual love and respect for the Nation had allowed them to be successful in their previous stops, to those who knew them well, it was clear that there was a monumental struggle for power going on behind the scenes.

They would sit shoulder-to-shoulder and conduct some of the most uplifting and enlightening classes you could imagine. They would get on the phone and handle everything from National FOI conferences to grilling and properly relieving a corrupt official in a distant temple. But once the work was done, they couldn't be further apart.

Kaaba, whose influence in the Nation was growing with every successful mission, was quietly sizing Daniel up. He was still one of the hardest working Brothers in the Nation, and considered himself on par with Daniel when it came to knowledge and wisdom. He wasn't so impressed with Daniel's teaching that he gave him a pass when it came to actual physical labor.

Rightfully so, he saw that Daniel could be doing a lot more than he was doing. He still wasn't prepared to call him out directly, though. He would apply pressure to those around Daniel who typically would bend over backwards to keep from making a negative report on the grandson of Allah.

Like me, many of the Brothers had more than a couple of real experiences where Daniel either helped or gave the strong appearance of looking out for us. This established a loyalty that many were not quick to betray.

This only incensed and fueled Kaaba even more. The more Brothers tried to cover for Daniel, the harder he would work to try to get him, even if that meant taking down his supporters one by one.

It was nothing for him to hold Brothers in interrogations for hours and days, twisting them in all types of shapes mentally and emotionally trying to get something, anything that would incriminate Daniel.

These investigations would always get back to Daniel and most of the time, he was able to maintain his Teflon-like aura.

Increasingly though, they served the purpose of isolating Daniel.

If he was distant with the Brothers in Connecticut, he was a downright ghost by the time he got to Detroit. Even though he and I still had our chemistry, he was clearly feeling pressure. He left nothing to chance, running the streets with me less than a handful of times in over a year in Detroit.

He would work out and play ball with me and Ray, but even that had to be justified. Kaaba wouldn't try to dictate his motion directly, but if he knew we were going out with Daniel, then he would give us hell. By this time he was National Lt., which meant his rank dictated that he was responsible for the motion of every brother in every temple.

Before long, the bitter rivalry between Kaaba and Daniel was driving a divide right down the middle of the FOI locally and nationally. This all was despite the fact that Daniel had long ago declared Kaaba as his successor as the head of the FOI.

While most of the Brothers would have been taken aback by such a compliment, Kaaba took it for granted. It was the truth, after all, and Daniel was doing him no favors by stating what had been made obvious by Kaaba's knowledge and motion.

Daniel had built relationship after relationship by being so good at understanding what was important to each Brother and giving that to them. He correctly had estimated that power was Kaaba's greatest desire, but overestimated his own ability to establish any degree of loyalty or even a most basic level of comradeship from Kaaba.
He couldn't deliver the kind of power that Kaaba was after. He was here to be God, not someone's official or friend.

Kaaba had been around him enough to know all of his vices and how he operated intimately. Whatever he had experienced under Daniel and his departed mother, Moreen, had effectively killed whatever love or compassion he may have had in his heart for him.

Daniel knew as Royall Family he had Royall's ear, so even though he was clearly irritated by Kaaba's antics, he was secure in his position. Oftentimes, he served as a secret advisor to Brothers (like me) who were the targets of Kaaba's political meandering, giving us just the insight or spiritual or mental support to fend off the next round of mathematical bullying.

Say what you will about Daniel's work ethic, he did not take lightly the mistreatment of the members of the Nation. Where Kaaba appeared to view the members as obstacles in the way of the building of the Nation,

Daniel emphasized that they WERE the Nation itself, not the buildings or the businesses.

The irony in all of this is that despite the contemptuous relationship, both would utilize the same principles of Mathematical Thinking to show how the other was tripping. Both would quote Royall to support their position and show how the other was out of step with how we were supposed to conduct ourselves. And of course, both would put on a happy face and pat each other on the back in front of the members and only bare their teeth when behind closed doors.

So progress was made, but never quite as much as was possible. The instability that lurked below the surface of their relationship created a disharmony amongst the temple itself. I considered each Brother a friend, so when their potshots at each other would pop up in private conversation, I would let it roll off my back.

I had a major issue with the lack of respect that Kaaba had for the members, especially the Brothers. He generally regarded the FOI at large as useless. On one occasion I told him I needed to go to Heaven in order to refresh my thinking and make sure I was in step with Father's teachings after years in satellite temples. His advice to me was that if I went back to Heaven, I would feel like I was God already because the Brothers in general were such fuck ups. I couldn't imagine how you could genuinely seek to help or lead those who you had such a low opinion of.

Daniel was unfailingly personable, seemed to genuinely care for every member young, old, male, or female. Even the ones NO ONE seemed to like, he could find and point out some redeeming quality about them. He was not above using said relationships to his advantage; in fact it could be argued he was as or more political than Kaaba, just more covert.

Despite these politics going on in the background, Detroit was making progress. In addition to the numbers being up, membership and attendance in class was growing. Charity was at an all-time high. We had so many teams going out, there was hardly a section in the Detroit Metro area that we were not hitting. We were, in fact, the number one fundraising team in the Nation, without a temple or an official business to speak of.

We were making no real progress with opening an actual bakery, however. Bro. Minister had offered us the use of his other building, but Kaaba was stonewalling any suggestion of that.

His relationship with Joe was as bad as ever, and he was making less and less effort to hide it. While Joe had Father's ear and could push certain agendas, Kaaba was all too willing to pick up the phone and show in detail and example how Joe was wasting the Nation's time.

Unfortunately for him, Bro Minister was operating on a level that rendered him out of Kaaba's league. Though he had gladly stepped aside on matters having to do with local temple business, Joe's deep business connections were presenting unmatched opportunities to the UNOI.

He had arranged meetings with diplomats and businessmen from several Middle Eastern and African countries and companies, with the National Secretary James 2X and some of Royall's wives. Kaaba could call Joe all the names he wanted in Royall's ear; this type of action was right out of prophecy. The UNOI was about to take off around the globe and it was relationships like these that were going to set the whole thing off.

Back stateside, he had plugged into a company that built energy efficient homes from foam. This was, at the time, the latest in home building. Not only did this cut the price to build a home in half, but the material to do so reduced home energy costs to a fraction of what they would normally be.

Home building and alternate energy sources were right up the Nation's alley. Even more so was the earning potential that came with business deals that were always coming along through Brother Minister.

Perhaps due to his own politicking, Kaaba was oblivious to the fact that elsewhere in the Nation, forces where plotting on his motion. In fact, before long he would find himself the center of attention of those in high places.

As much as Kaaba's constant pushing rubbed me and others the wrong way, it felt good to have him on your team because you knew he was going to give 100% to see the idea successful.

The more places he went, the more successful these places were.

Heaven.

Atlanta.

Wichita.

Detroit.

It's the very reason people like me who were serious about growing the Nation were clamoring for him to get him sent to their area.

Like most Brothers, Kaaba didn't have a problem with it. It was the sign of a job well done on his part. He was in the business of kicking ass and taking names and business was record-breaking.

His only request that he dare not request aloud; the last thing Kaaba wanted was any part of dealing intimately with the Royall Family, in particular, the Wives.

For all his mathematical astuteness, he understood that the regular laws, principles, and their application did not apply in the same way to the Family.

We all knew this.

One terse word from a Family member and you could find yourself on Class A, with duty in the dish room for a month. It didn't matter how mathematical your position was or how off the wall theirs was.

It didn't matter how humble and respectful your demeanor, or how out of pocket they got with you.

The hierarchy was clear and established.

Most of the time, this didn't effect things too much directly.

For most of us it was a far off reality because we would rarely encounter the Royall Family in our daily motion.

For those in satellites like Detroit, the most we had to endure was a phone call or two every once in a while.

 Maybe, you might have to deal with the Wives in a counseling session with your wife, or maybe they were in a class that you were in.

Short of that you only see them in passing, on the way to or from Nation's businesses or meetings. You might have to help them in or out of the car if there were no Brothers on duty with them, but for the most part, you were in two separate worlds.

On the rare and excruciating occasion you had duty with them, it would change everything about how you conducted yourself. Amongst the Brothers, and even to some degree the majority of the Sisters, you could be yourself. If you had a sense of humor, you make a joke, play with someone, share a laugh, you know, things we humans do to make the time pass.

But if the Wives were around you held your tongue, because whatever you might say was open for psychological analysis. The way you walked or sat down in a chair would be commented on and compared to the way that Royall sat down, or stood up or held his fork, or sat his napkin on his lap.

The major test would be how you responded to this attention. The wise thing? Whatever they said Royall did, you do. Immediately and with the proper spirit. Move too slow and at best you would have to explain your hesitation on the spot. At worst they would tell YOU why you hesitated. And then call the local official (who would NEVER back you up) to report and make sure it was reported to Royall.

Move too quickly and you looked like a chump and they knew they had you whether they said it or not.

All too often it was clear these episodes were nothing more than a means of the Wives entertaining themselves.

Kaaba, wise Brother that he was, made it his business to be nowhere around when the Wives showed up. Once he got a hint that they were coming to a city that he was in, he was making his plans to be somewhere, anywhere else before they got there.

In the Wives he saw yet another entity that ran counter to his personal agenda, not to mention his ego.

They say idea that the enemy of my enemy is my friend.

The Wives had undertaken the project that was going to be the latest Food for Life Supreme Restaurant in Newark, NJ. The Brothers had been crisscrossing the Nation getting things moving so this would be the Wives' opportunity to show their stuff.

This was to be a project to dwarf the other businesses the Nation had going. The artwork, money and resources that were being poured into Food for Life Supreme were unprecedented.

Not only had every temple in the Nation been asked to commit a weekly donation to the project, but Brothers were already in New Jersey going out into the community to raise funds. Despite Miss White's best ranting and ravings and picking and prodding, the Brothers still were not producing at the level she saw fit. Granted, they were going out for 12 hours a day driving all over the place selling baked goods, but they were not bringing in enough income to get the restaurant open. Well, this was simply unacceptable.

At some point either she, or someone near her began to consider Kaaba's well-documented reputation of getting the most out of the FOI.

And that's when THAT call came in.

The Wives would like to know if Kaaba was willing to come out to Jersey.

This was significant.

First, despite what he really wanted to say, there was NO WAY Kaaba was going to turn down a personal request like that from the Royall Family. No one would.

For years, he had been fielding calls from Brothers who had run-ins with the Wives and telling them what he would have done. In fact, he was one of Amanda's chief advocates when she had her run-in with Miss White. Telling her she was right and just needed to change how she was expressing herself.

Now he would have to put his money where his mouth was.

What was also significant about this "request" was that they WEREN'T requesting Daniel.

In reality, the feeling was probably mutual.

Daniel coming didn't fit their agenda, not only because he was not the task master they were looking for, but also because he was fully capable of standing up to and responding to whatever pressure they might send his way. Heaven forbid he actually pull the cover off of whatever irregularities they had going. He certainly wasn't ever going to stand by and allow them to run amuck over the Brothers. After all, he had Royall's ear just as much as they did.

On the flip side, they knew Daniel as well as he knew them. If temple politics were trumped by national politics, imagine how high the stakes were in the politics of the Royall family.

They knew about his smoking habits and his disappearing acts and there was no way he could get away with that around them for an extended period of time, especially with an opportunist like Kaaba around.

For us locally, Kaaba leaving represented a significant amount of responsibility and work that was going to be left unattended. In his place, we found out we would be getting one of the youth Brothers, Darren, a budding mechanic. So in effect, we were taking the top soldier in the Nation and replacing him with a 15 year-old. Granted, a hard-working 15 year-old, but still this was absolutely no contest.

What I didn't immediately take into account was the political ramifications of Kaaba leaving for Jersey.

As National Lt., Kaaba held a lot of sway as to which resources were permitted to go to which temple. Losing him meant losing a pivotal force when it came to commanding any significant help.

Another time in the Nation, Daniel's presence would have gone a long way in garnering the type of support it would take to get us to the next level. But the pressure that was coming from Kaaba's ever increasing influence had Daniel focused on keeping his nose clean more so than making moves in the Nation.

The entire time they were together Kaaba had never levied direct accusations, but consistently planted seeds of doubt about Daniel. Now, Daniel had unwittingly found himself in the position of having to prove himself because of Kaaba's departure. Now he was would be responsible for what did or didn't happen in Detroit. If there was any drop off in any way, it would give some validation to Kaaba's constant sniping.

All of this unfolded right before Independence Day Celebration, when all of the temples from across the Nation would make the annual pilgrimage to Heaven to commiserate on the progress being made spiritually, mentally and physically and of course, hear Royall give his annual address.

By this time, the Independence Day had graduated to a grandiose affair. For the young movers, shakers, heavy hitters and heads of the temples, it was a chance to play catch up. It had all the feeling of a class reunion as Brothers you once shared bunks and crappy duties with showed off new family members (be it wives or babies), exchanged gossip, and "can-you-top-this" tales of buffoonery from our various corners of the Nation.

From the moment I arrived in Heaven, I heard hints of Daniel not returning to Detroit with us. As of late, he had been spending less and less time in the city, always having to return back to Heaven for one task or another. This wasn't unusual. As far back as Connecticut, he had regularly traveled back and forth across the Nation to address his various duties as the head of the FOI and the most significant male Royall Family member next to Royall.

Lately, he had been gone with such regularity that he really seemed removed from everything that was happening in Detroit, so when he mentioned not returning as we nonchalantly rode around Kansas City, I didn't really have a strong reaction. He wasn't exactly a huge influence when it came to the physical labor that needed to be done in Detroit. Our relationship was strong enough that I knew I could continue to lean on him for spiritual/political advice no matter where he or I was in the Nation. In fact, more and more, his absence served as barrier to progress because he didn't trust us to make decisions without him, but he was never around.

Daniel leaving was beginning to sound less and less like a bad idea.

It was the final day of meetings at Independence Day when I found myself walking across the lobby of the hotel in "downtown" KCK where the majority of activity would take place that weekend. Coming out of the ballroom with a concerned look was Alan. I looked at him curiously.

"I have to go back to the barracks and pack my items. I'm going to Jersey."

I laughed, "Yeah right, stop playing. Who told you that?"

"Seriously. I just spoke to Sister Jocelyn. They had a big meeting this morning to see where everyone would be going. I'm going to Jersey. Anthony is going to… " He said pointing back at the ballroom.

I didn't stay to hear the rest of the conversation. I stormed away looking for somebody, anybody to tell me something. When I couldn't find anyone, I called Kaaba, Yunus, and Daniel repeatedly until one of them picked up. Somebody needed to tell me something. Here we were fighting, scrapping to make progress, and the one moment we are supposed to be recharging our batteries, we are simultaneously being gutted.

Finally, Kaaba picked up. I asked the obvious and what I got in return was silence.

"No one told you?" he finally said.

After a long pause, he explained that there had been essentially a draft. The heads of each Temple and Study Group met and picked which members they wanted to bring to their particular area. I spoke to Kaaba, Yunus, Daniel, all repeatedly that weekend, as well as exchanged pleasantries with most of the other Temple heads and had heard nary a peep about such a meeting.

I called Amanda to find out if she had been informed as the temple secretary. Brother Minister? Bilal? No one from Detroit had been told anything. And while no one saw fit to inform us about the meeting, they made absolutely certain to tear out the heart out of the Temple. Not only were Kaaba and Alan going to Jersey and Daniel staying here in Heaven, but Ray had been "drafted' to go out to Connecticut. The ultimate insult to injury being the very Brothers I had spent the most amount of time with that weekend, playing ball, shooting the shit, were the very ones sinking the knife into my back.

I immediately went into damage control, telling Bro. Minister our best bet was for him to call Father to protest these moves. Father's response was to tell us to speak with the same people who had cut us out of the deal in the first place. After phone calls individually and on conference with Yunus and Kaaba, I was getting nothing more than a bunch of jokes. Whatever was going on with Daniel, he was less than focused on what was happening, referring me back to Royall, who only refer us back to...

And that's where we were. Only after a sufficient amount of hemming and hawing, bitching and moaning did we even get a guarantee that Brothers would be coming from...somewhere...eventually...to replace the six out of eight full-time members that had been ripped from Detroit.

One of the primary duties of the Minister is to give the vision to the members. After losing more than half of our workforce, I was having a hard time seeing our success, myself.

Nonetheless, we didn't have a choice. It was said in and out of the Nation that attitude reflects leadership. I had been dealing with the doubts and subsequent actions of those who felt like there was no way I was going to be successful In the UNOI. How was this moment any different? I was never going to be able to match wits with anyone politically. I was probably going to always rough around the edges, you might be able to out talk, out politic me, maybe even outthink me, but who was going to outwork me?

We were still Detroit and it wasn't in our character to just lie down, despite what may have been happening in the Nation's court of public opinion. Many had predicted our collapse before we had even gotten this far.

We had been set-up. In a Nation full of Mathematical Thinkers, some of the sharpest minds you could imagine, there is no way that they made plans for our members without even a passing thought of who would replace them where they were. They didn't care.

I found out through the grapevine that my name was being mentioned as the next to be shipped out. Brother Juan called me excited one day about me and my family coming to North Carolina to help him get things going there. Problem was he was getting ahead himself. That statement had been made in confidence to him by those wagering on our eventual collapse.

Rumors of our demise were greatly overstated. With an "us against the world" mentality, we managed to maintain the same number we had before Daniel's departure. Despite it all.

Those waiting on the other shoe to drop would have to keep waiting. Preferably with their breath held.

It was one of Kaaba's last political salvos fired at the back of Brother Minister that ended up undermining any effort to shut down the Detroit Temple. His disdain for anything having to do with Brother Minister led him to enlist the Brothers who were going out in the community to start looking for bakeries or restaurants to rent. Although the company line was that we were going to send for the construction crew to convert one of Joe's buildings into an eatery that was going to happen over Kaaba's dead body. And Kaaba generally didn't intend on dying ever.

It was shortly after we arrived back from Celebration that Bilal called me one day to talk to me about a bakery on the east side. After arranging an appointment to look at the building, we learned that it had all of the latest top-of-the-line equipment. Compared to the paltry equipment that was constantly being shipped and recycled from business to business in the Nation, this Bakery was downright futuristic.

Of course, simple facts were never enough; in the Nation we had learned to look for signs even if sometimes they weren't there. The right presentation to the right people could make a proposal go from a "no way ever" to a "this must be the fulfillment of prophecy."

On that note, this bakery was less than a block away from Courville, the street where Joe had first presented the UNOI to his children and subsequently, the city of Detroit. It was on that very street where Amanda first told me about Solomon the prepared one and the great work he was doing in KCK. We had walked past that space no less than thousands of times collectively.

Though we had long ago moved from that neighborhood, it was still in the middle of a major section of our fundraiser and sat across the street from one the barbershops where we sold our cookies. When the owner of the bakery opened up the business, the guys in the shop wasted no time letting us know that our sales were in major trouble since there was a bakery right across the street. How great a show of power would it be to take possession of this business that the Brothers were so sure would shut our route down.

Even with all of the equipment, the asking price was extremely reasonable. And that was before we starting negotiating.

I was well aware of Joe's capability as a businessman, having been around him since my hustling days on the streets of Detroit. I had learned a good deal from him. I had seen him finagle everything from movies to fireworks to fish dinners to cookies to discounts on hotel bills.

But I had never, nor have I seen since the gut wrenching, arm twisting, teeth pulling, negotiating job that he put on the owners of the building. The original asking price was $2500 a month with a deposit of 5000, and for everything we were getting, that was actually not bad at all. Joe's first offer? $1000 and half price rent for the first year.

It took everything I had to keep from tackling the man. I just knew he was going to blow it for us. The owners looked at each other. One was taken aback but didn't say anything, just shook her head. The other got visibly angry. Possibly ill.

They protested.

He countered with half off the deposit, no rent for the first three months, $1500 for the next nine months, and then $2000 after that. The male owner got even angrier. The woman didn't say anything.

I began to see what he was doing. With each offer, Joe was offering very little ground, but he was finding the soft spot in the negotiating team. In other words, he was trying to find the point at which he could separate them, and then he would really start busting their balls.

Truth be told, I actually felt bad for them, because it was painful to even watch, and he was on MY side. When it was all said and done, he had shaved $1000 off the price of the rent, and cut the deposit in half. We also would be getting the first six months of rent free.

Impressed.

I was telling anyone who would listen about the way Brother Minister had dug in on those owners.

Though we had an agreement in principle, there was still a lease to be ironed out, which meant paper had to be sent back and forth between our legal department in Kansas and their lawyer about 200 times.

While that process was taking place, I got word from my mother that she and my grandma were moving out of town. I love my mother as much as the next guy, but I only saw her slightly more than I was seeing her before I came back to Detroit, which is to say not much at all.

Her exodus was significant in this case because she was leaving behind a three-bedroom house. Her primary concern was making sure that someone lived there in order to prevent crack heads from coming and stripping the place bare.

For that reason she was willing to offer it to us if we simply covered the cost of the mortgage, just a few hundred dollars.

Having somewhere to actually put members would go a long way in supporting the fact that we needed more bodies. As far as we were concerned this was another sign, the universe lining up in order to bring about our success.

I made sure to make note of this progress not only in my reports to Royall, but also weekly Ministers' meetings, and in any National venues hoping to generate some dialogue about what was happening in Detroit and put some pressure on the National Structure. I was learning the importance of building "public" sentiment for the projects you wanted completed in the UNOI. The more people you could get to buy into the hype of what you were doing, the more times you get your temple's name mentioned in conversations with those in power, the more support would come.

Restaurants were cropping up everywhere. Carter had the Restaurant in Atlanta raking in money hand over fist, Brother Juan had found a sandwich shop in Raleigh, Yunus had expanded the bakery in Cincinnati, and Cincinnati was opening a new restaurant in Dayton. Existing operations in Maryland and Wichita had been updated and were rolling. Even in Heaven where the Diner had NEVER made money, the fundraiser was producing.

And Jersey? Jersey was about to change the whole damn game. The Restaurant in Newark was up and running and was the crowning achievement of the UNOI. Everything about it looked to be out of a dream world; the food, the equipment, the art work. Every brick on the face of the building had been individually painted by the Nation's art department. What resulted was a beacon that attracted visitors from all over.

All of this energy and activity had brought the Nation to 118th and Lennox. It was a location that used to belong to the original Nation of Islam but had closed. What could be more idyllic? Right in the heart of Harlem, New York, UNOI's Food for Life Supreme.

Even though the UNOI had no official activity in New York, New York had been a hotbed for Black Muslim activity since the days of the Messenger. Malcolm and Farrakhan had both served as minister of temples in Harlem. As the NOI split into ever increasing factions and sects, New York would be the proving ground where many of these debates are waged to this very day.

Royall himself had run-ins with various groups and leaders like Melchizedek who went so far as to tell Royall he couldn't set foot in the city again.

To open a business right in the heart of Harlem would be orgasmic for Royall. By this time the majority of classes, were taking place on a national conference call. A significant portion of that conference call was spent giving blow by blow details of the progress being made in New York. THAT was building sentiment and it just so happened that the ones in New York, Kaaba and the Wives, were the ones setting the agenda for class.

After a National class where members would ooh and ahh at every description and every possible spiritual significance was pulled out of every pedestrian occurrence, the secretary would announce a National call out for funds to get Harlem up and running.

In the case of specific needs that carried specific price tags, like the deposit for the building or custom marble table tops, each temple would be asked to commit to an actual dollar figure and would be pressed until they kept their word on that commitment. One could beg out of such donations, but if you were looking for help like we were, that was political suicide.

"How dare such and such put the priorities of that temple over the priorities of the Nation?"

"Why, it showed how out of touch with Father's thinking they were."

The last thing you wanted to be accused of is pursuing your own agenda rather than Royall's. You also had to consider the Study group was expected to continue sending its regular charity. Just like a regular person expected to tithe and still be able to make the ends meet, some way or another we found a way through.

Oftentimes, the laborers would find ourselves in the position of a couple trying to figure out to spread too few pennies across too many bills at the end of the week. We would debate everything from ways to not spend as much money to ways for the fundraiser team to make more money. With the money that did come in, we would be locked in a bitter debate on how much to send and how much, if any, to keep.

When pledging time did come around, it was important to me for us to make donations the same as any of the major cities that had a business and a bunch of members. We needed to be seen as relevant as any place in the UNOI, lest we be lost in the shuffle of all of these businesses sprouting up.

At the same time Bro. Minister and most of the other laborers argued that there was no way that we were going to be able to make any progress locally unless we stopped sending money in, at least temporarily. This was probably true, but what many were not considering was what a damn unpopular move that would be politically. We no longer had anyone on the inside of the upper echelon of the Nation to speak on our behalf. And while we had to practically set ourselves on fire to get credit for the progress we were making, none of our detractors were going to miss a chance to wring their hands and say," Look at Detroit; they aren't even sending in charity."

The expectation, perhaps plan, was for us to fall off.

Kaaba was gone to Jersey. Daniel was increasingly occupied with his own survival in the Nation. All of our full-time help had been stripped from us.

The initial suggested solution to the pillaging of our ranks was to attempt to pressure the part-time members to come full-time.

Yeah right.

The idea that members were going to put in a "request" to go full-time, and then instantly go from slacking part-time members to dedicated full-time members was a joke.

Most of the best soldiers in the UNOI had to go through at least some time in Heaven before they were mentally and physically prepared for the work that went with being full-time.

Time in Heaven represented not only time to learn the laws and principles that governed the Nation but also the opportunity to adjust to things, like putting in a request to go on an outing, or requesting basic needs like food and toiletries or turning over all your money and material possessions. It was no small feat to adjust from the "me-first" mindset that this world teaches us, to truly understand what it meant to submit entirely to do the will of Allah and put the Nation first.

In Heaven there was a structure set up to facilitate this transition. In Detroit, that structure began and ended with me.

It was one thing managing people who had already agreed to submitting to such a system, but I had no interest in being in the role of police/baby-sitter to those who didn't quite grasp the concept.

The same people who were dragging their feet to send us help wouldn't dream of trying to get anything started in a city without a team of three or four veteran Brothers from Heaven, minimum. Yet here they were expecting us to keep things rolling with a rag tag bunch of part-full-time Brothers who had never gone through a day of Heaven.

Oddly enough, we did.

Somehow, someway, we kept it all together.

Bilal piled more responsibility onto his already loaded plate.

He and I started going out in the community solo in order to make sure that we could have as many teams as possible.

Amanda would start selling breakfast to the members who came over for duty.

Brother Minister would start taking the cookies to the gym with him.

The Brothers who couldn't commit to going out in the community would simply buy wholesale amounts of cookies at only slightly discounted prices. Their plan was to sell them while out on their grinds, but most of the time it just ended up being yet another form of charity. We would find bins of cookies in their trunk that they never got around to or bothered to sell. But that never stopped them from buying them.

The numbers decreased only slightly.

After months of back and forth between our respective legal departments a deal was finally reached on the bakery lease, and with Royall's permission we signed it. Most of the time when a business opened in the UNOI, there was much fanfare; a huge National announcement, interviews of that temple's members to describe the new entity, pictures posted on the Nations websites.

Suffice it to say, we got none of that. News that we had the bakery was greeted with more shock than excitement. Like, "Really? That was approved? Does Father know?"

To which I responded in kind.

"Yes he does, and now so do you. Detroit is Temple number 1 for a reason."

By this time, I was becoming less and less concerned about being politically correct to a structure that seemed to be blackballing us at every turn. My attitude was if Allah said I was good, then they couldn't tell me nothing.

After months of stalling on the part of the National laborers, help was on the way.

Brother KC had been banished from Connecticut a year or so after I left and was chilling in Heaven behind the scenes.

Despite being very experienced and knowledgeable, KC was not a hot commodity. He was a hard worker, but his effeminate mannerisms made him an easy target to many of the FOI. He often found himself an easy and frequent punching bag. He didn't do himself any favors by falling into deep emotional funks once pressure came. This emotional state would show itself in his work and eventually, he would find himself back in Heaven.

I'll take him.

I knew Detroit would be the ideal situation for KC. He would be free to come in, do his duty, and then be left to his devices. In most cases, that meant hanging out with the Sisters, sleeping, or surfing the world wide web on his precious laptop.

For all his talents in the bakery, KC was of zero value in the community, and that's where we needed the most help.

Like with KC, we were left to pick from the very best of the members no one else wanted.

In truth, there was absolutely nothing wrong these people, but just like any social group, once the majority of the Nation thought of you as and treated you like a screw up, it wasn't long before the average person took on that persona.

Bro. Minister Thomas was at one time one of the top Ministers in the Nation. He was the type of man whose positive, easy going energy could be felt from the moment he walked into a room. This also made him an easy target in UNOI.

He was probably the grandest example of the divide between the teachings of Royall and the Messenger I could imagine. When it came to the Messenger's teachings, he had a deep, deft understanding of them. Like many true soldiers of the First, he could share endless experiences of things he had done in the First. Like many soldiers from the First, this ended up being both a blessing and a curse.

There were many disconnects between what Royall was teaching and what the Messenger taught.

Royall said his teachings were the fulfillment of the Message. Since many of the elders had been taught by the Messenger, they would not be able to adjust to what Royall was teaching.

(Hey I'm just telling you what he told me).

This led to many conflicts with members of the First and those who were being taught exclusively by Royall. This conflict met with deadly consequences when Bro. Minister Thomas's wife had fallen ill, and under instruction from Royall's wives, he did not seek medical attention for her. Like a faithful Minister, he sat back and waited on an impending upturn in her health that Royall predicted.

That turn never came and he sat and watched his wife die.

This predictably left him a shadow of his former self; the smile still hung there on his face, but he never quite regained the emotional balance that had made him a successful Minister for decades. This tragedy didn't earn him the sympathy you might expect, as it was surmised that if his wife died it must have meant a) he/she had done something to take her out of Royall's' protection, or b) it was Father's will and she was removed so that Thomas could do his duty to Allah.

Sigh.

The political wheels of the UNOI continue to turn around him, and once motion came to Atlanta, it was not long before he found himself on the outside looking in. Deemed not assertive enough to be of any real use, he was on the first thing smoking to Heaven to cut hair in the barbershop.

Brother Ronnie was a different story. He was nobody's easy target. Also from the First, he was a Brother I had always had a fondness for. A man's man, he was like an older version of the Brothers I had grown closest with in the Nation. He would run through a brick wall for the idea, but you could easily see he was a street guy. If the gold tooth that showed when he smiled didn't betray it, then the hustler's mentality once he started talking definitely did.

He was the type of Brother who was always rotating on new ways to bring funds into the Nation or produce a new product that would free us from having to spend money in unnecessary places.

He was two or three decades older than what I had in mind, but Ronnie was the closest thing to what I was looking for. He went out into the community and handled his business without me needing to draw him an intricate map of what places to go to. He just wanted me to point him in a direction, literally.

There were Brothers from Detroit that didn't attack the streets the way Ronnie did. Some Brothers who actually made their money on the

298

street, born and raised in on the East side would ask for a shop by shop detail of where they should and shouldn't go on fundraiser.

While all too willing to take tips on a hot shop, the real heavy hitters in the Nation practically shunned any type of direction when it came to going out. That was part of the fun, especially in a new city, to go out and break new ground. We didn't really care to know what shops had rejected you. It was a matter of pride to go into a shop that had rejected everyone else and turn them into a customer. That was Ronnie.

He carried that same pit bull mentality into class. Like Thomas, he had a vast knowledge of the Messenger and the knowledge of the First, but what separated him from most was that he also had a very good grasp of what Royall was teaching. Even more importantly, like a good Brother from Heaven, he had no problem correcting something said or speaking up when he saw something out of order.

Both Ronnie and Thomas had brought with them their wives, Sis. Theresa and Sis. Cheryl. Having wives always added to the value of the Brothers coming because now we had two additional members to assist with prep and otherwise. It wasn't what we had before but dammit, it was progress.

But even with the help we would be getting from KC, Thomas, Ronnie and their wives, the biggest steal came from a different source all together.

All the way across the Nation, Brother Trevor (remember him?) had been dispatched to Mobile, AL. One of Royall's favorite sons, Trevor's success in Mobile was considered a forgone conclusion. The autonomy that came with starting a business where there was no motion appealed to Trevor's dictatorial style.

What it seemed he didn't understand about life outside of Heaven was that he couldn't make the part-timers do anything. He could ban and fire all the Brothers he wanted but there was no surplus of willing Brothers next door at the FOI house to come and take their place.

This reality didn't cause him to make any allowances in his approach, and in no time at all he was burning out of his help, in particular, his wife, Judy.

One major dynamic of being married to a powerful Brother in the Nation was that a Sister had proof positive, usually from the mouth of Royall himself, in addition to the respect that would come from other members that, hey, this is a powerful brother over here.
The impetus was on the Sister to be especially submissive.

Royall was Allah.

Allah recognized me as one his favorite sons.

So get in there and make me a bowl of cereal!

Now, a brother didn't have to be especially wise to understand that there was a balance here.

Yes, you were wise and powerful having been prepared by Allah himself, but your wife had also been prepared for you by Allah.

So it was also in your best interest to treat her accordingly.

After all, since you are SO wise, and SO powerful, then you should be able to cause her submit peacefully.

Gosh, that sounds so simple, doesn't it?

Invariably, the Sister would question the Brother about something or in a way that he felt was disrespectful.

The Brother, having been thoroughly convinced of his Godhood, would rebuke the Sister for not having the proper posture or respect.

The Sister having not been raised in the Nation would take it back to the hood on that fool and then before long, they would be on the phone with one of the Wives, or Father. Or worse, one would put in a request for a divorce, which more often than not would be accepted.

For all of Royall's talk of making things brand new, the Nation had a divorce rate of well over 50%. This was compounded by such a small population that meant many of those seeking companionship in the Nation would have to sift through the ashes of other failed marriages to find a prospective mate.

You could know a member for years and not realize that he/she used to be married to that Brother/Sister over there.

At some point, this scenario reared its head in Alabama.

Trevor had found himself a second wife and whatever was going on in the house Judy, was having none of it.

Never one to back down (from a Sister) or mince words, Trevor let it be known that she was welcome to go, and before he could finish the sentence good she was on the next thing to Heaven.

A slim sister with a bookish look, Judy happened to be KC's younger sister. As she arrived in Heaven, her brother was preparing to leave to Detroit.

Amanda was approaching the end of her pregnancy with our youngest son, who, by the way, we had conceived in the midst of all of this. She had been consistently been putting in requests to have a Sister come and assist her with the traditional six-week period, during which the mother and baby are allowed no contact outside the home.

We must have sent in a good amount of charity that week, because we found out that Judy was on transportation coming with KC. It was made clear, in big bold letters, that THIS WAS TEMPORARY, as she would be going back to Mobile before long.

That was the company line, but I had experienced enough in the Nation to know that temporary was often temporary.

In talking to Kaaba, I was able to surmise that she and Trevor had been on the outs for some time. She had requested a divorce he had given his emphatic approval.

Of course, it was never that simple.

Much like Amanda with me, Judy was a major part of what Trevor did in Mobile. He was a hardworking, spiritually minded Brother, but Judy's attention to detail and kind spirit balanced out his tendency to go to the extreme. They may have been ready to split, but you were never out of a relationship until the Royall Family said you were.

Although I understood her stay to be temporary, I was stoked beyond belief to be getting a Sister of Judy's caliber. She was a veteran in Heaven, which meant she knew how to do it all, cook, bake, secretarial duties. She was especially adept at taking care of and teaching the children. In addition to all of that, she was exactly the type of Sister the Brothers loved to be around; in other words, she knew how to correct your missteps without stepping all over your ego. A talented Sister could tell you what you should be doing and make you feel like it was your idea.

Judy's feet had hardly hit the ground and she immediately began taking responsibility for the MGT, the youth, the prep schedule, baking the cakes, and of course, helping Amanda in preparation for the baby. As much as I respected her before her arrival, I gained an even greater appreciation for Judy and all her capabilities once I saw her in motion.

I also knew that with my history and her ambiguous relationship status that it was best that I kept my distance.

It was one thing for me to cavort with lost-found women, but there was no way in fifteen Hells that I was ever gonna be accused of doing anything improper with one of the MGT, obviously not a married/unmarried one.

Nonetheless, the chemistry was apparent. Judy was about duty and still knew have to have a good time in doing so. Her presence even helped my relationship with Amanda.

In scenarios that we had come to accept as normal in our relationship, she began to play the active moderator for that which was lost in translation. I would watch Amanda storm into the bedroom, and chalk up the rest of the night as loss. Judy would slink into the room, and twenty (maybe more like thirty) minutes later, Amanda would be apologizing for flying off the handle.

Or I would miss something I should have done, Judy would point it out to me and how it affected my household, and I would fix it, making sure to apologize and thank my wife for her patience. While I felt I had to keep my mouth shut, it was hard to miss the chemistry that Judy had with our family. I knew we were in a different place when one day Amanda insisted that I take Judy to the Main Library on a "date."

Ok first of all, inappropriate.

Secondly, schweeeeet!

This was as unprecedented as it got. Even before I had ever shown any signs of cheating, Amanda was a seriously possessive wife, who once called me into question for holding the door for the wrong sister. Even if she was using the word "date" jokingly, it was incredible that she would be comfortable making such a joke.

But the feeling was mutual.

Judy made no secret of the fact that she was happier than she had been in a very long time, eventually coming to Amanda to address what would grow into an enormous elephant in the room: the second wife thing. Shortly after their discussion, the details of which are unknown to me to this day, Amanda approached me about the idea.

I told her yes, I had thought about it.

How could I not? Here was this beautiful Sister in my home who gets along famously with my wife, my children, and me. She is serious, dedicated, and knowledgeable about this idea.

But, I followed, too much was unclear about how long she was gonna be here, her marital status, hell, OUR marital status. I would be lying if I said it wouldn't be a dream come true, but I knew that it was better to address such things with my motion. If that was supposed to happen, then Father would see to it that it happens.

No doubt, this situation with Judy, Amanda, and I was a surprise to us, but I would come to find out we weren't the only ones shocked.

It turned out that Judy was permitted to come to Detroit as a deterrent to divorce as much as she was to assist Amanda. Despite our consistent growth and the acquisition of the bakery, Detroit was still regarded by many as the worst place in the Nation to be. And those who knew better were not about to stick their necks out to tell anyone different.

The thinking must have been to send Judy to Detroit, let her see Prostell's and Amanda's marriage and then she will appreciate what she had in Trevor.

Only thing is, once she finally had her follow-up hearing it was just the opposite.

She loved Detroit.

She loved us.

She loved how we interacted.

She didn't want to go anywhere.

She was happy.

Worst thing she could have ever said.

By the time she hung up the phone from her conference she was bawling. She made her way up to Amanda's room to be comforted by one of the very people it had been shared were unfit for her to join as a family. It was Father's will that Trevor be her husband.

As much as it hurt me and I wanted to reach out and comfort Judy, I didn't.

I couldn't.

Especially now that Royall's will had been made clear. Though none of us had openly discussed the possibility of Judy marrying into the family, at the very least she was a very important part of what we were doing in Detroit. Yet again, we were being shoved to the bottom of the totem pole.

"Really? Who wants to stay in Detroit?" was what she had been told by the National official. A National official who, like most of our critics, had never been here one day.

Nonetheless, a politically popular opinion always trumped nonpolitically popular fact.

Amanda saw the same thing I saw; we were consistently getting the short end of the stick, despite pouring all that we had into this idea. But what else was there to do but to keep fighting?

They had been doubting from the first time I got the phone call to come to Detroit. Hell, they had doubted since before I even set foot in Heaven. Yet and still, I had come through all of this with results. It pissed me off that people thousands of miles away, who had never even had a real duty in their lives could dictate the fate of things in Detroit, based on the opinion of something they overheard from someone who had been here once.

The laughable part being that the more the rest of the Nation turned their nose up at Detroit, the greater progress we made. Despite it all, the bakery opened up at 16411 East Warren Avenue.

We tried to wait on assistance from the Art Department with the interior decor of the bakery, but once it was clear that our requests were going to go unanswered, we held a joint FOI/MGT class to paint it ourselves.

While just about every other business had a huge call out for money and supplies to get started, we would have no such favors. By this time we didn't expect any.

We earnestly went about the business of expanding the bakery.

No matter what anyone had to say about what was or wasn't going on in Detroit, I wasn't about to chase it. They could gossip and take shots all they wanted. I had been around long enough to know the numbers tell the story.

With Bilal, Ronnie and Thomas going out to sell daily, I took the opportunity to greatly curtail my time out in the community.

My primary reason for this was to dedicate my full energies to the idea of promoting the bakery as its own viable entity above and beyond what the Brothers were bringing back from the community.

This included canvassing the neighborhood to let all the residents and business owners know we were there and ready to serve them.

We also joined every community organization we could, even going before the Detroit City Council to promote the program of Food for Life Supreme (the pseudonym that all of the Nation's new ventures had taken in order to appeal to a wider audience of patrons and donors). I would work to make sure that whatever the bakery brought in that day would more than replace what I might have made driving around that day.

My second reason, and the one I dared not share was I didn't want to mess up. I knew I was still amongst the very best when it came to going out with a car full of product and coming back with pockets full of cash. My problem was cash might not be the only thing I picked up while I was out.

By now, I was no longer in denial. I had a problem and/or needs depending on how I was looking at it that day. The more I went out amongst all the beautiful Detroit women in all those hair salons, the more likely I would succumb to the temptation that they presented.

I was on my last leg as it related to that, and now there was a lot more than my own position at stake. We were embroiled in the middle of a bitter battle for us as a temple to have the right to continue to promote this idea. If I went down, it would affect EVERYTHING in Detroit.

During all this time, I had still juggled the attentions of various lost-found women in order to supplement what I felt like I was missing at home. Like any official worth his title, it was no problem for me to justify it. I was a tireless servant to this idea no less than 18 hours a day. So if I found thirty minutes to spend on something for myself, I knew the other 23.5 hours went toward Nation building. Just as long as I didn't allow my thing to affect anyone else. My duty was done, the lost-founds had no complaints, and I was good until the next time I couldn't control my urges.

No harm. No foul.

At least until the lines that separated my passion (Nation) from my pleasure (Nature) began to blur.

Lost and Found

And then the other shoe dropped.

I suppose it is fitting that it was my own actions that came back and ended my time in the Nation.

I have come to learn in or out of the Nation it didn't matter.

No matter how big you try to build your so called enemies up in your own mind, they only have the power against you that you give to them.

Political and character assassinations hadn't worked.

Conspiracy had not worked.

Even the doubts of those closest to me were not enough to deter me from progress.

In the end the only one with any power to stop me was ME.

And now I stood in shock, having just cost myself the only thing that mattered to me in the world. I had worked every day for no less than 18 hours a day for the past six years to do my part to build this Nation.

And now I had to stop.

Sit still.

Chill out.

Don't touch nothing.

I was numb.

Since the only way I could contribute was to get a job, in less than a week I had a job doing taxes.

I figured that if I was going to be "away from us" status, then I was going to do that better than anyone before had ever done it.

Because of how I had learned to think, I was a fast study and the managers raved how I went about my business. I was disgusted by their praise.

A week ago, I was one of Allah's chosen people, teaching classes that were saving the very lives of people, traveled coast to coast conducting the business of the Nation, I even had Allah's number in my cell phone. I was supposed to get excited because they liked how I handled a keyboard?

There were no words to properly describe this demotion.

I had gone from Brother Minister Prostell X to Royall, Allah in Person to Prostell the tax consultant.

Cue the rim shot. This was a joke.

I would go to work all day long and not a single word that any person said to me was worth ANYTHING. These people only talked about money, bills, phones, cars, bad rap music, i.e. nonsense. What could I possibly have to talk to them about? We weren't even from the same reality.

These people were lost-founds, slaves to the very corrupt and unjust system that drove them to their deaths. And couldn't be happier about it.

Even when I came home, I was still in a state of solitary confinement. I made a simple bunk on the floor in a vacant downstairs bedroom at the house. My children coming into my room to kiss me and spend time before bed was the only source of inspiration in my day.

Even if they had wanted to, no member was permitted to discuss Nation's business with me or even be in my presence unjustifiably. Never did I realize the important role that everyday casual conversation about Father, his teachings, major and minor happenings in the Nation played in keeping one anchored in the idea.

To fill this void I studied; books, tapes, the internet.

There were a number of Royall's interviews on YouTube. To my surprise, I found quite a few interviews with Royall that hadn't been aired in Heaven or anywhere else. So I studied those.

It was just what I needed. They were new to me and as always I felt like Royall was talking directly to me.

But something funny happened. Nothing huge, actually, rather small.

Maybe Royall saying in passing that he did not have more than wife.

Maybe he referred to God as someone other than himself.

Perhaps bragged on a business or entity that was no longer open and was never really viable.

I had been in enough verbal sparring matches with NOI members, Christians, Five Percenters, Jehovah's Witnesses to know that there were a million justifiable reasons why one might not share every detail of truth with a person.

Sometimes you had to adjust your message to make sure it had maximum effect for your audience.

"Can't feed steak to a baby," as the saying went.

When looked at individually these things really didn't mean a whole lot.

The denial of a wife or two.

A teaching or quote from the Messenger that didn't quite line up with Royall's teachings.

A law or principle that didn't quite apply the same to the Royall Family or official as it did to a member.

Instructions or teachings that I had passed on to the members that hadn't sat right with me either in their logic or their righteousness.

One by one, a wave of doubts and unanswered questions that had been there all along, but because of the constant motion of Nation Building had been pushed to the very back of my consciousness.

Well, now there was no motion, no class to be taught, no cookies to be baked, no fish to be sold. I had nothing but time on my hands. Time and my thoughts.

How much of our life is like that? So many things we are not at peace with, but we never bother to think about because we are so busy with life.

Even interactions I had with the Nation on Farakhanfactor prior to coming to Heaven came floating back to my mind.

I visited the site of those conflicts to revisit the blind accusation volleyed against me and others by UNOI representatives including Royall himself.

Now I had six years of experience INSIDE this group the weigh against their comments.

Not just their comments, but even the things I was selling myself.

Unlike most of the thoughts I had about the Nation over the past years this was all going on inside of my head, as opposed to a classroom setting.

One major characteristic of life in any social group, be it in the UNOI or America at large, is the phenomena of "groupthink."

Events happen, then "we" as a group, whether it be in a math class, at the water cooler, watching the news, etc. have discourse to put some perspective, and definition to them.

"Did you see Lebron's game last night?"

"Did you see how Obama did Romney at the debate?"

"Did you hear

This collective consciousness can be very healthy, needed, in fact. But if we are not careful, too often we find the agenda of a few shaping the way we view the world.

We start identifying with groups or icons and using their perspectives to frame our worldview.

Instead of saying A) this is what my experience is so B) this is what IS, we begin to have the habit of saying A) this is what IS, so B)this is what my experience is.

Did that make sense?

Sure it did. Read it again.

Well, on "away from us" status, there was no one there to help me adjust the facts that were bouncing around in my head.

Even still, I wasn't ready to declare false an idea that I had lived and died for. I had to look no further than myself and the man I was to see the proof that Royall MUST be Allah. Who else could make so much with so little?

This internal struggle was just another sign that something was wrong with me that even God himself couldn't fix.

I must be predisposed for wickedness and wrongdoing, because even Royall couldn't change me and he is Allah, but then if he is Allah, then wouldn't he be able to change me? In fact, didn't he make me? And if he made me, why would he make me evil? Why would he put me in position to try to be righteous if all I would do is let myself and everyone else down?

I was teetering on the brink of insanity.

I would go through the motions at work daily pondering thoughts of if I would ever be worthy of this idea, would Detroit survive in my absence, did God hate me, what would the Hellfire look like as it rained down from the sky on me?

Until finally something snapped.

I couldn't do it anymore.

No matter how much I loved the Nation, my family, the man Royall had made me into, and the work we were doing, I just couldn't do it anymore.

Without the work to make it all real, there was no way the ideology could hold up to my constant pondering.

The idea of eternal life was often trotted out anytime those amongst us began to have doubts, fears, or questions. The teachings stated that we would have it all; money, good homes, peace of heart, contentment of mind, friendships in all walks of life.

But what is the point of eternal life if you have to spend it trying to be something you are not with people you don't necessarily want to be around? If I dreaded duty with some of these people for a few hours, how was I going to manage eternity?

Outside of my own children, the people I loved to be around where the lost founds. Even the few brothers and sisters I had a fondness for where finding themselves on the outside of the Nation.

I began to plan my exit.

If I was going to go out it would have to be through the front door.

I had conducted more than my share of classes where we took apart the latest defector and how they made their exit from the Nation, Brothers who left and took money and/or vehicles.

One family had gone so far as making a coordinated exit across two time zones, all calling their local officials at the same moment and then not answering the subsequent calls that would follow.

Worst of all were the ones who would leave and then try to go to war with the Nation, posting negativity online, reporting the Nation to the authorities for child labor violations, even joining forces with Royall's declared rivals, like Moreen, Son of Man, etc.

I figured my first phone call would go to Brother Minister Joe.

Not only was he the Minister of the Temple with a direct line to Royall, but he was the man who had introduced me to this idea in the first place.

"As salaam Alaikum, Brother Minister. I was calling to let you know that I have decided that I am not going to return to the Nation after my 90 days is up."

I went on to thank him for everything he'd done for me over the years, and ask him to thank Royall for me as well. He said he would, and that he was sure I would do well in whatever I decided to do.

I let him know that since food was just about all I had done since joining the Nation that I planned on to take up catering. Door-to-door sales, just like he had taught me.

He said he understood and wished me luck.

I didn't really expect any resistance from him, but I was surprised how peaceful the interaction was. Despite his love for the idea, Joe was a realist and lived in the real word. Aside from that, I am sure he was relieved to have me out of his hair. Not only had I been the source of much heartache to his daughter, but I had let the Temple down in grand fashion.

My next phone call was to the National Secretary in Heaven.

No answer.

I called back.

No answer.

I cursed. I really needed to take care of all of this at one time.

Fuck it. I called Kaaba.

We had not talked since the day I reported myself in the bakery.

He answered.

I gave the greetings. "I tried calling Bro. National and wasn't getting an answer. I am calling to let it be known that I have decided that I am not going to return to the Nation after my 90 days is up."

He cut me off before I could even get the words out good.

"Yes Sir, I got it. As Salaam Alaikum."

I didn't know if he was disappointed in me or just disappointed that he would not be the one who got to decide my fate.

I put it out of my mind.

One more phone call to make.

"Prostell what are you talking about!?! Are you CRAZY!?!?"

Amanda's reaction was predictable.

We had more than our share of drama, but who wants to see her Baby Daddy burn up in the Hell Fire.

I assured her I had thought it over and I had no interest in pulling my family away from Royall's protection, but I knew it was time for me to go.

If nothing else would effectively spell out the end of our time as a family, this did. We had been through the cheating, lying, but being in the Nation was the non-negotiable with Amanda.

This realization would push me into an even deeper, darker funk.

I had officially splintered my family.

I don't know what I expected when I made my decision to officially separate from the Nation, but this was Hell. I made arrangements to rent a room from a family member, began to busy myself with the business of running my own Catering Company, Three Brothers Family Catering.

By now the process was second nature to me.

Being in Detroit, I had no shortage of clientele, but I made sure to steer clear of the places that I knew the Brothers would go to sell. If I did stumble upon their route I would implore the customers in the shop to make sure that supported Food For Life Supreme before me.

I explained that I had decided to do my own thing, but what they were doing was still a very worthy cause.

Slowly but surely, I began to get my groove back. I was connecting with friends who had been begging to hang out so long that they had given up on me. I would spend the weekends with my children, as had been worked out between Amanda and me.

I wasn't quite happy, but I wasn't staring up at the sky waiting for it to rain fire on my head any more.

And then right on cue, the bullshit.

I am getting out of the car in front of Source Apparel on Woodward.

It's the lunch rush and I'm running a little late, so I am loading up the car with food when my phone rings.

"Yes"

"Prostell this is Kaaba, I got Brother Captain Rodney on the line."

Telltale sign of B.S.

"Yes Sir, what's going on?" I reply expecting nothing good to come from this call.

"I got a report that you are selling food. In particular, in the shops that the Nation goes in. And also that you are using accounts to purchase items in the Nation's name. Do you know anything about that?"

"Absolutely. When I called Brother Minister about leaving I shared that I was going to be selling food. I would have shared it with you, but you rushed off the phone."

Kaaba gave an exasperated sigh. "Prostell, are you familiar with what happened with Brother Emory and the Brothers in North Carolina?"

Emory had made his exit from the Nation about a year before me, sick of the games and politics. In order to support his family, he started making and selling cookies, which the members in North Carolina were not selling yet. That didn't stop the FOI military from declaring him a traitor for hostile cookie sales and running his name through the mud in the Nation.

"I am, but I need to let it be known, I have made it clear to the customers that they are to continue to support the..."

"First of all, Prostell we don't need you to do us any favors. Second, what you are doing is very dangerous, and could be taken as a direct challenge if you aren't careful..."

It was one thing to make these sort of calls when I was in the FOI and you were the ranking officer, but I wasn't in the Nation anymore. Most of all, I wasn't doing anything wrong, and in fact, I was still promoting the UNOI at every turn. I wasn't having this conversation.

"Well this is what's happening. I am NOT representing myself or my products as a part of Food For Life Supreme, I am not shopping in the Nation's name, I AM selling food, in particular to those customers who call me and say they want my food. In fact, its lunch time now, and I am standing in front of a shop as we speak, so unless you guys got something different I got to go."

I hung up.

Yes. That did feel good.

I was out of his jurisdiction. Any more back and forth was a waste of his breath and my time, and my loyalties to the military no longer kept me from saying so.

I continued about my business for the rest of the day putting that conversation out of my head.

I never saw the phone call I got the next day from Amanda coming.

"Prostell what did you do?" She sounded sick.

She could only be talking about yesterday's conversation.

"Wow, really? He told on me?"

"What happened?"

"Nothing. Kaaba and Rodney called like they were crazy. I told them what I was doing and that was the end of it. You know how they are. I knew they wouldn't like that. Oh, well."

I was slow, I didn't get it. She took a deep breath.

"Father has instructed that I am no longer allowed to let you see the children until you make that right."

"Excuse me?"

"You have instructions to call Kaaba if you want to change that."

I didn't say anything.

"Please, Prostell, just call. For me"

For. Her.

Every inch of my being screamed bloody murder.

I had underestimated the depths Kaaba would go to in order win an argument.

I can't say I had rational thoughts as much as I had thoughts of pain.

The pain I was feeling.

The pain I needed them to feel.

Pain to anyone whose pain might adversely affect those causing me pain.

She went on to say the explanation that had been given to her was that "The children belong to Royall and no one else; not even their biological families would be permitted to put them in harm's way."

It was said in my conversation that I had been disrespectful to the degree that showed I was a danger to the children.

That I had been disrespectful to two of the most notorious tyrants in the Nation.

Sitting here now, I suppose my not giving a damn about what they were talking about must have done great injury to their egos.

So they pulled out the stops on me.

With everything that had gone on, this was the first moment that I showed open disdain for the Nation as a whole. Amanda was clearly fighting for me and my children's relationship.

It is hard for those who have never been in that situation to understand, but I knew if I was still in the Nation and the shoe was on the other foot, I would have done the same thing.

She may not have been able to identify with my leaving the Nation, but she never had anything but love and respect for me and my children's relationship.

I swallowed my pride, anger and everything else.

I called Kaaba.

I laid down my weapons at his feet.

"Look, I just need to know what I need to do to see my sons."

It didn't sound right for me to be asking another man.

Knowing he was in the driver's seat Kaaba played coy.

"I don't know. If you had conducted yourself differently on the phone before then we wouldn't be here."

"I understand. I was frustrated. I think we both can relate to that. I don't have any interest in going to war I just want to see my sons."

Kaaba took a long pause.

"Well, that's not up to me. I'ma have to check on that and get back to you. Matter of fact, give me a few days, and if you don't hear anything from me, call me back."

Purgatory.

With each passing day, my anxiety over the situation grew and grew.

Would the Nation really keep my children from me indefinitely over cookie sales?

How much of this was Royall and how much of it was Kaaba?

Would I be able to keep myself from retaliating in dramatic fashion?

Finally, three days passed and I called.

No answer. I left a message.

I gave it a couple hours, and called back.

I called early.

I called late.

I was being played.

Days.

Weeks.

I called national headquarters to make sure he got the message and report that I was being ignored. I knew this was only slightly above pointless. Nothing carried less importance in the Nation than a member who had decided to leave.

Finally I got the call.

"The Mountain does not bow to the Wind."

This was the message Royall had given Kaaba to give to me.

I repeated it back.

"The Mountain does not bow to the Wind. What does that mean?"

"Well, what I took from it was that you need to be patient. Father is not going to be rushed."

I don't know where I got the strength or patience from, but I waited some more.

I occupied myself with reconnecting with friends who had long been trying to connect with me. Now outside the restraints and curfews of the Nation I could try to party/drink/smoke my cares away.

Or at least try to hold them at bay.

In the absence of a relationship with my children, I was buoyed emotionally by the relationship I did have with them before all of this, especially PJ. I knew they knew me. They had to know there was no way I would voluntarily not be in contact with them. Anyone who might make an effort to paint a negative picture of me in his mind would be instantly discrediting themselves.

My time in the Nation had built up my ability to deal with long absences from those I was closest to. That helped some, but this was so much different. These were my sons.

The longer this went on the more desperate I became.

Before long, I was parking up the street from the house and sitting for hours at a time. Hoping to catch some glimpse of my babies.

Unbeknownst to me, because of all the stress and drama, Amanda had put in a request to leave Detroit that was approved.

My children weren't within miles of that house which was a good thing, because as I sat in that car I knew that if I did see one of them with one of the other members, I would have a very hard time not skidding onto

322

the lawn, jumping out of the car, punching said member in the face, and snatching my child up.

I knew that experience would only add more trauma to the child's experience, so eventually, I would pep talk myself into driving away. Even then I would drive by the house a couple of times before I left the neighborhood.

I was renting a different car every week, so I wasn't sure if I was being detected, but by then I didn't care. I prayed one of them would run up on me physically. They thought that phone call was disrespectful. Someone would be paying in the physical for all my anguish.

My thoughts turned to the "protection" that Royall was providing to the members. More than once I calculated how much gas money and time would be required to show up in Heaven and "test" out just how protective that protection was.

But I knew that wouldn't do anything but make me even more powerless. That story didn't end with me being with my sons again, so I gradually let it go.

One thing was for sure, there was no longer need to hold onto any romantic ideas of peaceful coexistence.

If it was war they wanted, then who was I to turn the other cheek? That wasn't the FOI way. Up to this point I had avoided some of the more lucrative stops for food sales in order to avoid stepping on the Nation's toes. These were places that I had established and built a rapport on behalf of the UNOI.

Now I was ONLY going to the places I knew where vital to their daily success. I was not surprised to find out that they had made sure to let it be known that I was "kicked out" of the program. They would go on to tell customers that "They were taking their chances" by buying food from me.

Bad idea.

Detroit respects hustlers, not haters.

I was genuinely touched when shops I had known for years told me they had banned the UNOI from ever coming in their place of business again for making such comments. The Nation was actively trying to tear me down, but all around the city, my customers, my people were letting it be known that the love was real.

I was after all Detroit's son. No amount of time in the Nation was going to change that.

The divorce between me and the UNOI raged forward. I called Bilal to let him know that the members staying in my Grandmother's home needed to go and they had two weeks to do so.

They called me to let me know I needed to sign over whatever Nation's property that was still in my name. I was only so happy to oblige.

It was around this time I got a letter from friend of the court; i.e. child support.

This just kept getting better and better.

I was incensed.

I hadn't heard from Amanda for a few weeks, so this I assumed must have been why.

She KNEW she was wrong.

So not only was the Nation, that was supposedly here to uplift the Blackman, woman and family, denying me of my right to see my children, but on top of that they have Amanda file child support on me?

There was a hearing date and everything. Not only was this a new low, but it was stupid.

I didn't work a job with a traceable income. Was their goal to just get me thrown in jail for non-payment?

I filed the envelope under "shit I'm not about to deal with right this second."

I had a business to run and money to stack.

I knew not to go to war until my money was right, so I was working and trying to figure how I was going to A) get my boys back and B) make them regret picking a fight with me in my town.

It wasn't until the hearing date passed and I received another notice in the mail that I actually recognized the golden opportunity in what had been an apparent setup.

Not only was this hearing to setup payments but also visitation.

VISITATION!

I would pay whatever they could come up with as long as I got to see my boys.

I started studying the law like an imprisoned brother about to come up on his appeal date. I must have come to that building ten times before that hearing date to get all of the information I needed to have a successful court date. Finally the day came.

I was there when the building opened. This would be my moment of truth.

I got there super early, checked in, and took a seat staring out the window at Detroit's skyline.

As parents and public defenders filed in and out of the small family court rooms, I heard a familiar voice behind me.

"Prostell, what is going on?" Amanda was standing there looking at me with a baffled expression.

325

She may as well have been juggling flaming swords riding a unicycle. I was expressionless and I had no interest in a single word she had to say.

"You really don't want to talk to me right now."

She looked even more confused and after seeing I wasn't budging, she stormed off. Minutes later we were standing in front of a judge. I knew right where I wanted to go. On the papers that had been filed we were listed as unmarried.

"My wife…"

The judge stopped before we started.

"Your wife?"

"Yes, your Honor, we are legally married."

Amanda chimed in, "No we aren't, your honor.'

I laughed, "That's silly. Of course we are. I can run across the street and get a copy of our marriage license."

The judge looked irritated, as though they ever look any other way.

"Ok, if you can prove marriage that changes some things. We are going to have to reconvene to a later date, but you need that document." She turned to the court clerk, "What do we have available in three weeks?"

I jumped in.

"Yes Ma'am, your honor. The thing is, I haven't seen my children since March." It was July 24th.

The Judge looked at Amanda, "Is that true?"

Desperate not to violate Royall's instruction, she went way out her character, "Your honor, he has a history of abuse towards me and his home is not a safe envior-"

"Is any of this recorded in police reports, restraining orders, anything?"

Amanda looked dejected, "No Ma'am."

"Ok, if he was safe enough to marry and make three babies with, he is safe enough to see them now."

As the judge rattled off the rest of the instructions, I still wasn't relaxed. I wouldn't feel at peace until I had my sons in my arms.

I didn't at any point have any resentment in my heart toward Amanda. I knew what position she was in and her belief that this man was Allah and had the power to take children from her or worse, was the only thing that could ever get her to take this stand.

I also knew from being in the UNOI, Royall still reserved the right to tell the member forget what the judge said and make them disappear to another undisclosed location in the Nation.

I picked up a couple of car seats and called my uncle Clint, a former Marine. I needed to make sure I had a witness for whatever might or might not happen. He was older and experienced enough that I knew no matter what happened he wouldn't lose his cool.

I pulled up in front of the Nation's home at the prescribed time. Considering I was a bundle of nerves, I held it together quite well.

I rang the bell. Brother Anthony 6X, originally from Detroit, now a music instructor in Heaven, or so I thought, answered the door.

His face didn't betray his intention as he asked me to wait outside.

The next thing I knew, my youngest son was standing in the doorway. Before he toddled over to me and wrapped his stubby little arms around my legs I had lost it. I only partly heard his bigger brother as he called out, "Daaaaaaddy!!!" bounding across the lawn from next door, joining our hug.

I was done.

I cried and held my Sons, and they held me back.

The strong hugs coming from those little bodies told me everything they didn't know how to say.

"Daddy, we love you."

"Daddy, we missed you"

"Daddy, we been looking for you."

Yes Sir, Son, me too. Me too.

.

Even as my frame shook with tears, they didn't break the hug or even look concerned. Everything was as it should be.

Amanda explained to me that PJ was not in town, he had stayed in Maryland. I had figured as much.

Among any of his siblings, even the older ones, I was least worried about PJ.

More than anyone else, he had been by my side day after day in the community, on the road, at duty.

There was nothing they could tell him that would cancel out the reality of who he knew his father was.

He and I would catch up soon enough. For now I was content in allowing this moment to be what it was ; a beautiful, divine reunion between a father and his sons; a reward from the universe for my patience and perseverance.

It was this moment for me that was the final nail in the coffin as it related to any superior quality of the UNOI or Royall.

For months, my children were kept from me under the guise that Royall had to protect them from me lest I do some irreversible harm to them. Yet this principled stand by Allah himself was moot once the Friend of the Court in Detroit, MI stepped into the picture. In that case, it was no big deal.

I had come to Royall/UNOI respectfully as a Black man, looking to reconcile the situation peacefully for the sake of the children and that wasn't even worth responding to.

But some White lady in a black robe declared, not asked, that I was to see children immediately and the UNOI only asked how high they should jump.

We would return to court much more peacefully next time.

The Nation had no interest in investing the resources necessary to "protect" my children from me in a court of law, so Amanda and I would get back on the same page, much to both of our relief.

She asked if I had a problem with her and the children moving back to Maryland on the Nation's farm.

I didn't.

PJ would eventually come to spend time with me before they would head back out to Maryland.

Within two months he would be calling me asking to pick him up in Dayton. Somehow or another, my ten year-old son, who could walk into any business you pointed him at and charm the socks off of everyone in a mile radius had managed to get himself kicked out of Nation's care.

Within a couple months, Tammy would call me from Alabama letting me know she was ready to come home. By the time the summer hit, Amanda had put in her request to go part-time again.

Within months my departure, Detroit closed up the bakery and suspended all local motion.

I regretted that.

The remaining full-time members, including Judy, were scattered across the Nation.

Over the course of the next couple years, this pattern prevailed in the UNOI. Members whom you just knew would endure until the end would drop like flies. Whether personal grudges, vendettas, or political hits, many of the Brothers responsible for making things happen around the Nation would drop off inside a three-year period.

Carter.

Emory.

Me.

Morris.

Even Daniel would eventually bow out, relinquishing full control of the FOI to Kaaba, who was now Supreme Captain. He had achieved a very high level of power and autonomy, but to those who now stood on the outside looking in it seemed his chief goal was to dismantle the FOI.

With fewer and fewer members to ride, high ranking officials and Royall family members began to turn their sights on one another. Changes were coming fast and furious.

Or so I heard.

I had moved on with my life. My only regret was not being able to communicate with Alan and Ray before I left to let them know they had options. I wasn't interested in dragging them out with me if they wanted to remain in the Nation, but I knew walking away could be a scary thing and if they wanted to do that I had their back.

Despite my personal experience and feeling, I knew that the children of two crack addicted repeat convictions could be in a worse place.

I knew one way or the other eventually, we would be standing face to face again.

In the meantime, I began to move my life forward. I had a surplus of knowledge and experience that I was eager to put to work. Much of what we did in the UNOI was done under the guise of community service, but it was always about helping the Nation, first and last. If the community wanted help they should join the Nation.

Finally in places like Kuumba's Cove, Nandi's Knowledge Cafe, The Inner City Sub-Center, and any place that would have me, I started putting the skills I had developed to work. Even though I was no longer in the Nation I still maintained a 'fulltime' mentality. This was my life's work and I would treat it as such. Only now I didn't need anyone's permission or approval to do it.

I also started getting involved in Poetry. A friend had bought me a ticket to a poetry show, and truth be told, I wasn't impressed. As a true revolutionary who had been out here 24/7 for the past 7 years, a lot of it sounded like some amateurs who had read some books and were trying to sound deep talking about things they had never experienced. Sounded like part-time members to me.

Luckily for me I stuck around long enough to know that wasn't the case.

You had your share of posers but people like Lashuan Phoenix Moore, the Black Tie Poetry Collective, Tawana Honeycomb
Petty, amongst many others showed the power of words that where followed up and in many cases inspired by actions.

Stepping on stage, I was reintroduced to the spoken power truth could have and the importance of sharing the light and power that had been gifted to you.

Soon, that became my ministry. I started the Nommo Power of the Word Poetry Series with the help of Awaken Detroit and Daune Smith that would quickly become a juggernaut in the Detroit Poetry Community. Open Mics turned to features, features turned to out of town show dates, which turned into tours.

Time moved forward.

Our separation was probably one of the most honest moments of Amanda's and my relationship. Not knowing what is going to happen is sometimes more peaceful than knowing for certain something bad is going to happen. We still don't always see eye to eye on many things, but she is a great friend. This, of course, in addition to being a better mother than I would dare ask for to my sons.

I suppose it would be easy to sit back and think about those first few days on Courville and experience some sort of regret. What if that beautiful girl on the porch across the street had been like so many other beautiful girls that I never built up the nerve to even talk to? What if she was just a lady who used to live across the street from my Mom one summer? What if I had finished school, graduated and went with my original plan to be a teacher in the Detroit Public Schools?

But I don't regret a moment of it. I cherish my entrance and journey through the UNOI as much as I do my exit.

Early on in my life I prayed to God that He guide me in choosing an education that would allow me to have the greatest positive impact I could possibly have for my people.

The last decade of my life has been anything but traditional, but it has been nothing if not an education. I have discovered many laws and principles; some have stood the test of time, others showing themselves to be flawed. I have been blessed to meet, have duty, befriend and love many people from many places, some of whom I will know for the rest of my life.

But most important in all of this, I discovered me. I know my strengths. I know my weaknesses. I am finding more often than not they are one in the same. But they are mine; to hate, to love, the judge, to forgive. My burden and blessing.

You want to hear the ironic part of all of is this?

I feel today like I am in Heaven. I have a beautiful wife and wonderful children. I have activities that I am passionate about that add so much to my life. My life is an open field of opportunities and I am constantly blessed with new experiences in new places with new people.

I am still very much about service, but I understand that the act of serving benefits the server as much as it does the served. There is no separation. No them and us.

I have met friends from all walks of life from 80 year-old Jewish grandmothers, to artists from Iraq and Afghanistan, to legendary freedom fighters, to White kids who grew up with money and never knew a Black person until recently.

I have learned that I do not have to surrender or hide away the parts of myself that might make other uncomfortable, but I also do not have to where them on my sleeve in order to have a relationship with these people.

Most often I have been delighted to find a part of myself in many of them. Equally rewarding has the experience of finding parts of myself in me that I didn't know existed until some of these interactions.

Much of this is because of my experience in the Nation, even if it means I know what does not work for me because I tried it there and it failed.

I live a simple life and do not waste energy pursuing material "gains" that only end as burdens, because in the UNOI we learned to live a full life without these things.

On the other hand, we were taught that the Black man is God and the White Man is the Devil, and I have learned in and out of the Nation that the only God and Devil I have to fear is the one that resides in me.

We live in a world that manufactures fear and hate. It does this by constantly finding new ways to show us how we are separate, how we are different from another. Find any group of people anywhere on the planet with more than two people, and they have found some way to draw lines in the sand, real and perceived, to differentiate themselves from one another.

I honor those things that make me unique and that I have built, but no more or less than I honor those things that connect me to others.

So. Yeah I was in a cult.

It wasn't all bad.

As for Royall, you will not hear me speak ill of a man who set up a system that saved the lives of so many, including myself. Many of his harshest critics or those even hearing of him for the first time might call him crazy or worse. I think you judge a man by what he does. Many so-called revolutionaries and men of God can't be bothered to give five minutes of their time to a fellow human.

Whether you agree with the theology or not, Royall set up a system that provided food clothing and shelter. More than that, he gave us an opportunity to know what it is to accomplish great works; be Fathers, Mothers, Sisters, Brothers, the value of keeping one's word, the incredible things we can accomplish individually and collectively. To put it short, he showed us what we can do and I will FOREVER be grateful for that.

Today is not possible without yesterday.

Acknowledgements

I thought long and hard about writing this memoir. Ultimately I am at peace with the fact that these are my experiences and I am within my rights to share what I have lived. That being said, it is my will that these words have been taken in the proper spirit.

I have many mixed emotions about my time in the Nation in general, but what is overwhelmingly positive was what I received working with those in the ranks of the FOI and MGT.

I met and soldiered with so many great and amazing Brothers and Sisters that it literally brings tears to my eyes. These are not tears of regret or sadness, but of joy and appreciation.

Penning these words brought to the surface many emotions: shame, guilt, frustration, anger to name a few. But none of these feelings supersede the LOVE that I have for those who I soldiered with.

I am blessed to have been able to reconnect with so many who gave and continue to give all that is within their power to see our rise. Even in our pains and struggles, we have been divinely prepared. No matter what businesses close, no matter where you or I go on this Earth, we ARE the Nation.

I do not know what the future holds, but I do know none are more qualified to take this new world and place it squarely on our shoulders.

Except for KC. With his bad back he really shouldn't be lifting anything.

To my incredible best friend, life partner, muse and wife, Abigail.

The events in this book unfolded over the course of eight years and changed my life. I met you and knew in less than one month that my life had changed forever. I thank you for being here, for tolerating the odd hours that words come to me, for maintaining the household during my distant forays into my mind. All of this of course does not even begin to mention you are one of the greatest artists I have met and I eagerly await the day I can support you in whatever mediums you choose to make the world more beautiful

My children.

AC, JH, TH, NT, SA, AS, TR, CMB

Everything before this has been for you. Everything after it will be too. You ALL teach me so much every day, and ask for so little exchange, just hugs, kisses, and three square meals a week. There are not enough words in the language to tell you how deeply I love you, so I will just say go to bed.

My Father, if a good name is worth more than gold, thanks for more money than I could ever spend in a lifetime. My Mother, I should call more. Truth is I never feel far from you because so much of my spirit is YOU, and no thats no excuse, Imjusayin I Love You.

The Hopewells, Hopwoods, Watkins, Jones, Williams, Ehiemeres, Kuykindalls, yup.

Detroit Poetry. Hip- Hop. Conscious Communities. mmhm

Denver, Orlando, Cincinnati, Columbus, Earth, yeah.

Dimonique Boyd for your expertise and advice. Anyone supporting this project including and especially buying this book.

Thank you.

See you next go round.

-P

www.ingramcontent.com/pod-product-compliance
Lightning Source LLC
Chambersburg PA
CBHW071406090426
42737CB00011B/1366